ENDORSEMENTS

"Much has been discussed and written about concerning the missional-incarnational movement in recent years. While many agree on the orthodoxy of this movement, only a few seem to take the practice of this movement serious. Renew: A missional movement for the "none, done and undone" serves as a missional-incarnational primer highlighting the practices of living with a missional purpose. This is a practical handbook for anyone wanting to alert their neighborhood or community to the rule and reign of God."

—**Terry Ishee,** *Director of Online Residency and Hub Programs for Forge America*

"Church planter Robert Butler offers his personal experience of sharing the Gospel with the 'nones', 'dones' and 'undones' in our culture. With courage and conviction, he declares that the love of God is available to every person on earth. With intimate detail, he addresses topics that every person can relate to, from friendship and marriage to poverty and war. This is an essential resource for everyone who has a passion for sharing the Gospel in this age."

—**Rev. Martin Lee,** *Director of Congregational Development and Church Planting for Northern Illinois Conference of The United Methodist Church*

"The world is desperate for deep people who admit, commit, submit and practice the principles of Jesus. Bob Butler does. Bob really knows Jesus, and you can too. The question is not "What if I die tonight?" The question on most of our minds is "What am I going to do about tomorrow?" We need a way to live fully into Christ-likeness. Bob has given us a helpful practical guide to grow deeper in our faith. I am thankful for it!"

—**Rev. Dr. Mark Foster,** *Founding and Sr. Pastor of Acts 2 Church Church Planting Coach, Edmond, Oklahoma*

Thanks...

THE SHEER ACT OF putting thoughts to paper has been a spiritual experience all its own. The project has brought me closer to our triune God. This book is for His glory. Any credit for its content or its effect on the lives of the those willing to use it goes to Jesus. It was our Lord who brought a great number of people into my life who have assisted, encouraged and challenged different aspects of the book. They deserve mention.

First, I'd like to thank my wife, Diane. She has supported and encouraged this project since its inception. I am not sure this book would have ever been finished without her.

Second, I'd like to thank Kevin MacDonald and Dwayne Turner for their efforts in proofing each section and discussing the topics with me before bringing them to the Romeoville RENEW group on Thursday nights.

Third, I need to thank the Thursday night RENEW Group Leadership Team (Karole Masters, Mike Onken, Brian Riordan, Paula Riordan, Jim Lloyd, Cheryl Lloyd, Jim Osborn, Kathy Osborn, Mike Gyuricza, Stacy Gyuricza) and all those who have attended our Thursday night events. The topics and the discussion questions had you in mind. Your comments and our debriefs have been invaluable.

Fourth, I need to thank Karen Klaus for her encouragement and her experience.

Finally, I need to thank Rev. Ronn Smith, The Sanctuary Church (Romeoville), Exponential, Hugh Halter, The Forge America tribe, The UMC and the new leadership team at The Center (Itasca, IL) for their support.

RENEW

*A Missional Movement for the
"None, Done and Undone"*

ROBERT BUTLER

EQUIP PRESS

Colorado Springs

RENEW

Copyright © 2018, Robert Butler

All rights reserved. No part of this publication may be reproduced, distributed, or transmitted in any form or by any means, without prior written permission.

Published by Equip Press, Colorado Springs, CO

Scripture quotations marked (ESV) are taken from The ESV® Bible (The Holy Bible, English Standard Version®) copyright © 2001 by Crossway, a publishing minis-try of Good News Publishers. ESV® Text Edition: 2011. The ESV® text has been reproduced in cooperation with and by permission of Good News Publishers.
Unauthorized reproduction of this publication is prohibited. Used by permission.
All rights reserved.

Scripture quotations marked (KJV) are taken from the King James Bible. Accessed on Bible Gateway at www.BibleGateway.com.

Scripture quotations marked (NASB) are taken from the New American Standard Bible® (NASB), copyright © 1960, 1962, 1963, 1968, 1971, 1972, 1973, 1975, 1977, 1995 by The Lockman Foundation, www.Lockman.org. Used by permission.

Scripture quotations marked (NIV) are taken from the Holy Bible, New International Version. Copyright © 1973, 1978, 1984, 2011 by Biblica, Inc.® Used by permission.
All rights reserved worldwide.

Scripture quotations marked (NKJV) are taken from the New King James Version®. Copyright © 1982 by Thomas Nelson, Inc. Used by permission. All rights reserved.

Scripture quotations marked (NLT) are taken from the Holy Bible, New Living Translation, copyright © 1996, 2004, 2015 by Tyndale House Foundation. Used by permission of Tyndale House Publishers, Inc., Carol Stream, Illinois 60188. All rights reserved.

Scripture quotations marked (NRSV) are taken from the New Revised Standard Version Bible, copyright © 1989 the Division of Christian Education of the National Council of the Churches of Christ in the United States of America. Used by permission. All rights reserved.

First Edition: 2018
Renew / Robert Butler
Paperback ISBN: 978-1-946453-47-1
eBook ISBN: 978-1-946453-48-8

EQUIP PRESS
Colorado Springs

CONTENTS

	Renew: A Movement for a Broken Ecclesia	9
	Foreword	13
	Introduction	17
1.	Missio Dei	21
2.	Unconditional Love	25
3.	Father	31
4.	Prayer	35
5.	Will of God	41
6.	Society	47
7.	Defects of Character	53
8.	Temptation	59
9.	Politics	65
10.	The Church	71
11.	Enemies	79
12.	Renewable Forgiveness	87
13.	Error	91
14.	Unbelief	97
15.	Friendships	101
16.	Marriage	107
17.	Family	115
18.	Women	123
19.	Wrath	129
20.	Riches	135
21.	Poverty	141

22.	Giving to Man	149
23.	Giving to God	157
24.	War	165
25.	Non-Resistance/Boundaries	171
26.	Rights	177
27.	Character	183
28.	Death	189
29.	Love	195
30.	Work	201
31.	Teaching	207
32.	Disease	213
33.	Kingdom of Heaven	217
34.	Hell	223
35.	Falsehood	229
36.	Judgement	235
37.	Faith	241
38.	Sacrifice	251
39.	Holy Spirit	257
40.	Pleasure	263
41.	Purpose of Life	269
42.	Jesus	275
43.	Moral Ideas	279
44.	Good News	283
45.	The Supernatural	289
46.	Technology	295
47.	Sex	301
48.	Idols	311
49.	Cults	317
50.	Kindness	323
51.	Violence	329
52.	Complacency	335

Appendix A : Discussion Guide Questions   341

*RENEW IS A MISSIONAL EXPRESSION
TO REINVIGORATE THE AMERICAN CHURCH*

Remember the movie *Kindergarten Cop* where Governor Arnold Schwarzenegger shouts "It's not a too-mah"? Well, in this case, it is! For many years now, we have felt the American "church" is broken. The word "broken" comes as a shock to many. Those within the establishment will quote Jesus' words and talk of the church as God's bride and therefore, foolproof. We disagree. What God originally intended as the ecclesia has been altered so dramatically by us that it's time we admit our mistakes. The American church is in need of a complete redesign.

The numbers tell the tale. Millions leaving the institution over the past five decades. No real growth. The majority of the next generation finding Christianity irrelevant. The culture of a post-Christian America is even at odds with those aspects which form cornerstones. As a result, those who are left gather weekly only to be reminded of how our once-mainstream lifestyle has failed to address the larger questions brought forth from the enlightenment era. The church needs to be re-positioned to meet the world outside its doors.

The culture is skeptical and longing for authentic community. The days of trusting institutions or well-educated people is gone. The Internet has also changed the way we get information. We have more at our fingertips than ever before, but we don't know how to discern the truth. We are ever-knowing and never-understanding. We have more ways to connect than ever before and we are more alone than ever. A recent statistic claimed in the last ten years the average American has gone from three close friends to two. We have an ever greater need to be known and to know others intimately, but less willingness to share.

As we look around for what is working in the culture, we see the successful phenomenon of smaller communities of faith. They closely resemble the twelve-step recovery model. They are often labeled missional or billed as alternatives to the mainstream church. They are loosely based networks (small denominations really) of Christian outposts across America. Like the recovery format where enlightenment comes as a simple process: admit, commit, submit and practice the principles of Jesus. These expressions admit lives worth living require a triune God and others. These expressions are quick to ask for commitment and the surrendering the old to start anew. They require submission of one's will to a caring God. They practice a new-found life in an accountable group and practice it in the world outside the group. The simplicity of the process culminates into an experiential spiritual awakening.

The phrase "spiritual awakening" comes with some skepticism today, but the roots point to a spiritual program worked through the Oxford Group in the 1930s. They centered their teachings on a small book from 1902 called, *The Principles of Jesus* by Robert Speer.[1] The author proposed four absolutes and then expanded the teaching to over 50 weekly discipleship topics. It is an incredible — albeit dated — text for those wondering about the relevance of Jesus in all areas of a person's life.

Equipped with this information, we began to live one missional expression for the "none, done and undone" in our communities. The "nones" are those individuals with no religious context, the

---

1   *The Principles of Jesus*, Robert E. Speer, The Westminster Press, 1902

"dones" are those individuals who have been in the belly of the current American church and the "undone" are those who have all but checked out of this life because of what they have or are enduring. Our missional expression is affectionately called RENEW. It encompasses the best of all great movements, heralds back to the original movement of Jesus and longs for the rule and reign of God to once again become viral. We are a missional expression seeking to discover a life worth living which truly offers a foretaste of heaven.

FOREWORD

RENEW is a missional expression and part of the larger movement to redesign the American church.

A little over eight years ago, a few of us began to plant an outpost for Christ in the far western suburb of Oswego. We literally started without a plan and believed our reputation would be enough of a brand to bring people to the facility. We had the arrogant idea the rest of the area churches had failed in reaching the community. After all, less than 20 percent of the people were attending a faith community and only one church had any real growth in the area in the last ten years. We weren't all that original. We followed the formula given at so many of the church planting conferences and in sixteen months launched a new church in the middle of a cornfield. Over three hundred showed up on launch day. One year later, we had land, more parking and a great Sunday morning product. Yes. I said product. It was a weekly production that took a lot of resources so people could come pick up their spirituality on a Sunday morning and drive off. We were the latest brand people were talking about. However, some of us had begun to sense something wasn't right. I'll never forget reading my first missional book and bringing the concept to the church lead team hearing: "Yes, it's exciting but you can be missional and small. Or you can be attractional, encouraging and make it large." The point was clear. The leadership may deride the current state of affairs in the Church but we're not ready to change anything other than offer a better product than everyone else.

A few years later, the entire launch team would disappear. The early adopters would be replaced by more institutional people. The old church ways would be implemented and coordinated, and the Sunday morning ritual sterilized. The church would still champion the idea of being a missional church in two locations. However, the church planting truth that whatever you do to bring them into the facility must be maintained or they will leave as fast as they came had begun. Today, the second site is less than half its launch size and the first location which once stood over 800 in attendance has fallen by two-thirds.

We still believe in the Church but there must be a better way.

The RENEW idea was born out of this experience, our reluctance to accept the status quo and the understanding that the American institutional church of our fathers is crumbling. While we admit some church expressions are thriving, many are only the result of transfer growth of those who are discontent. While the 'cool' factor may bring them in, we know there's not a fog machine, a strobe light, a celebrity pastor or a worship band that can reverse the decline. The time has come for a wholesale change.

The group we believe has done the greatest investigation and learned the most through practical application is the Forge Network. Michael Frost, Alan Hirsh, Lance Ford and Hugh Halter have been championing movement to extend God's Kingdom and reign through solid orthodoxy, praxy and pathy. The American culture has made it clear to those gathering on Sunday: The good news is only good if you are willing to proclaim it *and* live it daily. Forge provides a host of residencies and trainings across the world. RENEW is a missional expression in a great sea of expressions to authentically reach, teach and create true followers of Jesus. Anything less taints the message and enforces the American Christian hypocrite stigma.

RENEW encompasses the best of all great expressions and heralds back to the original movement of Jesus. We are part of the larger movement seeking to discover a life worth living which truly offers a foretaste of heaven. We are focused on reaching the "none, done and undone" in every context. The "nones" are those individuals with no religious context, the "dones" are those individuals who have been in the belly of the current American church and "undone" are those who have all but checked out of this life because of what they have or are currently enduring.

The following fifty-two chapters are the discussion primers. They represent an effort to synthesize orthodox theology with cultural conundrums to help individuals and groups become more thoughtful in the practice of the Christian faith. We believe all the topics lead the group to a more orthodox understanding of Jesus. We subscribe to the Christian theological mainstream. Our book is meant to be read, wrestled with and discussed. We suggest this book be a group project with multiple levels of spiritual maturity present during the discussion.

Our first RENEW group consisted of over fifty individuals. We are now in the second year of meeting together on weekday evenings. We have seen all types of people and viewpoints. We have laughed, cried, argued and even agreed to disagree. The process has been life giving. We have often wondered about those first Christians as we discussed the differences between Christian thought, the human condition and cultural bias. Those first Christians must have debated a lot. We have covered the topics within this book twice. We have expanded some of the sections, re-wrote others and added a few new topics because the original idea led to more questions. A second book with more topics is underway.

We have found RENEW works as a weekday conversation. For some, RENEW is their only Christian connection. We affirm this. For others, RENEW augments their Sunday morning commitment. We affirm this too. Our purpose is to advance the Kingdom.

Our original group is a collection of many individuals and theologies. We have gathered on a weekly basis for dinner, details and discussion for a long time. Our gatherings are roughly two-to-three hours long. We also strongly suggest each group further their weekly learnings by encouraging connections with outside institutions to apply the teachings through service. RENEW is changing lives in the gatherings and outside.

If the pattern sounds familiar it should. It combines the best of the Wesleyan movement of "bands" and "classes" along with vital aspects of accountability, apprenticeship and missional service.

I hope you will take the time to review the chapters and the study guides. These teachings are not meant to be read and put on a shelf. They are meant to advance a movement in your area to RENEW the souls of individuals who are looking to discover a life worth living. If you enhance section for your groups edification, please consider sharing it with us so when we can consider adding your thoughts and content to further others growth as a Christians.

We define 'a life worth living' as a life with two core relationships — God and others — at the center of every thought, discussion and action.

INTRODUCTION

Changing times create dissatisfaction. Dissatisfaction without action leads to desperation. Desperation leads to innovation.

The "Church" in America for the most part needs total redesign because it:
- No Longer fits the culture of post-Christian America.
- Represents a declining trust with institutions, as well as their importance and allegiance
- Fails to recognize the growing belief of the irrelevancy of the gospel
- Rarely speaks to the cultural movement away from the moral teachings of Jesus
- Fails to articulate the benefits of gathering regularly to learn and discuss the spiritual.
- Falls short in the areas of arts, public discussion and technology.

The "Church" needs to be re-positioned to meet the world outside its doors.

We have more ways to connect than ever before and we are more alone than ever. A recent statistic claimed in the last ten years that the average American has gone from three close friends to two. We have an even greater need to be known and to know others intimately, but are less willing to share.

Old is new again.

If we are to address what is working in our culture, the phenomenon of twelve-step recovery has made its mark. A loosely based denomination of sorts with outposts in every town in America where the format to enlightenment comes with a simple process: admit, commit, submit and practice small group community. The simplicity of which is stunning and culminates in spiritual awakenings.

Equipped with this information, a love for sharing the gospel and willingness to not sit idle, we formed a ministry for those people who are:

- "Done" — with what we call church in "America
- "None" — claiming no religious preference when asked
- "Undone" — drowning in life by their actions or the actions of others.

We call this special gathering RENEW.

RENEW encompasses the best of all great movements and heralds back to the original movement of Jesus. RENEW gathers on a weeknight for a dinner, details and discussion.

Dinner

We begin with a free dinner and childcare for everyone. We ensure the time is enriching and filled with ways for people to connect with one another.

Details
After dinner, we gather in an area to hear the details of a relevant topic of spirituality. This part of the evening will contain a variety of the arts to increase the awareness of the topic.

Discussion
We then break out into groups for discussion. We currently have a:
- Spirituality group where we dive into the Christian understanding of the topic
- Men's group
- Women's group
- Unique recovery group for both the addict and the family

Service
Finally, to cement the weekly learnings, each group is asked to connect with an outside institution to apply the teaching through service. RENEW is already changing lives.

If the pattern sounds familiar it should. It combines the best of the Wesleyan movement of "bands" and "classes" along with vital aspects of accountability, apprenticeship and missional service. The updated program book includes discussion starters and guides to connect with those who self-identify as the "none, done and undone." It changed lives over 100 years ago and it's changing even more now.

CHAPTER 1

MISSIO DEI

*Renewing relationships begins when His mission
reshapes our desire and prepares us
for a better one alongside Him.*

Every year since 1950, people have decided to leave the dominant faith in America. The interesting point is that they are not publicly changing their faith. It's not a priority or value anymore. I often wonder why some people go to church or temple or the mosque while others don't or won't? I've heard people say:

- People are busier these days.
- There are more family activities on the weekends.
- There are children's sports on the weekends.
- We only get two days off, so why would I want to spend it in church?
- I get more out of reading my Bible alone than I do going to a church.
- I commune better with God when I'm in nature.
- The local church seems more concerned with ancillary issues than fostering my relationship with God.

All these comments are real for some and excuses for others. However, my point is that the riddle of why people don't value coming together never gets solved.

The Jesus I read about was about introducing others to His Dad. He was about relationship. He spent extensive amounts of time with God. He humbled Himself to be a servant. He modeled it for three years with twelve apprentices. He took them everywhere and showed them everything they would need to know before they asked. He demonstrated that love in action equals relationship. It was the type of relationship that stimulated a desire to know more in the hopes of encountering a living God.

Missio Dei means "the mission of God". Many believe this is the story behind the story. God's will for us all is that all would come to know Him. The word "know" is not just information. It recognizes our need to grow in our understanding and experience of the relationship, so we can discern when and where to get involved. An involvement that puts into play the two greatest commands (love God and love others) so the people around us will open their hearts to the possibilities that God's love has for them.

What does it mean to love someone? The Greeks had multiple words for love, but in English we have "love." As a result, songwriters have struggled with this topic for years. Love is just too hard to define. However, one thing is for certain, love is the cornerstone of every good relationship. It's as true for the people you meet, as the God you revere.

The larger question is how we can best live "love" as a lifestyle. Discovering this is what RENEW is all about.

We can never give away what we do not have. If you are good relationally today, you are an anomaly. It is the most critical aspect of being successful and yet so many are terrible at being in a relationship with others. We're not talking about being an extrovert or an introvert. We are referring to the ability to demonstrate love for another in a way they feel valued, known and heard. Social media is a great advancement in the use of technology. It's useful for keeping connected to those in your social circles, but it doesn't foster authentic relationships or personal growth, unless you consider emojis a growth area. Rarely does a person share their most intimate thoughts online. They share what they want the world to hear or see. The motives behind a post or picture or video are fascinating, but you will never discover the truth about an individual without first talking with them, belly button to belly button. Trust is hard to develop electronically. We can argue about the power of teleconferencing but ask a person to close a multi-million-dollar deal over SKYPE or ZOOM and my point will be made. Trust is formed when people gather. The most precious aspects of any of our lives require us to be in relationship.

RENEW is founded on the vision that to discover a life worth living, you must first be in relationship with both God and others. Once either relationship begins, the authentic and compassionate nature of human beings fosters a greater understanding of the world around us.

Everything we do at RENEW is about fostering growing relationships. We gather around a table to eat because it lowers the barrier to interaction with others. We provide topic cards for an easy opening. We then move into a time we've called the "experience" so people can get themselves centered in the peace, joy and hope of this life. We offer music, art and a story to help everyone begin to think more critically before we break out into smaller affinity discussion groups. The experience is also about diffusing the tension of the world and infusing an everyday topic with a spiritual twist through the intersection of a spiritual and physical consideration. The final component is service. We encourage each person who comes to RENEW to serve somewhere. It could be the neighbor down the block, the local mission or another not-for-profit. We recognize God works in these areas every day. He fosters our relationship with Him in these times and helps us to continue the expansion of our relationships, so others might discover a life through living as well.

It really is the most basic of concepts. It's easy to say and far more difficult to follow through because, inevitably, if it's of God there will come a time *when it gets hard.* This is not a bad omen but a realistic one. It's the moment the flesh (our will) begins to fight against God's will. This is not the time to disconnect. These are the moments to walk in faith. As the folks in recovery say, "don't quit before the miracle happens." In the same sense, don't stop the renewing of your heart, mind, soul and strength when the near future looks tough. This is when the real renewal begins because it reshapes your desire or prepares you for a better one.

The group discussion guide for this topic is in Appendix A on page 342.

CHAPTER 2

UNCONDITIONAL LOVE

*Loving God and others
is an action of perpetual creation*

What does it mean to love someone, something or some activity?

It can't all be the same. I can't love chocolate the same way I love my son. I can't love lifting weights the same way I love serving others. I can't love getting every green light on the way to work the same way I love hearing my wife laugh. I can't love the smells of a beautiful summer morning the same way I love a clean car. It just doesn't seem right.

The Greeks had multiple words for love, but in English we just have "love." Song writers have struggled with this topic for years. I think it's because when we hear the word "love," we get so tangled up in emotions, we are not sure what to make of the word. As the saying goes, "Love is many splendored thing" with "many" being the focal point. Love is just too hard to define within our language. However, one thing is for certain, love is the cornerstone of every good relationship. It's as true for the people you meet, as the God you revere.

I have a confession to make. When I was in my teens and my twenties, I walked away from God. I believed the Billy Joel song, "Only the good die young." I believed all those people going to a church building were fools. I believed the media when they used Karl Marx's famous statement, "religion is the opiate of the masses" as a rallying cry that I was smarter than the average bear.[1] I knew if I could just plan better, work harder and catch a few breaks, I would succeed in life. I believed by living this way, the "cosmic baker" would bless whatever I did. It wasn't until I ran so hard that I crashed and burned that I saw the flaws in my philosophy of life.

The soul searching that followed pushed me to answer the question, "If I'm not in control, who is and why are we here?" If you want to talk about a journey, try pondering that question for a while without alcohol or drugs. There are a lot of ideas in the world. However, the one which made the most sense at the time was, "God is love." It was a simple concept with huge ramifications that grew over time.†

Now, there are many through the ages who have wrestled with the statement, "God is love." I was even listening to a Christian radio program recently whereby a teacher/preacher was not happy with this proclamation. He was convinced this statement, like Marx's, was actually a half-truth. A deadly half-truth that God would disagree with and he went on to prove his point using scripture. I wondered as I drove if the person on the radio had ever really loved anyone unconditionally. You see, I believe deep, unconditional love can give us a glimpse of God's love for each of us.

---

1   *Critique of Hegel's Philosophy of Right,* Karl Marx, Cambridge Press, New York, 1970

I'll never forget when my son was small. I was watching him at our home when I turned my back for a minute. I heard a horn honking in the street. I turned to see my son in the street with his nose a few inches from a car bumper. I ran, grabbed him and put him on the driveway, waved to the neighbor and then swatted his rear. I didn't hit him hard enough to hurt him. But I surely scared him and me. I will never forget his look. I then got down on my knees and explained how much I loved him and why it scared me so. It was revolutionary to learn love includes discipline, obedience, sacrifice and even consequences when we reject the love being offered. The Christian understanding of God builds this into its teaching from its primary source, the Bible. It's a love story — but not a sappy love story they make into a movie that your wife or girlfriend makes you go to on date night. It's a real story of a God so confident, perfect, just and loving, that He creates a world out of love, creates plants, animals and yes, even humans. He then watches us fail, like a loving parent watching his youngest learn to ride a bike without training wheels. And then when we fall, he comes to each of us and provides for us out of love.

I want to share with you a little snippet of scripture which has profound implications for all of our faith journeys. It comes from the Bible and it's written by a guy named Mark. Mark was an interesting guy who wrote the facts, and just the facts, as he could remember them of his friend Jesus. Listen to this …

> [28] One of the teachers of the law came and heard them debating. Noticing that Jesus had given them a good answer, he asked him, "Of all the commandments, which is the most important?" [29] "The most important one," answered Jesus, "is this: 'Hear, O Israel: The Lord our God, the Lord is one. [30] Love the Lord your God with all your

heart and with all your soul and with all your mind and with all your strength.'³¹ The second is this: 'Love your neighbor as yourself.' There is no commandment greater than these." ³² "Well said, teacher," the man replied. "You are right in saying that God is one and there is no other but him. ³³ To love him with all your heart, with all your understanding and with all your strength, and to love your neighbor as yourself is more important than all burnt offerings and sacrifices." ³⁴ When Jesus saw that he had answered wisely, he said to him, "You are not far from the Kingdom of God." And from then on no one dared ask him any more questions. Mark 12:29-34 (NIV)

Now, there is a lot in this passage. I want to add some background, so you see this. The Jewish leaders of this era didn't like Jesus or want to believe He was the Messiah. Sure, they were praying He would come for a number of years, but Jesus didn't fit the bill. They believed an all-powerful God would come and free them from oppression and choose them to run the joint. Since Jesus didn't have the right lineage (or so they thought), they discounted Him and just like the whistleblower at the office or a cancer in the body, they wanted Him gone. They proceeded to try to catch him in lie or stating something foolish, so they could discredit Him. It's kind of like our political candidates when they are interviewed. The press asks a question so they can make a headline. The only difference between today's pundits and those of Jesus' time is the question carried more cultural clout. The questions in this text are coming from the community's spiritual leaders.

Jesus is asked by the community leaders, "What's the greatest commandment?" This was always a "talk show" debate back in the day. People would call into radio stations to talk about it. The

Roman comedians of the day would joke about it. However, Jesus was not amused. He shared from the core Jewish teaching, the Shema — words no good Jew would ever forget. They repeated them twice a day. They were the words spoken by God to Moses, so as Jesus answers, you can see every Jew nodding, including the cultural leaders.

The scripture then really pinpoints the Pharisee and Scribe's arrogance, "you are right." I mean, really think about that for a second. The scribe is telling Jesus he got the answer right. Jesus?! The one that more than a billion people claim was God in the flesh? But when I dig a little deeper, we all do the same thing. When God does what we like, we claim he gets it right. But when God doesn't do what we want, we begin to think God must be the one who is wrong. The reality is, we all have a God problem.

We all do it. Truth and confession time: I have been angry at God before. He didn't answer the prayer. He didn't keep me from temptation. In James 1:13-14, *"When tempted, no one should say, 'God is tempting me.' For God cannot be tempted by evil, nor does he tempt anyone; but each person is tempted when they are dragged away by their own evil desire and enticed."* He tells us God will not keep us from temptation. He didn't stop the tragedy. He didn't hear my cries. I developed resentment and you want to know what he did? He watched as I acted like a two-year-old at the grocery store. I would cry, scream, fall on the floor, throw things and act inappropriately. He would stand back. Just waiting for the right moment to ask if I had had enough, was I willing to try it His way?

We don't want to admit the God of the universe is bigger than our understanding of Him. He doesn't need you, your approval, or your understanding of His actions. He loves you unconditionally; He wants you to have a relationship with Him, not for His benefit, but yours.

Once you realize there is a God and you're not Him, the next question is revolutionary. Why did He create us? Some theologians will state He created us out of an abundance of love. An unconditional love that wants more for other than for one's self. The kind of love that inspires the other person so completely that they want to return love and share the love with others. It's the kind of love born out of relationship and that motivates you to reciprocate. You can't help yourself.

I'll never forget a time when a good friend became a great friend. We were both entrepreneurs. He had been at it for a number of years and every time I needed advice, I went to him. One day, I was wrestling with the idea of renting a warehouse and he told me to use his. I asked how much. He offered it for free for three months and then $1,000 dollars a month thereafter, which was about $5,000 below market price. I couldn't believe it. He didn't ask for anything in return. He just wanted to help me. When he was having issues in life and he needed to talk, I didn't think twice about rearranging my schedule. He'd been such a support before, how could I turn him down? The reality is, it never crossed my mind to not be there for him.

You see, loving God is this type of proposition. It's a spiral upward. When I recognize God loves me, I begin to return the love and God is already giving more. If you really want to RENEW your life, you need to recognize God's unconditional love for you, accept it and then get ready to reciprocate. Once you accept His love, get imina in ways you can't even imagine.

The group discussion guide for this topic is in Appendix A on page 343.

CHAPTER 3

FATHER

Jesus lived in relationship with His Father fully knowing His creative power as well as His all-encompassing dignity and so can you!

Have you ever heard the phrase, "What would Jesus do?" There were bracelets made with this phrase on them years ago. This was and is an entire line of Christian trinkets today. People would strive to answer the question according to how they personally believed Jesus would act. Unfortunately, most never consulted anyone on their perception of what Jesus would do in any situation, so a lot of people have done that and justified it with the greatest justification of all: Jesus would do this!

Now, please read this with all the force I can on muster on a page of ink. There were plenty of good deeds done and lives changed because of asking the question. However, I would wager to say a whole host of people never studied how Jesus made decisions or the process by which we might want to consider how to walk through our lives today.

I believe if rubber bracelets were around at the time of Jesus, His might have had one that said, "WWHG" — what will honor God? And for those who are thinking, "well isn't that the same as WWJD?" I would respond no, because Jesus could tell us how He determined every word and action. He prayed. He meditated. He fasted. He understood. He was unwavering. He lived without fear.

If we look at Jesus' actions and teaching, we see He didn't wait for a circumstance to arise to ask the question, like so many of us. Jesus didn't keep God at a distance, like some cosmic "elf on a shelf." He was in conversation with Him daily. He didn't do anything without prayer and meditation. It wasn't a drive-by prayer or a wish list or gossip list but a full or conversation. It was a relational moment between Jesus and His Father. Now, some in the room are looking for the loophole in my logic and already thinking, "Well, I'm not Jesus. I've never heard from God. I feel like I'm yelling in the house and no one is home." To which I would say, a relationship is not founded on commuter calls (a five-minute call until something else gets your attention) or directions on what He should do next — like you have something on the creator of the universe. Jesus was intensely relational with everyone — good and evil. (Read Mark 5:12-16) How's that possible? Let's read on.

Authentic relationships require time and effort. They are forged in the hard times and the tough discussions. Do you remember your first love, the endless conversations, wanting to know everything about them, endless texts, long telephone calls, or times in silence as you sit on the phone trying to reveal one more aspect of their personality? What if there was a manual for that person and you could have had access to it? Would you have read it first, or read it to clarify the things you didn't understand? I believe I would have wanted to read it at some point, so I could have loved them better.

It probably wouldn't have changed how it ended but it might have explained a few of the things that hurt so much.

Jesus had God's playbook. He was intimately connected. We have it, too. He memorized it. He lived it. He wore the bracelet (*WWID — What would I do?*). Jesus was so in tune with God he used the term "Abba," a familiar term which means daddy. Jesus never addressed God as the almighty God or infinite or eternal one. He was connected. He understood the role he was to play in the spiritual war being waged. He constantly wanted to please the Father because He knew him. He chose to live in this type of relationship fully knowing God's creative power as well as His all-encompassing divinity.

Jesus lived in reverence, which means filled with awe. The cool part is we can, too. How, you ask?

Simple. Renew your approach. Try just spending some quiet time with Him. Turn off the media stimulation for a few days or weeks or months. Read a book about Him. Visualize Him in the room with you. Speak your doubts, concerns and even what you find hard to believe. Confess your heart — positive and negative. Afterward, sit silently with eyes closed listening to the sounds of life around you. Ask Him to reveal himself over the next few days and then look for His hand in every facet of your life. He is ever-present. The psalmist says, all of nature screams His glory.

If renewing your life is the goal, then establishing an authentic relationship with God is the key.

The group discussion guide for this topic is in Appendix A on page 345.

CHAPTER 4

PRAYER

Prayer offers us the opportunity to dialog with God

A man's daughter had asked the local pastor to come and pray with her father. When the pastor arrived, he found the man lying in bed with his head propped up on two pillows and an empty chair beside his bed. The priest assumed that the old fellow had been informed of his visit.

"I guess you were expecting me," he said.

"No, who are you?"

"I'm the new pastor at your local church," the pastor replied. "When I saw the empty chair, I figured you knew I was going to show up."

"Oh yeah, the chair," said the bedridden man. "Would you mind closing the door?"

Puzzled, the pastor shut the door. "I've never told anyone this, not even my daughter," said the man. "But all of my life I have never known how to pray. At church I used to hear the pastor talk about prayer, but it always went right over my head."

"*I abandoned any attempt at prayer,*" the old man continued. "*Until one day, about four years ago, my best friend said to me, 'Joe, prayer is just a simple matter of having a conversation with Jesus. Here's what I suggest. Sit down on a chair, place an empty chair in front of you, and in faith see Jesus on the chair. It's not spooky because He promised, 'I'll be with you always.' Then just speak to Him and listen in the same way you're doing with me right now.'*"

"*So, I tried it and I've liked it so much that I do it a couple of hours every day. I'm careful, though. If my daughter saw me talking to an empty chair, she'd either have a nervous breakdown or send me off to the funny farm.*" The pastor was deeply moved by the story and encouraged the old guy to continue the journey. Then he prayed with him and returned to the church. Two nights later the daughter called to tell the pastor that her daddy had died that afternoon.

"*Did he seem to die in peace?*" he asked.

"*Yes, when I left the house around two o'clock, he called me over to his bedside, told me one of his corny jokes, and kissed me on the cheek. When I got back from the store an hour later, I found him dead. But there was something strange. In fact, beyond strange — kind of weird. Apparently, just before Daddy died, he leaned over and rested his head on a chair beside the bed.*"[2]

Do you pray? Is your prayer life so real you see Him in the room? Does the creator of the universe respond?

There's a great Alcoholics Anonymous saying, "The only ones who don't believe in prayer, are those who have never tried it." If

---

2   Source: unknown.

you've tried prayer and the results didn't meet your expectation, I would like to make a few suggestions to help you renew your connection to the greatest power in the universe:

Prayer requires:
1. ***Intimacy.*** God wants more than few random comments from us to Him. He wants us to have an active relationship with Him. He wants to spend time with you and me, both individually and collectively. Do you miss your time with Him when you fail to stop and connect? Did you know studies have shown multitasking dramatically reduces your ability to concentrate on the objective? So, praying and driving might not be really praying. When someone talks to you and looks over your shoulder, do you feel they are engaged with you?
2. ***Humility.*** God is not a personal genie. He is the creator of the universe. We should stand in awe of His power and recognize who we are coming before. Personally, I love getting on my knees or even spread out on the floor. I'm an experiential learner. By kneeling or lying prostrate, I've created a submission moment. It is a physical action whereby I say I am not God and if He wills, He can take me out.
3. ***Purity of heart (motivation).*** Prayer rarely is about my will or my neighbor's wish but about knowing and doing God's will for the expanse of the Kingdom. I've prayed for people to live and for healing to occur only to be disappointed. I've later realized

my motivation for the prayer was not for the King but for me. I wanted the person to live because I didn't know what life would be like without them. I was afraid.

4. **Faith/trust**. When you pray, do you believe God always answers? Be honest here. When you pray for your neighbor's cat, do you really think God is listening or cares? When you pray for a sporting event result, do you believe God cares? Do you believe or are you praying because it's the last chance? A Hail Mary pass to heaven hoping God catches this one?

5. **Unity**. Prayer is the tool the creator of the universe gives us to communicate with Him and come to know how we can best walk with him to do his will.

6. **Longing for a God's response.** Have you ever prayed and thought there is no way this will come true? Lottery? A cancer ridden relative? Our logic sometimes gets in the way of our faith. Logic is built on a set of known aspects of life, most of which are temporal or physical in nature. However, the spiritual realm does not work under these constraints. It has its own set of guidelines. We have theories, but they are just that: theory.

7. **Consistency and vigilance**. Does the person who calls once a year know you? Does the relative who you see at the family reunion know your needs? Relationships require consistency and vigilance. It's the same with prayer — regularity and persistence.

8. **Pause.** Relationships are fostered when we set aside time to listen. "Drive-by" prayer doesn't offer this moment of reflection so be cognizant of your willingness to share your heart. I will never forget a good friend passing me in the hall as I said, "how are you?" He turned and asked, "do you really want to know?" Relationships require a willingness to spend time listening.

Prayer is the cornerstone to renew your relationship with God. Prayer is our opportunity to dialog with God — the creator of the Universe. It's our excuse to come before Jesus — the redeemer of our souls. It's our chance to call upon the Holy Spirit to intervene. So, don't delay. Take five minutes right now. There is a one-week prayer challenge in Appendix B (4) if you would like a quick start guide. Otherwise, pray for the needs of the nation, the community, your family and then listen for the small still voice. God wants to renew the relationship by hearing from you.

The group discussion guide for this topic is in Appendix A on page 346.

RENEW

CHAPTER 5

WILL OF GOD

Jesus is calling us to assist Him with the 'in-breaking' of the Kingdom now and throughout eternity.

I grew up in a great family. My dad had a great job and my mom stayed home with us kids. We were the stereotypical suburban middle-class family. We had a nice house; two cars and we took two week vacations every summer. The key phrase I heard growing up was, "you can do anything in this life if you work hard enough." It probably came from my dad and his father because they both lived and worked their way out of poverty and the Depression by building homes. I inherited this attitude, so it's no wonder I grew up with the theology of "pray to God but row towards shore." That is, believe in God, but you still have some personal responsibility to make life good. I owned the hat, "Life is Good" and I am sure my friends thought it was glued to my head to hide my ever-receding hairline at the time. But what does the phrase "life is good" mean? Before I was a Christian and maybe even for some time later, I'm not sure I really knew. I can remember when I owned my business looking at the profit ledger at the end of the month and thinking, "Is this all there is?" You see,

> For a capitalist, the goal is to make money or a profit.
> For the narcissist, it's to receive accolades.
> For the moralist, it's about being good.
> For the spiritualist, it's about finding enlightenment or peace or light.
> For the environmentalist, it's about taking care of all that is on the planet.
> For the hedonist, it's about pleasure.
> For the humanist, it's about being the best kind of human you can be.

And yet, none of these ways to living life, really end up — as Blaise Pascal said — *"able to fill the deepest yearning in our soul."*[3] They each leave us wanting. They don't really do anything other than occupy us. It's like mankind has this internal craving and in order to fill it, western society creates a series of different Sit 'n Spin games to keep us busy. Do you remember Sit 'n Spin? It's the game you pull on one side and move around in a circle but go nowhere. You feel like you're doing something because there is movement, sometimes there's laughter and even a sense of purpose. However, you never really get anywhere. The Sit n' Spin

---

[3] "What else does this craving, and this helplessness, proclaim but that there was once in man a true happiness, of which all that now remains is the empty print and trace? This he tries in vain to fill with everything around him, seeking in things that are not there the help he cannot find in those that are, though none can help, since this infinite abyss can be filled only with an infinite and immutable object; in other words, by God himself."
Blaise Pascal, Pensües VII (425)

is the perfect example of many of our lives. So, why do we feel stuck? Why aren't we moving forward? Why aren't we successful? Because we fail to pursue God's will for our life.

So, what is the will of God for us?

The scripture in John 6 gives us an answer; let me provide a little background to the writing that follows. Jesus fed 5,000, prayed for his disciples, walked on water, moved the boat to safety without anyone noticing and practiced direct communication with the Messianic tribe that had been stalking Him. In this conversation, Jesus uses the image of the bread and their hunger to make a point about His ability to fulfill their deepest desires. John 6: 34-40 says,

> Sir," they said, "always give us this bread." Then Jesus declared, "I am the bread of life. Whoever comes to me will never go hungry, and whoever believes in me will never be thirsty. [36] But as I told you, you have seen me and still you do not believe. [37] All those the Father gives me will come to me, and whoever comes to me I will never drive away. [38] For I have come down from heaven not to do my will but to do the will of him who sent me. [39] And this is the will of him who sent me that I shall lose none of all those he has given me but raise them up at the last day. For my Father's will is that everyone who looks to the Son and believes in him shall have eternal life, and I will raise them up at the last day." (NIV)

The reality is clear. God is not a capitalist, communist or socialist. Jesus is trying to make the point that He is the fulfillment of the Jewish prophecy, the Messiah, the Lord and the Son of God. The good news being communicated in this gospel passage is that the time has come whereby Jesus is calling all who claim to be followers of His, to also be participants into the in-breaking of the Kingdom now and throughout eternity.

Out of the passage we just read, there are four distinct ideas that Jesus discussed that we need to elaborate upon.

1. *"For I have come down from heaven not to do my will but to do the will of him who sent me."* Jesus did not come to make people religious, but to fulfill God's will for all creation.
2. *"And this is the will of him who sent me that I shall lose none of all those he has given me, but raise them up at the last day."* God's will is that none of those who come to Christ will be lost. In fact, he is quite specific.
3. *"For my Father's will is that everyone who looks to the Son and believes in him ..."* All those who look to Jesus and believe in Him (that is, place their trust in Him as demonstrated by their worship, obedience and the receiving of the Holy Spirit's empowering presence).
4. *"... shall have eternal life, and I will raise them up at the last day."* We will not only have this abundant life in the here and now, but also be raised up by Jesus at the final judgment.

Christian faith is not a lifestyle issue, it's a matter of the heart; it's a surrender of one's will. It's not as simple as choosing shoes or music or which color you like best. Jesus came, suffered, died, and rose again for all of us so through our belief and repentance we shall know Him intimately. So, the question is, how? How do I live out the will of the God who created me, died for me and who restores me?

I think there are three components which are interwoven in our lives to help raise and sustain our faith:

- Devoted: This is placing your relationship with Jesus at the top of the priority list. An hour of private study is a great start; however, why settle for little when there is so much more? A great start would be to review Chapter 4 on prayer and commit to adding more.
- Relational: This is a life where other people are more than just acquaintances. It means diving into a life where you get to know folks. As a friend of mine says, if you don't stick out your paw, you will never touch or be touched in this life. You have to be willing to invest in others. Remember, Jesus simplified the mission to unconditionally love God and others.
- Kindness: This has a lot to do with our time, talents and resources, but it has more to do with our hearts. I will never forget a great volunteer and friend saying to me once, as we served together, "you really can't out give God can you?" Every time I try, He rewards me more than I could ever imagine with exactly what I needed.

A *renewed* life is one where we realize God's will for us is to fulfill His call on our life. We must believe God is bigger than our dreams, our stuff and even the hole in our soul.

The group discussion guide for this topic is in Appendix A on page 348.

RENEW

CHAPTER 6

SOCIETY

Our role as we emulate Him is to live among the individuals he places in our lives to demonstrate His love!

How would you classify many people you call friends? How many friends do you have who are Christian? Muslim? Jehovah? Mormon? How many come from other countries or ethnic backgrounds?

Here are four interesting facts about our society as a whole:

1. America is less culturally diverse than you might think. Although on pace to be a "majority-minority" country by the early 2040s, wherein no one ethnic group dominates the population as Caucasians long have, studies show America is not particularly diverse on a linguistic, ethnic or cultural level, compared with many other countries.

2. Among developed nations with complete, reliable statistics, the U.S. has the highest teen pregnancy rate, according to a recent report from the

Guttmacher Institute. Statistically, out of 1,000 girls ages 15 to 19, 57 percent are pregnant at any given time.

3. The United States incarcerates more people than any other country. According to the International Centre for Prison Studies, the country currently has more than 2.2 million people behind bars. That works out to about 22 percent of the total global population of inmates, shocking when considering that the U.S. supports just 4.4 percent of the world's population.

4. A 2014 study in the journal *The Lancet* confirmed, again, that the U.S. is the most overweight country on Earth. Compared with 38 percent of men and 36.9 percent of women worldwide who are overweight or obese, 70.9 percent of men and 61.9 percent of women fall into that category in the United States.

5. Each American throws out about 4.4 pounds (2 kilograms) of trash every single day, according to the Environmental Protection Agency's latest 2012 figures. When the country's population is accounted for, that means some 1.4 billion pounds (635 million kg) of trash gets tossed in the U.S. daily.[4]

Don't all these statistics almost make you want to pack up and go to a secluded place? Renewing our lives and history has proven this unwise.

---

4   https://www.livescience.com/51448-startling-facts-about-american-culture.html

"The Holy men of the middle ages deemed the deepest knowledge of God incompatible with a free life among men. They withdrew, accordingly, from the movements of the world, and in cloister, cell and cave sought the Holy life. 'The greatest saints,' says Thomas A Kempis, 'avoided the society of men when they could conveniently, and did rather choose to live to God in secret.' And he goes on to quote the saying of Seneca, 'As often as I have been among men, I returned home less a man than I was before.'"[5]

While this is a true statement, would we be more spiritual beings if we segregated ourselves? I would suggest the answer is "*!#@ no!". In truth, being in society with all its foibles forces us to rely more deeply on our connection to God, Jesus and the Holy Spirit. The hardship of being around selfish and self-centered people forces us to lean into God. Jesus provided a perfect example.

Throughout His ministry on earth, Jesus maintained a connection with the Father so He would know the highest and the best. As such, he moved freely among all men and seemed comfortable in all of creation's presence.

Jesus didn't seclude himself from the world. He walked within it as a regular man with family and friends from a small town. We only need to look at where He began. His first miracle was at a family wedding. The scriptures say:

---

5 *The Principles of Jesus*, Robert E. Speer, The Westminster Press, Chicago, 1902 p.25

On the third day, a wedding took place at Cana in Galilee. Jesus' mother was there, **2** and Jesus and his disciples had also been invited to the wedding. **3** When the wine was gone, Jesus' mother said to him, "They have no more wine."**4** "Woman, why do you involve me?" Jesus replied. "My hour has not yet come."**5** His mother said to the servants, "Do whatever he tells you." **6** Nearby stood six stone water jars, the kind used by the Jews for ceremonial washing, each holding from twenty to thirty gallons. **7** Jesus said to the servants, "Fill the jars with water"; so they filled them to the brim. **8** Then he told them, "Now draw some out and take it to the master of the banquet." They did so, **9** and the master of the banquet tasted the water that had been turned into wine. He did not realize where it had come from, though the servants who had drawn the water knew. Then he called the bridegroom aside **10** and said, "Everyone brings out the choice wine first and then the cheaper wine after the guests have had too much to drink; but you have saved the best till now."**11** What Jesus did here in Cana of Galilee was the first of the signs through which he revealed his glory; and his disciples believed in him. John 2:1-11 (NIV)

Jesus was not a party animal. He's not pictured in a toga because he lived a fraternity house lifestyle. He was a normal guy who loved those around Him. They worked with Him. They knew Him as a carpenter. He was Joseph's son from "over by there." (Chicago Grawboski accent preferred.) (Check out Luke 15:8-10, 14:34-35; John 2:24-25; Luke 5:29-30, 15:1-2; Matt. 11:19; Luke 7:34.)

SOCIETY

He was a little different than most. He always did what He said He would. He had a peace about Him. He was not afraid of the political and religious elite. This persona would sometimes get him into dispute. He was greeted with anger, criticized for helping the poor and outcasts. He owned the label glutton and drunk as well as a friend of sinners. What labels ring true for you?

Here's what Luke wrote about one of his encounters:

[36] When one of the Pharisees invited Jesus to have dinner with him, he went to the Pharisee's house and reclined at the table. [37] A woman in that town who lived a sinful life learned that Jesus was eating at the Pharisee's house, so she came there with an alabaster jar of perfume. [38] As she stood behind him at his feet weeping, she began to wet his feet with her tears. Then she wiped them with her hair, kissed them and poured perfume on them. [39] When the Pharisee who had invited him saw this, he said to himself, "If this man were a prophet, he would know who is touching him and what kind of woman she is—that she is a sinner." [40] Jesus answered him, "Simon, I have something to tell you." "Tell me, teacher," he said. [41] "Two people owed money to a certain moneylender. One owed him five hundred denarii, and the other fifty. [42] Neither of them had the money to pay him back, so he forgave the debts of both. Now which of them will love him more?" [43] Simon replied, "I suppose the one who had the bigger debt forgiven." "You have judged correctly," Jesus said. [44] Then he turned toward the woman and said to Simon, "Do you see this woman? I came into your house. You did not give me any water for my feet, but

she wet my feet with her tears and wiped them with her hair. [45] You did not give me a kiss, but this woman, from the time I entered, has not stopped kissing my feet. [46] You did not put oil on my head, but she has poured perfume on my feet. [47] Therefore, I tell you, her many sins have been forgiven—as her great love has shown. But whoever has been forgiven little loves little."[48] Then Jesus said to her, "Your sins are forgiven." [49] The other guests began to say among themselves, "Who is this who even forgives sins?" [50] Jesus said to the woman, "Your faith has saved you; go in peace." Luke 7:36-50 (NIV)

Jesus recognized those of position and status. He did not favor them even though He had empathy for them. He never compromised His standards for their respect. His compassion was reserved for those who had been undone by life. The overarching will of God is for all His creation to know Him and live accordingly. Our role, as we emulate Him, is to live among the individuals He places in our lives to demonstrate His love!

Jesus leaned into His Father to Renew the world He encountered daily. Do you lean in?

The group discussion guide for this topic is in Appendix A on page 350.

CHAPTER 7

DEFECTS OF CHARACTER

Character defects or sins are a search for perfection in an imperfect world and body. Our renewal is dependent on our willingness to shed our personal desires for God's.

Have you ever done something or said something so out of your character that you later wince in shame, guilt or remorse as you remember it? If you haven't, I need to get to know you more because I have. I must admit I still have wincing moments even as someone who likes to think of himself as a Christian. When I do something I regret or feel ashamed of, I often find myself hearing the voice from the Talking Heads song, "How Did I Get Here?" What led me to this place? What were the rationalizations and justifications I used to believe it was okay? What was underneath the surface at the time?

Now, don't get me wrong. This willingness to go deeper to the root cause did not come naturally. There was a time in my life when I *wanted to make everything I did* either someone else's fault or demonic. I wanted to blame others for my predicaments or say the devil made me do it! The interesting piece of that strategy is it fails to pinpoint the one constant, ME, ME, ME! By always making it someone else's issue or the devil, I didn't have to take responsibility for my part. Yes. It kept my belief about myself intact, but it failed to allow in my evolution as a growing follower of Jesus.

In 1995, Harvey Keitel and William Hurt starred in a movie called Smoke. Harvey Keitel plays Auggie Wren, the owner of a tobacco store, Brooklyn Tobacco Co., which sits on the corner of Third and Seventh Streets in Brooklyn. One of Auggie's closest friends is a writer by the name of Paul Benjamin, played by William Hurt. At the end of the movie, Paul Benjamin, the writer, tells Auggie that he's been asked to write a Christmas story for the New York Times, but he's stumped. What's he going to write about? Auggie says, "I've got lots of Christmas stories. In fact, I've got a great Christmas story. Buy me lunch and I'll tell it to you."

Paul buys Auggie lunch and Auggie tells his story. "It's about me" says Auggie. "One day, I'm in my shop" — the Brooklyn Tobacco Co. on the corner of Third and Seventh — "when I notice a kid in the act of stealing a girly magazine from the shelf up the back of the store. I call out and the kid bolts for the door and starts running away. So I chase him." While he's running, something falls out of the thief's pocket onto the sidewalk. It's his wallet. Auggie stops running and picks it up. It's got the thief's driver's license inside. Now Auggie's got his name and address. The only other thing the wallet contains is three photographs. One of them is the thief as a young boy with his mother. It softens Auggie's attitude. This is just a kid who lives in a poor part of the town, who's struggled all his life to get by. So Auggie decides not to go to the police. Instead, he takes the wallet home and puts it on the shelf. And there it sits.

A couple of years later it's Christmas day. Auggie's got no friends or family to celebrate with, so he's sitting at home and his eyes fall on that young thief's wallet sitting on the shelf. "What the heck," he thinks. "I'm going to go around to that kid's place and give him his wallet back." So, he heads downtown, 'til he comes to the address on the driver's license. He walks up to a rundown building, rings the doorbell and waits. After a few moments he hears some shuffling, then an old woman's voice, "Yes, who's there?" I'm looking for Robert," says Auggie. "Robert" replies the woman. "Is that you Robert? I knew you wouldn't forget your Granny Joe on Christmas day."

She flings the door open and Auggie can see she's an old woman who's almost completely blind. She opens her arms wide, and next thing Auggie knows she's hugging him. "I knew you'd come Robert. I knew you wouldn't disappoint your old Gran." Well, what's he supposed to do? "What the heck" thinks Auggie, "I've got nothing better to do today. I'll play along." "Yes Gran, it's me, Robert."

He can tell by the look on her face that she knows it's not her grandson Robert, but she's living all alone and seems to need some company. So, she decides to play along, too. She welcomes Auggie in, and for the rest of the afternoon Auggie pretends to be her grandson Robert. He tells her how he's got a good job now, that he owns his own store, that he's met a lovely girl and they're going to be married. All this brings a smile to her face and she replies, "That's fine Robert, that's fine." Auggie decides to make lunch for the two of them, but when he goes to the cupboard he finds Granny Joe has no food. So he goes down the road and buys a chicken and bread rolls and salads, and brings it back for them to have lunch together. They open a bottle of wine Granny Joe has lying about and spend a wonderful afternoon together, Auggie still pretending to be her grandson Robert, and she pretending to believe he really is her grandson.

Later in the afternoon, Auggie needs to go to the toilet. He walks down the hallway till he finds the bathroom. He goes in, and as he's relieving himself he notices a stack of six Polaroid cameras by the window. Brand new, still the box. Six of them. He thinks to himself, "I've never had a camera before, but I'd love to have one." In a moment of decision, he decides to take one of the cameras. After all, the old woman won't know. She's blind; she's got no use for them. So, he picks up one of the cameras and heads back to the lounge room. When he gets there, Granny Joe has fallen asleep. He decides to let her sleep. He washes the dishes, cleans up the kitchen, picks up his coat and the camera, and walks out the door.

From that day on he starts taking photos of his shop, the Brooklyn Tobacco Co., on the corner of Third and Seventh. Every morning at exactly 8:00 a.m., whatever the weather, he walks across the road and takes his photo. Over fourteen years, he documents life in his little corner of the world. It becomes his hobby, his life's work.

A few years after the Christmas he stole the camera, Auggie decides to go and see Granny Joe again, to apologize for stealing the camera. But she's no longer living there. He guesses she's died, but his guilt pangs have not died with her. Fourteen years later as Auggie Wren tells his story to his friend Paul Benjamin the writer, he still feels guilty and ashamed for stealing that camera. The story says something about all of us, not just Auggie Wren. It captures the human dilemma. On the one hand, we're capable of extraordinary acts of love and generosity, like Auggie's gift of his presence to an old woman on a cold Christmas Day. But on the other hand, we're capable, in the same moment, of extraordinary selfishness, like Auggie when he steals a camera from the house *of a lonely old blind woman. In Auggie we see ourselves, in all our glory and all our shame.*[6]

Sin is not merely a sickness or a disease (although it has those characteristics). It is the use of God's gifts gone astray. The New Testament word for it is "missing the mark."

Recovery programs use the words "defect of character" because the founder knew that new people in recovery have/had a problem with God, as well as the idea of sin. To put the two words or concepts together would put them over the edge. So, being the wordsmith Bill Wilson (founder of Alcoholics Anonymous) was, he chose the words "defect of character" or "shortcomings" in some of the AA literature. I like "defects of character" because it suggests the same malady the story outlined. It's a defect in our thinking and understanding. We can be good one minute and troubled the next.

Character defects (or sin) are our wants of perception: It is a want for a completeness of life, a want for a change of environment, a want for a connection with something greater. Sin is a search for perfection in an imperfect world and body. It is open rebellion and an affront to God that we finite beings can ever fully know what God's will is for this place. It's the reason He came to us in the flesh. God broke through the veil of the spiritual to the physical, as Jesus, so that we would know the truth of this life (that there is more than what we see) and while we are here, a relationship with God through His son Jesus is possible. And if we're to be forgiven for our defects of character, then we must be willing to confess our shortcomings with another human and then be accepting of the offer of grace and mercy only He can provide.

---

6   *1001 Movies You Must See Before You Die*, 7th edition, A Quintessential Book, London, 2003, p. 839

We have learned that to renew a person's life requires an acceptance of one's defects, a willingness to humbly share those defects and to live in the solution. The recovery community does this exceptionally well though a personal moral inventory. They often refer to this as doing Step Four. The moral inventory requires a person write down all of their resentments, fears, sexual conduct and deep, dark secrets. After the initial attempt, it's suggested a person review the list looking for where the writer may have had a part to play in the event or relationship. It's recommended this exercise be shepherded by a knowledgeable guide and then eventually shared out loud. This process with another human is considered critical in discovering and overcoming the deepest of issues. In the New Testament, James suggests this action for all. It is deeply freeing, genuinely empowering and overwhelmingly spiritual. Becoming transparent to others and being willing to expose these defects as part of our lives places oneself on the forefront of renewing one's soul and discovering a life worth living.

The group discussion guide for this topic is in Appendix A on page 352.

CHAPTER 8

TEMPTATION

*Jesus never sought temptation,
but when it came, He relied on the Father to overcome.*

In the previous chapter, we learned sin is a part of our humanity. It's a search for perfection in an imperfect world and body. Sin is the refusal of the offer of all He came to earth for. It is open rebellion and an affront to God that only Jesus can forgive when we are willing to confess and be accepting of His forgiveness. This week, we discuss the other aspect of the sin equation, temptation.

In the spirituality breakout group, we started down the road of temptation and testing. What is the difference? Who's behind the temptation or test? Is it me, God or some other Spirit who tempts or tests? I'll come back to this, but first, we need to admit to ourselves that we are all drawn to different objects, actions and individuals for internal reasons.

The definition of temptation is:
1. a desire to do something, especially something wrong or unwise.

synonyms: desire, urge, itch, impulse, inclination

2. a thing or course of action that attracts or tempts someone.

synonyms: lure, allurement, enticement, seduction, attraction, draw, pull

Temptation is the desire to obtain that which you do not currently have. Its pursuit can cause serious internal and external issues.

There was great story from early 2001 that demonstrates this point. It was then that in India several villages were stricken by a plague of monkeys. The monkeys were so numerous they would invade homes, bite people and make off with food supplies. It was agreed the monkeys would have to be caught and relocated. The people in these towns resorted to a traditional method for catching them. They gathered their old milk bottles, tied them to the ground, and then placed something sweet, such as a lollipop, inside the bottle. Then, when a monkey came along and saw the sweet, he would place his hand inside the bottle. With the sweet enclosed in his palm, his fist was too big to get back out the bottle. The monkey would pull and push in an effort to get that sweet out, but he would not let it go, not even as his captors approached. And so the monkey was caught, literally with his hand in the candy jar!

Temptations in this life offer much of the same predicament. We, you and I, like the monkey, are presented with an attractive offer; we sometimes seize it even though we have seen others fail, and we won't let go until it destroys us.

Why do some let go and others do not? The answer lies in our truest desire(s). What would you trade your spiritual life for?

A great spiritual father once wrote: "For everything in the world—the lust of the flesh, the lust of the eyes, and the pride of life—comes not from the Father but from the world" (1 John 2:16 NIV)

Temptation comes because of our desire or will. Yes. There are forces which whisper, "it will be okay. Go ahead. It will all turn out in the end." They are everywhere. Subtle. Overt. Covert. Even downright bold. All trying to get you and me to believe this is person, place, thing, experience is what's missing. If only I had ...

So how do we overcome the temptation? How do we pass the test? What's the difference? First, the test of one's faith deals with our ability to be obedient when we are in Christ. We reject our wants in favor of God's direction. A test helps us see our relationship in a new light. A temptation comes from an external force and requires a surrender of your desire and will in favor of God's. You will have to surrender something you believe might bring you the piece that fills the void we all feel at the time.

- Satan tempts us to bring out the worst in us, but God tests us to bring out the best in us.
- Temptation will usually attack a weak spot; trials test our strength, as well as exposing a weakness we may have been unaware of.
- Temptations come from within; trials are sent from God. Therefore, when we speak of "trial," we see God's fingerprints; when we see temptation, we see our own—or the devil's.[7]

James 1:12-15 (NIV) offers the following in support of these comments:

---

7 http://www.charismamag.com/blogs/1524-spirit/devotionals/by-love-transformed/8578-the-difference-between-trials-and-temptations

[12] Blessed is the one who perseveres under trial because, having stood the test, that person will receive the crown of life that the Lord has promised to those who love him. [13] When tempted, no one should say, "God is tempting me." For God cannot be tempted by evil, nor does he tempt anyone; [14] but each person is tempted when they are dragged away by their own evil desire and enticed. [15] Then, after desire has conceived, it gives birth to sin; and sin, when it is full-grown, gives birth to death.

There is a story in the book I love to read of Jesus who came face to face with temptation. He was physically and mentally drained. How could He not be, He had been fasting in the desert for forty days. In this state,

1. He was enticed to use His own power to meet his needs. He rejected it on the knowledge that the Spiritual is more important than the physical.
2. A second time he was enticed. This time it was to force God to do a miracle to help. He rejected this suggestion through an understanding that God is not required to act on our suggestions. Jesus knew when we are in the will of God, God will protect us.
3. Finally, a third time, Jesus is enticed to take a shortcut to Kingship. He need only worship the created being. Jesus rejected the shortcut knowing/ believing the Father had more in store for Him. (Matt. 4:1-11)

The interesting point to the story is that this was not the end to the temptation. It would come again in different forms and during His final evening on earth. (Matt. 16:21-23)

TEMPTATION

Jesus never sought temptation, but it came. We should be aware temptation is a part of this life, whether a believer or not.

So, what is the secret of how to overcome temptation? It's an understanding that the will of God requires study of the word of God, an ongoing relationship with God and practical service for God to know when to surrender so we can be confident of His power in our lives. If you really want to renew your life, you must decide to choose Jesus over and above everything and everyone else.

Being connected to the Father ensures our strength to persevere and overcome and a renewing of one's life.

The group discussion guide for this topic is in Appendix A on page 354

RENEW

CHAPTER 9

POLITICS

Christ followers operate under an alternative understanding of governance which offers both freedom and challenges.

It seems we have forgotten that as a Christian, it doesn't matter who you voted for because as a follower of Jesus, you will eventually be at odds with the establishment.

Politics (from Greek: Politikó: Politika, definition "affairs of the cities") is the process of making decisions applying to all members of each group. More narrowly, it refers to achieving and exercising positions of governance — organized control over a human community, particularly a state. In its most basic sense, those who are participating in this process are called on to be servant (to serve) to the greater good or the populous.[8]

I was driving down the road and read a church sign with one of those sermons on a sign. The sign said, "It doesn't matter who is elected president, Jesus is still King!" At first, I thought it was a great

---

8   https://en.wikipedia.org/wiki/Politic

statement. However, I began to think about the person who has never been to church, who has been burned by church or who is of a different faith. The sign makes no sense and furthers the divide. The culture doesn't understand the story of God wanting the Jewish nation in 1060 BC to just have Him as their king and have the justice system administered by religious judges who had God as their ultimate authority. Most people driving by probably didn't know the people couldn't handle *not* having a human ruler. They wanted to be like every other nation, so God gave them *what they prayed for* and this time it was a human king who failed. And then another. And another. And another. Until God had enough and that it was time to set it right. Jesus, a true King, who serves instead of being served. A king who dies for His people and rises to make it clear who's really in control and there's more to live for than what we see and touch. A king whose Holy Spirit lives on through those who claim Him.

The origin of all governance exists to better serve. As followers of Jesus, we must look to serve others. How? Let's turn to the example as given to us in the accounts of His life.

First, **we** show Jesus is king by supporting the system in place that governs our society even with its flaws. Jesus, even when brought to trial by both ruling bodies of his time (religious and secular), let his actions speak. He didn't miraculously manipulate the system. He stood trial knowing it was a sham. And He was cleared of all three charges (Luke 23). Jesus remained a good citizen even though He knew the corrupt nature of human governance and knew it would cost Him His life.

Second, **we** show Jesus is King by obeying the laws and standing up against disorder. Jesus obeyed the laws of his time — Jewish and Roman secular. Jesus encouraged obedience to the law and shunned disorder. A great lesson for us came from the ruling party's question about paying taxes (Matt. 22:17-21). He knew it was a trap. If he said yes, He would be a traitor in favor of Rome. If He said no, He'd be a despised Roman sympathizer. The answer he gave kept him outside of both camps. I think it's important to note what Jesus did after answering so wisely. He didn't miraculously manipulate the system; He stood trial knowing the system was a sham and was cleared of all charges by the governor of the community.

Third, **we** demonstrate Jesus is King by calling upon Him to confront the governing systems seemingly too large to change. Jesus knew and understood certain reforms cannot be altered using political or physical means. He used spiritual forces in these times. He was *not* a civil reformer. He was a redeemer of life. Renewed lives express themselves in better government service. Evil always tempts in this process because power is involved.

Fourth, **we** live the phrase "Jesus is King" when we support democratic reforms to ensure the minority and the majority can be heard. Jesus laid the foundations for popular government. Remember, authoritarian government was the standard in religious and secular sectors. How different is the world in which we live? We all are empowered. We are responsible to act. Today, more than ever, one voice can start a revolution. We only need to look around the world. Ever since the onslaught of the expansion of worldwide media technology, the world is waking up to this fact. The story of the Orange Revolution solidifies the point.

In 2004 Victor Yushchenko stood for the presidency of the Ukraine. Vehemently opposed by the ruling party, Yushchenko's face was disfigured and he almost lost his life when he was mysteriously poisoned. This was not enough to deter him from standing for the presidency. On the day of the election, Yushchenko was comfortably in the lead. The ruling party, not to be denied, tampered with the results. The state-run television station reported: 'Ladies and gentlemen, we announce that the challenger Victor Yushchenko has been decisively defeated.' In the lower right-hand corner of the screen, a woman by the name of Natalia Dmitruk was providing a translation service for the deaf community. As the news presenter regurgitated the lies of the regime, Natalia Dmitruk refused to translate them. 'I'm addressing all the deaf citizens of Ukraine,' she signed. 'They are lying and I'm ashamed to translate those lies. Yushchenko is our president.' The deaf community sprang into gear. They text messaged their friends about the fraudulent results and as news spread of Dmitruk's act of defiance, increasing numbers of journalists were inspired to likewise tell the truth. Over the coming weeks, the "Orange Revolution" occurred as a million people wearing orange made their way to the capital city of Kiev demanding a new election. The government was forced to meet their demands, a new election was held and Victor Yushchenko became president.

Fifth, **we** *show Christ is King when we live a life worthy of the image of God each of us bears.* Jesus lived a life of non-resistance, but it wasn't the doormat type of non-resistance. It was a resistance where the dignity of human life could not be questioned. The world in which we live requires our participation to ensure that society is not delivered to those who govern who would suppress the truth of all humans — *we all are made in the image of God.* My wife and I went and watched the movie *Hacksaw Ridge* one weekend. It's the true story of Pfc. Desmond T. Doss, who won the Congressional Medal of Honor despite refusing to bear arms during WWII on religious grounds. Doss was drafted and ostracized by fellow soldiers for his pacifist stance, but went on to earn respect and adoration for his bravery, selflessness and compassion after he risked his life — without firing a shot — to save 75 men in the Battle of Okinawa. It was a great movie about standing apart from the acceptable norm and standing against the pressure of those who subscribe to those societal norms.

Jesus despised leadership that manipulates, compromises and lifts expediency above principle. To advance and renew society, we need to look to engage and not disengage. So, what are we to take from any election? Christ followers need to operate under an alternative understanding of governance which offers both freedom and challenges. Freedom to consciously object to those items in conflict with Christian belief and accept the challenge that comes with freedom. Christians need always be offering positive solutions (not criticism) to stand with the hurting, assure the minorities among us and begin to ask the deepest questions of all: How can I serve so God's will can be done and others be renewed in their faith?

The group discussion guide for this topic is in Appendix A on page 356.

RENEW

CHAPTER 10

THE CHURCH

Renewing the church requires we distinguish between the Church and the abuses that disfigure it. We must be involved in the continual refining of the culture surrounding it.

A high school girl wrote the following letter to a friend:

I attended your church yesterday. Although you had invited me, you were not there. I looked for you, hoping to sit with you. I sat alone. A stranger, I wanted to sit near the back of the church, but those rows were all packed with regular attendees. An usher took me to the front. I felt as though I was on parade. During the singing of the hymns, I was surprised to note that some of the church people weren't singing. Between their sighs and yawns, they just stared into space. Three of the kids that I had respected on campus were whispering to one another throughout the whole service. Another girl was giggling. I really didn't expect that in your church. The pastor's sermon was very interesting, although some members of the choir didn't seem to think so. They looked bored and restless. One kept smiling at someone in the congregation. There were several people who left and then came back during the sermon. I thought, "How rude!" I could hear the constant shuffling of feet and doors opening and closing. The pastor spoke about the reality of faith. The message got to me and I made up my mind to speak to someone about it after the service. But utter chaos reigned after the benediction. I said good morning to one couple, but their response was less than cordial. I looked for some teens with whom I could discuss the sermon, but they were all huddled in a corner talking about the newest music group. My parents don't go to church. I came alone yesterday hoping to find a place to truly worship and feel some love. I'm sorry, but I didn't find it in your church. I won't be back.[9]

Unfortunately, this letter expresses a regular experience for so many. People long for a connection to something greater than themselves. They enter a building expecting something different: people to be more caring, interested and, dare I say, loving. And what happens is that they are met with a group of people committed to something other than God. It can be a building, a geographic community, an ideology, a way of life. And it doesn't seem right; or, in everyday terms, it's broken.

What is the first thing you think of when I say the word church? Barna Research did a study in 2015 on the Millennial viewpoint. I believe it reflects a majority of our society's thoughts on church.

---

9   Source: Author unknown

The results say that those who don't attend any house of God perceive the church as: "judgmental (87 percent), hypocritical (85 percent), anti-homosexual (91 percent) and insensitive to others (70 percent)." Of those that do attend a house of worship, the percentages decrease — but not as substantially as you would think.[10]

As I survey the results, I wonder if the American word "church" gets in the way of the idea cast within scripture and even farther away from the original intent. Did you know the Bible only uses the word church three times (Matt. 16:18, 18:17)? It's true. The word itself means communal gathering. Jesus went to synagogue — a Jewish precursor to our form of church. It had rituals, pontificators and administrators. The biggest difference was it was the center of both religious and secular life. For a Jew, it was much more than a few songs, a few rituals and some teaching. It was the center of life. The people of this type of community clung together. Jesus was brought up in a connection like this. He respected his parents, displayed reverence for God and was a regular attendee. (See Luke 2:41-51, Luke 4:16, Matt. 12:9; Luke 4:33, 44; John 6:59; and Matt. 26:55.)

As much as Jesus was in the church of his day, Jesus was clear that he was not in favor of:

Bartering in sanctuary

"In the temple courts, he found people selling cattle, sheep and doves, and others sitting at tables exchanging

---

10   https://www.barna.com/research/what-millennials-want-when-they-visit-church/

money. So, he made a whip out of cords and drove all from the temple courts, both sheep and cattle; he scattered the coins of the money changers and overturned their tables" (John 2:14-15).

"On reaching Jerusalem, Jesus entered the temple courts and began driving out those who were buying and selling there. He overturned the tables of the money changers and the benches of those selling doves and would not allow anyone to carry merchandise through the temple courts" (Mark 11:15-16 NIV).

Pretension in worship

Be careful not to practice your righteousness in front of others to be seen by them. If you do, you will have no reward from your Father in heaven. "So when you give to the needy, do not announce it with trumpets, as the hypocrites do in the synagogues and on the streets, to be honored by others. Truly I tell you, they have received their reward in full. But when you give to the needy, do not let your left hand know what your right hand is doing, so that your giving may be in secret. Then your Father, who sees what is done in secret, will reward you. "And when you pray, do not be like the hypocrites, for they love to pray standing in the synagogues and on the street corners to be seen by others. Truly I tell you, they have received their reward in full. But when you pray, go into your room, close the door and pray to your Father, who is unseen. Then your Father, who sees what is done in secret, will reward you. Matt. 6:1-6 (NIV)

Formal Repetitious

"And when you pray, do not keep on babbling like pagans, for they think they will be heard because of their many words" Matt. 6:7 NIV.

False Holiness

So that it will not be obvious to others that you are fasting, but only to your Father, who is unseen; and your Father, who sees what is done in secret, will reward you. "Do not store up for yourselves treasures on earth, where moths and vermin destroy, and where thieves break in and steal. But store up for yourselves treasures in heaven, where moths and vermin do not destroy, and where thieves do not break in and steal. Matt. 6:18-20 (NIV)

Enslavement of Tradition

The Pharisees and some of the teachers of the law who had come from Jerusalem gathered around Jesus and saw some of his disciples eating food with hands that were defiled, that is, unwashed. (The Pharisees and all the Jews do not eat unless they give their hands a ceremonial washing, holding to the tradition of the elders. When they come from the marketplace they do not eat unless they wash. And they observe many other traditions, such as the washing of cups, pitchers and kettles.) So the Pharisees and teachers of the law asked Jesus, "Why don't your disciples live according to the tradition of the elders instead of eating their food with defiled hands?" He replied, "Isaiah was right when he prophesied about you hypocrites; as it is written:

"'These people honor me with their lips, but their hearts are far from me. They worship me in vain; their teachings are merely human rules.' You have let go of the commands of God and are holding on to human traditions." Mark 7:1-8 (NIV)

Shows of Piety

For Moses said, 'Honor your father and mother,' and, 'Anyone who curses their father or mother is to be put to death.' But you say that if anyone declares that what might have been used to help their father or mother is Corban (that is, devoted to God) — then you no longer let them do anything for their father or mother. Thus you nullify the word of God by your tradition that you have handed down. And you do many things like that. Mark 7:10-13 (NIV)

Emphasis on Externals

"Are you so dull?" he asked. "Don't you see that nothing that enters a person from the outside can defile them? For it doesn't go into their heart but into their stomach, and then out of the body." (In saying this, Jesus declared all foods clean.) He went on: "What comes out of a person is what defiles them. For it is from within, out of a person's heart, that evil thoughts come—sexual immorality, theft, murder, adultery, greed, malice, deceit, lewdness, envy, slander, arrogance and folly. All these evils come from inside and defile a person." Mark 7:18-23 (NIV)

The true church Christ desires is described by Paul in Ephesians 5:25-27 (NIV):

> Husbands love your wives, **just as Christ loved the church and gave himself up for her** [26] to make her holy, cleansing her by the washing with water through the word, [27] and to present her to himself as a radiant church, without stain or wrinkle or any other blemish, but holy and blameless.

Jesus distinguished between the church and the abuses that disfigured it and did not let His love for the former suffer because of His aversion to the latter.

Renewing the church requires we distinguish between the church and the abuses that disfigure it. We must be involved in the continual refining of the culture surrounding it.

The group discussion guide for this topic is in Appendix A on page 358.

RENEW

CHAPTER 11

ENEMIES

"To stand with defeat behind us, and to face Godward, knowing that every sin has left an impress on character that wil need vigilance of the awakened manhood to overcome, and yet know that the soul never stands alone, that the power to overcome is always within the grasp of the man who fights to win, gives victory."[11]

Have you ever really disliked someone? I mean the thought of them makes your blood boil. Or you see them and begin an internal convulsion. The adrenal begins to flow. Palms get sweaty and you begin to replay all the things they have done to you and then you move into the torture techniques you would love to use on them.

Probably the greatest American story of hatred and revenge was the Hatfields and McCoys. The folklore is based upon truth.

---

11 *The Principles of Jesus*, Robert Speer, Westminster Press, 1902. P.56

The Hatfields of West Virginia were led by William Anderson "Devil Anse" Hatfield, while the McCoys of Kentucky were under the leadership of Randolph "Ole Ran'l" McCoy. Those involved in the feud were descended from Ephraim Hatfield (born c. 1765) and William McCoy (born c. 1750). The feud has entered the American folklore lexicon as a metonym for any bitterly feuding rival parties. More than a century later, the feud has become synonymous with the perils of family honor, justice and revenge.

William McCoy, the patriarch of the McCoys, was born in Ireland around 1750 and many of his ancestors hailed from Scotland. The family, led by grandson Randolph McCoy, lived mostly on the Kentucky side of Tug Fork (a tributary of the Big Sandy River). The Hatfields, led by William Anderson "Devil Anse" Hatfield, son of Ephraim and Nancy (Vance) Hatfield, lived mostly on the West Virginia side. The majority of the Hatfields, although living in Mingo County (then part of Logan County), West Virginia, fought on the Confederate side in the American Civil War; most McCoys, living in Pike County, Kentucky, also fought for the Confederacy; except for Asa Harmon McCoy, who fought for the Union. The first real violence in the feud was the death of Asa Harmon McCoy as he returned from the war, murdered by a group of Confederate Home Guards called the Logan Wildcats. Devil Anse Hatfield was a suspect at first, but was later confirmed to have been sick at home at the time of the murder. It was widely believed that his uncle, Jim Vance, a member of the Wildcats, committed the murder.

The Hatfields were more affluent than the McCoys and were well-connected politically. Devil Anse Hatfield's timbering operation was a source of wealth for his family, while the McCoys were more of a lower-middle-class family. Ole Ran'l owned a 300-acre farm.

Both families had also been involved in the manufacturing and selling of illegal moonshine.

Between 1880 and 1891, the feud claimed more than a dozen members of the two families. On one occasion, the governors of West Virginia and Kentucky even threatened to have their militias invade each other's states. In response, Kentucky governor S. B. Buckner sent his Adjutant General Sam Hill to Pike County to investigate the situation. More than a dozen people died and at least 10 people were wounded. A few days after the New Year's Massacre, a posse led by Pike County deputy sheriff Frank Philipps rode out to track down Devil Anse' group across the border into West Virginia. The posse's first victim was Jim Vance, who was killed in the woods after he refused to be arrested. Philipps then made other successive raids onto Hatfield homes and supporters and captured three before cornering the rest in Grapevine Creek on the 19th of January. Unfortunately for Philipps, Devil Anse and other Hatfields were waiting for them with an armed group of their own. A battle ensued between the two parties, and the Hatfields were eventually apprehended. Two Hatfield supporters were killed, and a deputy, Bill Dempsey, was executed by Frank Philipps after surrendering. Wall Hatfield and eight others were arrested and brought to Kentucky to stand trial for the murder of Alifair McCoy, killed during the New Year's Massacre.[12]

Have you ever been the one hated? Disliked for something you did, or others have assumed you have done? An old girlfriend? Boyfriend? An ex? An employee? Again, I stand before you convicted of actions before and after I met my Savior.

---

12   https://en.wikipedia.org/wiki/Hatfield%E2%80%93McCoy_feud

Speaking of the one I call my Savior, Jesus was hated even before he was born. The king Herod hated him because of what the prophecy spoke of. His hometown folks wondered about him and at one point, others even tried to stone him because he dared to speak of forgiveness. A forgiveness so expansive even folks not of the Jewish tradition might be forgiven. The dislike and the popularity went hand-in-hand. The more he became popular, the more the elite religious leaders hated him. Jealousy and envy brought about charges of heresy, blasphemy and even insurrection. (Read Luke 5: 21, 30 and 6:7-11). How dare he heal on the Holy Day? This was the beginning of God's ministry. The rest of the story is history. *Hatred turned into uncontrolled madness that would end with Jesus on a cross, His mother, her friends and a few key disciplines looked on, wondering what could be so wrong about loving people?* Why would the traditions of the day stay in contradiction to caring for others born in God's image?

So, what are we to learn from His story?

1. Goodness is no guarantee a man will have not enemies. Expect it! Don't ever think you can please everyone. It's a sick disjunction of the modern day that anyone can or should try to please all people. In doing so, we deny a fundamental truth. All men and women will encounter people who will not care for you. They may even have rational reasons for their behavior. The tragic truth is the persecutor and the martyr are cut from similar cloth. Both believe they are right. Fortunately, we know one is suffering from an illusion, a deception, a lie. Truth and error are NOT identical. It is not relative. Those who serve a higher power will always unselfishly seek to move

creation toward a relationship with the King. All goodness needs to be judged through this rubric: Does this advance the Kingdom or detract from it?

2. God's will is not to invite the wrath of men. God's will is to dissuade men from their evil purposes (John 8:37-40). Along with this attitude, we are not to antagonize men, but we are to correct error, condemn shallow moral judgements (Matt. 5:17-48) and speak against hypocrisy (Matt. 7:5, 16) and insensitive behavior. He was direct without judgement, so they couldn't claim His instruction a was personal matter. He stuck to the issues at hand and avoided the public and private discourse which would arouse greater trouble (John 6:15; 7:11; 11:9-11; 12:36).

3. We are not to flee from enemies. We are to stand resolutely, move forward in the face of opposition and even despite it (John 7:25-26). We are not to be afraid of them. Whatever will be done comes with a cost and we may end up suffering in order to accomplish His will (John 7:6-7; 8:20; 13:1; 17:1).

4. We are to love our enemies. We are to be gentle in our suggestion they need to correct error to be just (John 18:19-24). Our hope is based in a faith that awakens them verses ever using violence (John 18:10-11, Matt. 26:53).

5. No enemy can conquer a Christian — except an enemy from within. Jesus was calm, dignified and heroic in the way He stood when many would have understood an outburst or even a claim this is not

fair. He understood the time of evil is short and soon enough all His enemies would be put under His feet and us alongside of Him (1 Cor. 15:25; Rev. 3:21).

Life or death was determined by the answer to a single question: Are you a Christian?

That was the question asked by an anti-Christian gunman who stormed into a classroom at Oregon's Umpqua Community College.

Eyewitnesses say the shooter targeted Christians. Christians were martyred for their faith, on American soil, a fact mostly ignored by most of the mainstream media and the White House.

Kortney Moore was inside the classroom. She told the Roseburg News-Review that the shooter ordered students to get on the ground — and then told them to stand up and state their religion.

"And they would stand up and he said, 'Good, because if you're a Christian, you're going to see God in just about one second,' Stacy Boylan said in a televised report. "And then he shot and killed them."

His 18-year-old daughter was struck in the back by a bullet — that traveled down her spine. She survived. Miss Moore, too, survived. Davis Jaques, publisher of the Roseburg Beacon News, said he received a text message from a student who said she was inside the classroom.

"The shooter was lining people up and asking if they were Christians," the message read. "If they said yes, then they were shot in the head. If they said no or didn't answer, they were shot in the leg."

Christians were martyred for their faith — on American soil — a fact mostly ignored by most of the mainstream media and the

White House. The New York Times *only mentioned that the gunman inquired about people's "religions" and one cable television news channel opined that the shooter's motive was unclear...*[13]

Robert Speers says it best in *The Principles of Jesus*: "To stand with defeat behind us, and to face Godward, knowing that every sin has left an impression on character that will need vigilance of the awakened manhood to overcome, and yet know that the soul never stands alone, that the power to overcome is always within the grasp of the man who fights to win, gives victory."[14]

Who must you overcome to stand in His presence again?

The group discussion guide for this topic is in Appendix A on page 359

---

13   http://www.foxnews.com/opinion/2015/10/02/day-christians-were-martyred-on-american-soil.html

14   *The Principles of Jesus,* Robert E. Speer, The Westminster Press, 1902, p.56

RENEW

CHAPTER 12

RENEWABLE FORGIVENESS

There is rarely a place where we are so like God as when we are lifted up to His nature and enabled to forgive one another as God for Christ's sake has forgiven us.

In the previous chapter, we read about Jesus and his enemies. Now, I'd like you to search your life for a moment you'd wish you could do differently: a behavior or an incident you'd like "do-over" or to get a "mulligan" on.

I'd like a mulligan on all the times I decided not to tell the whole truth and nothing but the truth to the priest when I was kid. You see, I grew up a Roman Catholic. My mom wore the spiritual pants in the family. We went to church every Saturday night. I can still remember my heart pounding leading up to communion. I also remember my first confession and sharing details of my life for actions I believed were "bad." However, it wasn't until years later when a friend jokingly told a story about sharing only part of his "bad" stuff and noting there was a loophole in the Catholic sacrament of confession and absolution that you were forgiven for all the sins for the period of time since your last confession after you did the big penance (a few Hail Marys and some Our Fathers I guess). I laughed at first, but I, too, remember minimizing my behavior to the priest to get a lighter sentence. It's funny to think about it now; however, I've had the most mature Christian ask, "How many times will God forgive my sins in this life? When does His forgiveness end?"

The last time this question was asked in a small group discussion, the room filled with silence as the people turned and looked at yours truly. After a little bit of silence, I asked the group to recite the Lord's prayer. We talked about the origins of the prayer in Matthew 6 and Luke 11. We discussed Jesus' words, "forgives us our trespasses as we forgive others." Interesting for its circular nature, but also, it's a command to forgive. Jesus dives in a little more forcibly in Mark 11:25 (NIV) when Jesus says, "And when you stand praying, if you hold anything against anyone, forgive them, so that your Father in heaven may forgive you your sins."

We then went into some other writing which has Jesus saying to Peter, "seven times seventy." Basically, equivalent to saying there is no limit (Matt. 18:21-22; Luke 17:3-4). What an incredible message of hope this brings. Think about this. If Jesus told them there was no limit to the number of times we are to forgive, it only makes perfect sense our Lord would demonstrate the same behavior with us. All your trespasses, sins, debts and defects of character can and are forgiven when you believe in and live as He did. Jesus forgave sins! It's one of the factors which really upset the Pharisees. Before this, it was believed only God could forgive sins so when Jesus forgave sins, they didn't know what to make of it. They were bound by the rules of the day (the law) and couldn't celebrate the good news that through Jesus this restraint was nullified. All now can be forgiven.

This has been a huge discussion with a friend for several years. She doesn't believe all can be forgiven. It came to light one day when we were talking about some mass murderer who was said to have found Jesus in prison before he was executed. I said, "If it's true, and only Jesus can judge his heart, he will be in heaven with us." She was not buying it. The discussion turned intense — different levels of sins came up. I asked her to prove that through scripture. She couldn't. We discussed consequences, but also forgiveness. I brought up Judas, who betrayed Jesus for thirty pieces of silver. Even as Satan entered Judas, Jesus said, "So Jesus told him, "What you are about to do, do quickly" (John 13:26). He didn't back away or expel him from His presence. Later, when Judas came with the guards to the garden, Jesus said, "Do what you came for, friend" (Matt. 26:50 NIV). Did you hear that Jesus said "friend"?

It's utterly inspiring to think of how God forgives. He forgave His murderers (Luke 23:24). He forgave Peter for denying him three times (Mark 16:7; John 21:15-19). He said, "If your brother or sister sins against you, rebuke them; and if they repent, forgive them." Did you read any conditions? Should we add any? The answer, of course, is no!

The word translated as "forgive" in Luke 17:3, is literally "to let off or to send away." It requires your willingness and God's grace. It's also the reason many a biblical scholar and many sensitive souls will debate a scripture that does say there is an unforgivable sin. The scriptures in Matthew, Mark and Luke vary slightly but the basic text says, "Anyone who blasphemes against the Holy Spirit will not be forgiven either in this age or in the age to come." Pretty intense, huh?

I believe Jesus is saying, if a man will not accept the forgiveness offered by the indwelling of the Holy Spirit, he has chosen not to believe in Jesus and, therefore, has sealed his own fate. That is what the blasphemy against the Holy Spirit really is — a hardening of one's soul that makes the perception or inclusion of the spiritual realm impossible. It's a sort of callousness that grows over time. It is not a single failure to do what is right or a single decision which is blasphemes. It's a consistent turning away which creates the effect.

Jesus always forgave. And in it, the greatest joy is found in forgiveness (Rom. 4:7). There is good feeling in forgiveness (Matt. 9:2). And the more Jesus has forgiven us, the warmer our gratitude and life is for all His creation (Luke 7:41-43). There is rarely a place where we are so like God as when we are lifted up to His nature and enabled to forgive one another as God for Christ's sake has forgiven us (Eph. 4:32 NIV).[15]

Who needs your forgiveness? With whom should you seek it?

The group discussion guide for this topic is in Appendix A on page 361.

---

15   ibid, p. 60

CHAPTER 13

ERROR

All error is connected to human understanding of the world in which we live. An understanding which has been so warped by the world and culture that we are incapable of seeing it at first.

The other day I was flipping the channels and I saw an old episode of a show called *Happy Days*. For those aren't old enough to remember, *Happy Days* was sitcom set in the late 1950s, when everything seemed to be simpler. The main characters were a guy named Richie and an idolized car mechanic with the name "the Fonz." This episode was one I remembered for years because it was all about the Fonz having to admit he was wrong. He couldn't even get the words out of his mouth. The laugh track would continue to be interjected as he tried to say the words. His inner being would not allow him to say the words.

Can you say them? "I'm wrong." I can, but it has taken several heart-wrenching mistakes. The one that comes to mind happened when I owned my own business and needed more space. I decided to hire a "friend" to build an office inside a warehouse. Not a bad idea unless you decide to do it without permits and without a licensed contractor. "What are the chances we would get caught?" Overruns and cheap labor made this a bad decision from the start. However, the moment the fire inspector came through and alerted the rest of the building department, I was in real trouble. In the end, I had to tear the entire structure out and take the loss on the chin. Try explaining a $30,000 loss to your wife for cutting corners. It was painful. I was overcome with feelings of being stupid, of not recognizing my own will run amuck, of having to admit I needed help to lead this business.

Have you ever been down this road? A place where your best decision-making led you to dread and misery? Of course, you have. We all have. The only being who hasn't is God Himself. But even He has been surrounded by it.

A. When God decided to become man in the form of Jesus Christ, He was surrounded by it. The error of intellectual opinion, the error of emotion and even the error of human will.
   a. He encountered intellectual error when the smartest people of His day (the Pharisees and Scribes) were blinded by blunders of human opinion regarding God's word.
   b. The error about Sabbath observance
   c. The error of the importance of ritual
   d. The errors of interpretation of the Torah, the Old Testament scripture
   e. The error in how the Messiah would come.
B. Jesus encountered emotional error. An error which stemmed from both a racial and religious pride. It was a pride so steeped in emotion that when it was challenged, the reaction would erupt in an anger so

fierce it would kill — not only the mind but the body as well.

C. He also met the error of human will. The worst, really, because it often disguises itself as moral behavior. A falseness which centers on the belief one can be perfect enough to not need the hand of a grace and mercy-filled God except in emergencies. It's the idea, kind of like an Elf on the Shelf. God is always present, but never intervenes except when called upon. Always watching but never interceding. If you act morally, then you will obviously not need to trouble God with any of your issues; He is pleased with you and will give you what you desire.

The interesting aspect of error is that Jesus encountered it not only in His enemies, but in His friends.

A. He encountered it in the disciples. The guys who had been with Him from the beginning. Three years they traveled with Him and on more than one occasion they demonstrated vanity and pride. Remember the discussion Jesus overheard between a few of the disciples trying decide who was the second in command? Or the time Jesus encountered the woman at the well and the disciples wondered what he was doing to talking to that half-breed slut of woman? Seriously, the disciples were full of it and *they* literally walked with Jesus.

B. He encountered error in the disciples all the time. He even had to correct on occasion. Do you remember the story from Luke 9:51-55? Jesus comes up to a

Samaritan village and Tom Bodett from Motel 6 forgot to leave the light on for him, so the disciples asked Jesus, should we call down fire on them? Can we, please? Seriously, I bet you Jesus wanted to have a Scooby-Doo moment there.

Seriously, the story of the village is interesting because it's one of only a few places where Jesus turns to and talks sternly to them. Jesus normally modeled:

- A. A patient and considerate response even when He knew the other person was in error. His responses were kinder and more thought-provoking versus judgmental. It's probably the reason he asked more questions in His interactions with others.
- B. He corrected those closest to Him privately.
- C. He took on public discourse carefully with logic and story.

There is this great piece in the book where Jesus is being challenged in Jerusalem at the synagogue. The people keep asking Him if he is the messiah. Tell us plainly if you are. He said, I have, but you are choosing to not listen. They get angry and want to kill Him by stoning. He eventually shares more and walks right on past them (John 10:24-39).

- A. He didn't compromise His value to accommodate others. Always tolerance for the human but not the idea.
- B. He accepted honest error and restored the individual quickly.
- c. He always focused on revealing the larger truth. He wanted to direct people to His Father because that is

the Father's will — all will know Him before he comes to reign.
D. He was careful to condemn public policy and not the individuals called upon to enforce cultural norms.

This last point is critical to our understanding of Jesus' role and therefore our willingness to engage the world around us. Jesus focused his engagement with the errors of this world by challenging those ideas which get in the way of people coming to a lasting faith in God. The best example of which comes in the teaching commonly referred to as "the sermon on the mount." We will look at the issues of Jesus' day in the spirituality discussion group tonight. The main point being, He wanted to debunk the cultural understanding of God's word in favor of His actual will.

Another great story of this comes out of John's book in chapter 8:31-59. Jesus is talking to some religious leaders who have chosen to challenge Him on his authority. He answers their questions and then moves through their objections swiftly using their own knowledge base. They still don't get it.

We now understand the reason for His presence. Jesus begins His relationship with the world with signs and wonders, moves to education through relationships and then onto action. It's the cornerstone of why God had to come to earth. All error is connected to human understanding of the world in which we live. An understanding which has been so warped by the world and culture that we are incapable of seeing it at first. It's not until we are willing to be renewed by Christ that we are even capable of seeing who and what we really are.

The group discussion guide for this topic is in Appendix A on page 361.

RENEW

CHAPTER 14

UNBELIEF

To blindly follow a stream of belief of another is not belief at all, but superstition.

Have you ever wondered what the creator of the universe thinks about our questioning of His created order? What He thinks about our unwillingness to admit He was behind it all? Would He be vindictive or harsh or hurt because of our lack of recognition? There's a preacher story that has been around for years and it goes something like this:

A professor of biology was an atheist. Every year, he began his lectures on evolution by asking if any of the students were religious. When they identified themselves, he boasted that by the end of his course, they'd all know evolution was the truth and would become atheists. Over the years, many a student lost their faith during his course.

One day, our atheist professor was walking through the forest, marveling at the wonderful world evolution had given us. His wondering was interrupted by a loud growl. He turned to see *a large, hungry and cranky grizzly bear charging toward him. The professor began to run, but it was no use, the bear was too fast. The professor tripped and next thing he knew the grizzly was standing above him, one foot on his chest, his paw ready to strike. With terror in his eyes the atheist professor realized he was about to experience survival of the fittest first hand.*

At that point he cried out, "God help me!"

Time stopped! The bear froze. The forest was silent. A bright light shone down upon the atheist and a voice boomed from the heavens, "You deny my existence for all of these years, teach others I don't exist and even credit creation to a cosmic accident. Do you expect me to help you out of this predicament? Am I to count you as a believer?"

The atheist professor looked up into the light, "It would be hypocritical of me to suddenly ask you to treat me as a Christian now ... but perhaps could you make the bear a Christian?"

"Very well," the voice said.

The light went out and the sounds of the forest resumed. And then the bear dropped its right paw, brought both paws together, bowed its head and spoke: "Lord, for this food which I am about to receive, I am truly thankful."

While a cute story, it does make you wonder.

Does the creator of the universe get upset with those who ignore, reject or nullify Him, or his work?

In a world created with checks and balances, like ecosystems or solar systems, does *not* believing in a creator leave one vulnerable to creating one's own theory of what "this" life is and then, because we are finite, it (the theory) can end with us? Like that of a good Al-Anon spouse, who loves their partner but waits, hoping their loved one awakens to the true essence of their malady before they pass.

On May 15, 1950, a group of students from Oxford University gathered for their weekly debate between atheists and Christians. Huddled inside the Junior Common Room at St. Hilda's College, the meeting was chaired by C.S. Lewis. A young philosophy student named Antony Flew presented a case for atheism. His speech was titled "Theology and Falsification". It doesn't sound very exciting, but it became the most widely published philosophical paper of the 20th century and Antony Flew went on to became one of the leading atheist thinkers of the 20th century. It has been said that: "Within the last hundred years, no mainstream philosopher has developed the kind of systematic, comprehensive, original and influential exposition of atheism that is to be found in Antony Flews' fifty years of ... writing".[16]

In 2004, Antony Flew dropped a bombshell — he declared he had changed his mind. He had not had a Damascus Road conversion experience. He had not had a personal encounter with God. He simply believed that the evidence from science and philosophy now pointed to the existence of a God. "I have followed the argument where it has led me," he said. "And it has led me to accept the existence of a self-existent, immutable, immaterial, omnipotent and omniscient Being."[17]

I've never claimed to be smart, but it does give me pause to wonder, if the most intelligent and diligent folks on the planet have consistently found a God at the end of their investigation, do I need

---

16   *There is a God*, Anthony Flew and Roy Varghese, Harper Press, New York, 2007

17   Ibid.

to do the same investigation? The answer is yes. To blindly follow a stream of belief of another is not belief at all, but superstition. We all must come to a personal understanding or relationship with God if we are ever going to answer the largest questions of life: Why am I here? What is my purpose? Is there another dimension to this life? Does this existence or life connect to the next? How?

Personally, I have wandered the journey from being a Christian in name only, to an agnostic hedonist and back again. The turning point happened when all my best thinking brought me to the floor of my condo, holding my dog, asking God to kill me. It happened again a few years later, when, looking at a profit and loss sheet I wondered, is this all there is? And then a third time, realizing the Jesus meant for us to be more committed to Him than to speaking and doing "religious stuff." It meant trying to establish authentic relationships built on trust with God, His Son Jesus and His Spirit while combining all of it with humans he directs my way. Relationships not built on what I get but what Jesus gives through me.

I suspect you will talk a bit more about belief and unbelief with your friends. Begin with the question, "What does it mean to believe in God?"

The group discussion guide for this topic is in Appendix A on page 362.

CHAPTER 15

FRIENDSHIPS

*Friendship is not what one claims to the public,
but the sacrifices one makes for the other.*

Do you find it easy to make friends or hard? How many close friends do you have?

I want to begin by asking you to think of two people with whom you share everything. Why two? Because the most recent surveys report true friendship has declined in the last ten years from three people to two? If you are a white male over fifty, this average number may even be less?[18]

Have you stopped to consider the effect Facebook, Instagram and Snapchat have had on our idea of what it means to be a friend?

Oxford anthropologist and evolutionary psychologist Robin Dunbar is famous for his "Dunbar number" — how many people an individual can really be friends with at any given time. His research found that based on the

---

18   http://psychcentral.com/lib/how-many-friends-do-you-need/

size of an adult brain, the average human can have around 150 people in his or her social group, and that anything more than that is too complex for most of us to process. Think of 150 as the holiday card list, the broad group of people with whom you want to stay in touch in some meaningful way. According to Dunbar, social media has only reinforced his conclusions. He explained that a recent analysis of one million Facebook pages showed that the layers of friendship (most intimate, best, good, just friends) are the same size as they are "in real life" (about 5, 15, 50, and 150). What seems to happen, Dunbar said, is that Facebook introduces "a few extra people" to the outermost layer of casual acquaintances (people you know but wouldn't send a holiday card), which can extend out to 500 individuals. Facebook confuses things by calling all of these relationships friends. But while Facebook probably slows a relationship's "rate of decay" — when you no longer meet in person — he suspects social media won't stop a more intimate friend (say, in the fifteen or fifty category) from moving into a further-out ring if there's no longer any face-to-face contact.[19]

If social media is not expanding our core relationships, does its presence enhance or take away from our ability to connect? Does a social medium give us a false sense of assurance that we are known and know others? Or is it all a terrible charade?

---

19   http://www.theatlantic.com/health/archive/2015/02/how-real-are-facebook-friendships/384780

Tanja Hollander realized in 2010 that she had 616 friends on Facebook — some she had never personally sat with or been to their homes. On New Year's, she decided to take two weeks out of every month and visit all her Facebook "friends" and take their picture or their family portrait. She crowdsourced the project and it will go on display in March of 2017. She claimed she needed to put meaning behind the number and context to the pictures, as well as the stories she would regularly read. The project itself has been eye-opening for her. Over 95 percent of the people were interested in having her in their homes and some 70 percent wanted her to stay with them overnight.[20]

The experience has been enlightening and she is excited to share the portraits of her friends on line at the New England Art show. However, the word friend is still yet to be defined. She still wrestles with the concepts of friend. She is not alone.

Ronald Lawrence, executive director of the Community Counseling Center of Southern Nevada asked the question, "Does the mish-mash of friend-friends, casual friends, work friends, friends of friends and friend-seeking strangers gathered on the typical Facebook users page constitute 'friends' in any practical sense? The answer to that is mostly no. You may call yourself friends. You may share a lot of things," Lawrence says. But, for Lawrence, friendship is built upon, and is nourished by, multiple levels of interaction beyond just words on a computer screen. "It's social, it's emotional, it's psychological and it's spiritual," Lawrence says, and "it's hard to experience those dimensions on a flat screen." In a friendship, "there is something ... that happens at unconscious

---

20   http://www.theatlantic.com/health/archive/2015/02/how-real-are-facebook-friendships/384780/

levels, and I actually believe that people have to be in contact with each other, in the presence of each other, to experience that friendship," he adds.[21]

True friendship requires relationship in which each party is connected in a way that they will give of themselves for the betterment of the other. Honestly, it's rare.

Kathy Poe and Esther Kim were best friends. They were also competing to represent the U.S. in Taekwondo at the 2000 Sydney Olympics. Working through separate sides of the draw, they both made it to the final of the Olympic trials. Whichever of them won would go to the games. Poe, however, dislocated her knee in the previous match and couldn't compete. Then came an incredible act of friendship. Knowing her friend's knee would be healed by the games, Esther Kim forfeited the match and her spot on the Olympic team.

"You will have the gold medal around your neck and I feel inside I have a gold medal in my heart," she said. "There are other ways to be a champion. A real martial artist is a champion every day in life, too." [22]

Ester elevates the understanding of friendship to the spiritual in that last statement. Friendship is not what one claims to the public, but the sacrifices one makes for the other.

---

21   http://www.reviewjournal.com/business/technology/facebook-changing-meaning-friendship

22   https://www.nytimes.com/2000/05/25/sports/on-the-olympics-two-athletes-an-injury-and-a-sacrifice.html

It revolves around a level of trust that the other party has your best interest at the same level or above their own. This level of trust is not natural. We struggle against it because of our own self-centeredness, the competitive nature of the society and the lack of our spiritual relationship to define our world. This last point is paramount.

As a self-avowed Christian, I am claiming a worldview when I call someone my friend. It's a view that the will of the creator of the universe takes everything into account and coordinates all the tangible and intangibles, so all would come to know Him. In so doing, He has all our best interests at heart. How can we be assured he has our best interests? Just look at the text.

- He loved where no love summoned him (Rom. 5:7-8)
- He gave himself where men rejected him (Matt. 23:37)
- He died for his foes (Rom. 5:10, John 11:49-50)
- In the agony of death, he cried out for forgiveness for His persecutors (Gospels)

The same unselfishness that ruled his entire life allows me to know He would not reject anyone who claims Him as a friend or savior. He even called all of us His children, praying for us and our future before allowing Himself to be taken and killed.

Do you have any other friends who act like Jesus did? Willing to claim you as a friend in your worst moments? Offering friendship without a thought of personal gain or benefit? Fearlessly dealing with those willing to be loved? Always inviting more intimacy and sheer numbers into the circle of friendship?[23]

The group discussion guide for this topic is in Appendix A on page 364.

---

[23] *The Principles of Jesus*, Robert E. Speer, The Westminster Press, 1902, p.72-75

CHAPTER 16

MARRIAGE

Marriage is for life, so we learn to experience the more important aspects of relationship.

There is a lot of talk in society about marriage in our society. A lot of cultural wars and vilifying of the other side. The reality is, marriage is viewed differently depending upon one's worldview. Americans are at a flashpoint currently where their worldview and their religious views are colliding. As a result, there's a lot of emotion and passion. So, if we take a step back and look at the four greatest religious worldviews as demonstrated by their leadership, we may discover our leanings. Did you know the following facts about the other great religions and their leaders view of marriage as polled from the internet?

- Islam's does not purport equality among the sexes or in marriage. In fact, Muhammad, the original leader, had thirteen wives, the last when he was in his fifties was six at the marriage and nine when it was said to have consummated

- ○ The Koran does not mandate inequality between men and women. Officially, men and women enjoy equal rights and duties in the practice of Islam and also equality in the marriage relationship. This theory, however, is often overridden by local customs and ingrained attitudes among communities. Such is the case in prohibiting polyandry while permitting polygamy, prohibiting interfaith marriage for women but allowing it for men, and allowing the practice of certain courtship rituals.[24]
- Hindus believe marriage is more cultural. It's better to marry someone from your class or village or a second cousin in an arranged marriage
  - ○ Hindu marriage joins two individuals for life, so that they can pursue dharma (duty), artha (possessions), kama (physical desires) and moksha (ultimate spiritual release) together. It is a union of two individuals as husband and wife and is recognized by law.[25]
- Buddhism believes marriage is more of an individual aspect and centers around the greater realization of oneself
  - ○ Marriage is a social convention, an institution created by man for the well-being and happiness of man, to differentiate human society from animal life and to maintain order and harmony

---

24   http://guidedoc.com/muslim-marriage-beliefs-rules-customs

25   https://en.wikipedia.org/wiki/Marriage_in_Hinduism

in the process of procreation. Even though the Buddhist texts are silent about monogamy or polygamy, the Buddhist laity is advised to limit themselves to one wife.[26]

Since I have disparaged these others, I feel it only fair to bring up a few of the mis-communications circulating about the Christian faith too.

Have you ever heard it proposed that some scholars believe Jesus was married? The movie *The Da Vinci Code* suggests it. A few scholars have even purported it to be true. Could it be?

The logic behind the accusation behind the assertion goes like this:
- It would have been rare to have an unmarried rabbi. Most were married at the time.
- It also would have been rare to have a woman in your discipleship following because it was a male-dominated profession and so having a female around must mean she was connected to the rabbi
- Finally, Jesus never addressed the issue of marriage by a rabbi or the benefit of being single

All of these are respectable, scholarly assertions. However, God's Word makes no mention of a married Jesus. The documentation and the facts just do not support the assertion. Now, if you believe Tom Hanks' character in the movie, the absence of any scripture referencing a married Jesus was the work of the church eradicating any written scriptural evidence. However, even

---

26 http://www.budsas.org/ebud/whatbudbeliev/237.htm

the popular historic writings closest to the time of Jesus, by both Josephus and Philo, validate the Christian practice of dedicating one's whole life. They also include surrendering one's sexuality in the pursuit of a more exclusive relationship with God. Rev. Dr. Mark Robert wrote in an article not too long ago,

"Both Philo and Josephus attest to the fact that Essene men remained single in the time of Jesus. But, one might argue, this kind of behavior was common only on the outskirts of Jewish society. Mainline Jews, if you will, would have looked down upon Essene celibacy. [27]

Jesus was not married, but he understood the institution and supported everyone's right to get married or stay single as a Jew. The true ballast for everyone was the advancement of their call to the service of God the father. (Matt. 19:12 comes to mind.) It never dealt with one's yearnings or leanings. It was assumed faithfulness to God came before one's physical desires and God does sometimes call people to be single and celibate to maintain their focus on Him and the doing of His will.

As much as we would like to believe we can pursue two things equally, the reality shows it to be a lie. We, as humans, must focus our efforts on single objectives. For someone who claims to be a Christian, it is to be a servant of the most high and do His will in the world. In this context, marriage is a secondary concern, to be reviewed, discerned and then put to rest. If decided upon, the parties enter a union with a similar singular focus — serve the Lord together as one (body, mind and soul). If decided against, the individual must let the matter go and pursue a different path for companionship and relationship.

---

27 http://www.patheos.com/blogs/markdroberts/series/was-jesus-married-a-careful-look-at-the-real-evidence/

Marriage should be considered a lifelong commitment which should not be broken. This is Jesus' view. Marriage is not an indulgence but a discipline. A discipline whereby a person learns consideration and forgiveness as part of the exercise of a singular belief in God's will in conjunction with His commands. Unfortunately, over 50 percent of marriages end in divorce for all kinds of reasons — some valid and some not. Jesus said it, "God hates divorce." Why? Because it breaks an indissoluble union with God. Christian marriage is supposed to be a spiritual commitment between three parties. God will not break the commitment. We humans on the other hand, are not great at keeping our side of the bargain. All the volumes of human history will show that. The only way we can keep our commitment is with His presence and guidance. Hence the reason unfaithfulness in marriage (adultery, as well as all other forms of intimacy outside of three-pronged relationship) was/is considered an acceptable reason for ending a union. It's only with this higher guidance we can offer love, mercy, grace, forgiveness, patience and kindness when our natural instincts are to be self-serving.

Civil law may allow for divorce, but the higher design is for lifelong relationship. Have you ever asked yourself why? Why would God want us to be in a lifelong relationship? Is it some kind of cosmic joke on the human race as one comedian proposed? Or did the Vancouver TED talk by sexologist Jessica O'Reilly entitled "Monogamist" get it right? [28]

She claims the 50 percent divorce rate is not a problem of compatibility, but of unrealistic societal expectations. Should we just admit the expectation of monogamy doesn't consider our sexual

---

28   https://www.youtube.com/watch?v=0sYguTPLpHE&t=605s

instincts or the benefits which come from variety? She suggests if we could just recognize the truth and accept the alternatives we might have marriages which last for a lifetime, like other friendships?

The problem with the alternative views on marriage is they fail to recognize the positives which come from endurance and overcoming both personal issues as well as worldly ones. How can the most intimate of friendships be experienced when we fail to discover the true benefits of intimacy which only comes through familiarity and authentic acceptance?

The perfect parable for this answer comes through a children's story book, written by Marjorie Williams entitled, *The Velveteen Rabbit*.

The Velveteen Rabbit tells the story of a stuffed toy rabbit given to a young boy as a Christmas present. The velveteen rabbit lives in the nursery with all the other toys, waiting for the day when the boy will choose him as a playmate. In time, the shy Rabbit befriends the tattered Skin Horse, the wisest resident of the nursery, who reveals the goal of all nursery toys: to be made "real" through the love of a human. One night we get to overhear their conversation.

> "What is real?" asked the Rabbit one day, as they were lying side by side near the nursery fender, just before Nana came in to tidy up the room. "Does it mean having things that buzz inside you and a stick-out handle?"
>
> "Real isn't how you are made," said the Skin Horse. "It's a thing that happens to you. When a child loves you for a long, long time, not just to play with, but really loves you, then you become real." "Does it hurt?" asked the Rabbit. "Sometimes," said the Skin Horse, for he was always truthful. "When you are real, you don't mind being

hurt." "Does it happen all at once, like being wound up," he asked. "Or bit by bit?" "It doesn't happen all at once," said the Skin Horse. "You become. It takes a long time. That's why it doesn't often happen to people who break easily, or have sharp edges, or who have to be carefully kept. Generally, by the time you are real, most of your hair has been loved off; and your eyes drop out and you get loose in the joints and very shabby. But these things don't matter at all, because once you are real, you can't be ugly except to people who don't understand." [29]

Marriage is for life, so we learn to experience the greater spiritual aspects of being in relationship. It's not external but internal; it's moments as well as shared experiences, both good and bad, which create a 'real' bond that lasts. All endured together during our time here on earth knowing there is a place beyond this where all will be revealed.

I know I have sidestepped the questions of sexuality and polygamy as it relates to marriage. Society, science and scripture provide a lot of food for thought on the topic. However, I do not have the time or energy to present both sides of the division that is splitting Christianity and our nation. It also doesn't seem correct to direct your thinking with my opinion until such time you have searched your own heart. I'd prefer you talk about this in each of your groups. I've provided several potential readings, scriptures and commentary from both sides of the debate for you to ponder.

The group discussion guide for this topic is in Appendix A on page 364.

---

29   *The Velveteen Rabbit.* Marjorie Williams, George Doran Publishing, 1922

CHAPTER 17

FAMILY

The indispensable root of all theology, family — family as an orientation for all humanity, a model for the everlasting link between humanity and God.

My disclaimer for the assertion is that my perspective on the world is fueled by my experience, reason, tradition and a text I believe was uttered by God and written by men for such a time as this.

Family life is changing. Two-parent households are on the decline in the United States as divorce, remarriage and cohabitation are on the rise. And families are smaller now, both due to the growth of single-parent households and the drop in fertility. Not only are Americans having fewer children, the circumstances surrounding parenthood have changed. While in the early 1960s babies typically arrived within a marriage, today, fully four in ten births occur to women who are single or living with a non-marital partner. While family structures have transformed, so has the role of mothers in the workplace — and in the home. As more moms have entered the labor force, more have become breadwinners — in many cases, primary breadwinners — in their families.

Because of these changes, there is no longer one dominant family form in the U.S. Parents today are raising their children against a backdrop of increasingly diverse and, for many, constantly evolving family forms. By contrast, in 1960, the height of the post-World War II baby boom, there was one dominant family form. At that time, 73 percent of all children were living in a family with two married parents in their first marriage. By 1980, 61 percent of children were living in this type of family, and today less than half (46 percent) are. The declining share of children living in what is often deemed a "traditional" family has been largely supplanted by the rising shares of children living with single or cohabiting parents.

Not only has the diversity in family living arrangements increased since the early 1960s, so has the fluidity of the family. Non-marital cohabitation and divorce, along with the prevalence of remarriage and (non-marital) re-coupling in the U.S., make for family structures that in many cases continue to evolve throughout a child's life. While in the past a child born to a married couple — as most children were — was very likely to grow up in a home with those two parents, this is much less common today, as a child's living arrangement changes with each adjustment in the relationship status of their parents. For example, one study found that over a three-year period, about three in ten (31 percent) of children younger than six had experienced a major change in their family or household structure, in the form of parental divorce, separation, marriage, cohabitation or death. [30]

---

30 http://www.pewsocialtrends.org/2015/12/17/1-the-american-family-today/

I have been challenged at times about the use of the word "Father" for my description of God. I can specifically remember sharing a few years ago in a church on a Sunday morning and must have used the word Father several times. After the worship service, a woman came up to me and expressed the pain she felt every time I used the word Father. She was in tears. I felt horrible. However, I couldn't apologize. I could only ask her about her pain. It came from years of abuse at the hands of a man who did little more than contribute to her arrival in the world. Her story was painful. I then shared that when I use the word, I have the different context of a good father who did his best. However, I also had the vision from scripture of the perfect loving and compassionate leadership figure. Robert Spear once pointed out that the entire Christian "theology may be described as a transfiguration of the family. God is the Father, man is His child; and from the Father to the child there is conveyed the precious message of paternal love."[31] This thought seemed to stun her. She looked at me as if I had rejected her. I went on to explain that Jesus used the family structure idea as a tool to describe what for many would have been hard to comprehend. Family had a different meaning 2,000 years ago in a sustenance culture. Families (relatives) were the core support in a brutal world. The father figure was the responsible person and the family had specific roles in support thereof. A good family was one that felt loved and cared for both physically, mentally and spiritually. She understood, but the pain still came through her face.

As we review the good news written 2,000 years ago, we can highlight several interesting lessons from Jesus' use of the family for a foundation of relationship:

---

31 *The Principles of Jesus*, Robert E. Speer, The Westminster Press, 1902, p.80

1. He spoke to God with the love and respect of a son (John 2: 16; 5:17; 10:15; 11:41; 12:27-28)
2. He gave glimpses to others of real intimacy and closeness he had with "Dad" — Abba (John 5:35; 5:20, 26;6:57;8:28, 38; 17:5)
3. He strove to be like His Father (John 5:19)
4. He thought of heaven as a home (John 14:2)
5. He related to others in a family way (Eph. 3:15)
6. Attended the family events — weddings, etc. (Luke 9:42, John 2:1-11)
7. Connected to the appeals by family members (John 4:49)
8. He was always aware of his parent's feelings (Luke 7:11-15)
9. He spoke of a Father's unconditional love (Luke 15:18
10. He appreciated the family home and the importance of those closest to Him (John 19:27; 20:10)
11. He found rest in the family circle (look at Bethany)

He respected his parents and took care of his mom until his dying breath.

The quote from Dr. R.E. Thompson says it best, "His elevation of patience and forgiveness to the rank of primary virtues in the Kingdom gave a new law of life to the Christian household."[32]

---

32 Ibid, p.81

The lessons are extensive when we look at this idea of God's use of the family to get across a much larger point — God wants an intimate relationship with each of us, but many of us don't know how to cultivate this kind of relationship. It reminds me of a story I read some time ago ...

When I first sat down there were two men sitting together quietly. One man appeared to be in his thirties. He was dressed in some old work clothes and still wearing his baseball cap. The other man I would guess was about 80. He had the most incredible face. The lines and creases gave him character. His white hair was messy from wearing a stocking cap he held on top of the table. He wore one of those red plaid shirt jackets that you might see on a construction worker. Heavy enough to keep you warm while you're moving about, but not too bulky to limit your movement.

But he didn't look like he was going anywhere. Neither was this conversation.

"Boy, I really worked up a hunger today, Pop. All that shoveling and sweeping the snow will do that," the younger man said. "Yeah, this is something," replied the old man.

Silence followed for the longest time.

Suddenly I heard the young man say, "Here they come," as he pointed toward the doorway. He almost looked relieved. Somebody who would join in and help get this conversation going. It appeared to me that the two people who joined them were a mother and teenage grandchild. The woman sat next to the younger man and Pop stood up to let the grandchild slide in place. "Hello, Dad. Good to see you," she said as she sat down.

"Yep," the old man replied.

Silence. Even longer gaps than before.

"I feel real good," the old man said proudly. "Oh, you look good Dad," the younger man said. Then, one by one, the others agreed.

Silence.

The waitress approached and took their breakfast orders. Grandpa excused himself. "Gotta go to the bathroom. It happens a lot when you're old," he said. As soon as he was out of sight, the younger man said, "God, I don't know what to say to him. We just sit here looking around. He never talks." "I know what you mean. God what do you say?" the woman added. "He's old. What do you talk about with an old man," the kid joined in. Oh, no. Here I go. I can't just sit here and listen to this. I'm going to say something, swallow hard and wait to see if they tell me it's none of my business. "Ask him about his childhood," I said as I continued eating. "What? Pardon me? Were you talking to us, sir?" the woman asked.

"Yes. It's really not my business, I know. But do you realize what he has to offer you? Can you even begin to understand what this man has seen in his lifetime? He most likely has answers to problems you haven't even discovered as problems in your life. He's a gold mine," I said.

Silence again.

"Look, talk to him about his childhood. Ask him what the snows were like back then. He'll have a million stories to share. He's not talking because no one is asking," I told them. Just then he came walking around the corner. "Oh, boy. I feel much better now. You know I haven't been goin' good in a while," the old man told them. They all turned and looked at me. I shrugged my shoulders. Okay. So old people also talk about the facts of life. And going or not going is a major thing when you're old. You take the good with the bad. After a long silence the young girl said, "Paw Paw. When you were a kid were the snows this bad?"

"Gees, honey. This is nothing like the snows I had when I was a kid. Did I ever tell you about the snowstorm that covered my house?" he asked. "No, Pop. I don't think I ever heard that one myself," said the younger man. Now for the next twenty minutes the old man was in his glory. At one point he even stood up to show them how high the one snow drift was. Throughout the entire meal everyone chimed in with more questions. They laughed, and he lit up like he was on stage and the play he was acting in was his life story. Just as I was about to leave I heard the old man say, "You have no idea what this has meant to me. All these years I never thought you were even interested in what I had to say."

"Oh ... well, I guess we just didn't think you wanted to talk," the woman said.

"Well nobody bothered to ask me anything. I just figured I was boring or something.

It's been a tough life you know. Ever since Ma Ma died I really had nothing to say." He paused for a moment. I could see him nervously wringing his rough life worn hands together. "You see, her and I were like a song. I made the music and she ... she was the words," he said. Like tough guys of his time are supposed to do, he held back any visible emotion, sniffled and wiping his eye he said, "No sense talkin' if you ain't got the words." As I turned to walk away I looked across the table. I saw the young girl wave and smile at me as she put her arm around Paw Paw's shoulders. She didn't have to say a word.[33]

---

33   Bob Perks © 2001. Used with permission.

The story elevates a few main points about our relationship with God:
1. All family relationships, including the one with God, can be dry and boring unless we are willing to open ourselves up to discovering a wiser understanding of the world from those who were here before we were. To open up requires asking a few questions and listening for the answers.
2. God, like an earthly father, wants to share His knowledge with His children as well as their offspring and so on and so on. It is a gold mine for both parties of lessons learned and experience explained. However, wisdom must be requested. In so doing, respect is conferred and the giving of oneself becomes primary for both parties.
3. Communication is key in all relationships and without it, relationships cannot exist for long.
4. Everyone has a need to be known and family's love helps to define the priorities of this life.

The group discussion guide for this topic is in Appendix A on page 365.

CHAPTER 18

WOMEN

Jesus never recognized inferiority of women and his actions demonstrated equality between the sexes.

A short time ago, I watched a series of marches by woman all over the United States. They were utilizing their right to protest. And while many had a different understanding of the purpose of their presence, the underlying factor for participation was fear. Fear the United States would revert back to a prior understanding of women; an understanding that treats women like a second-class citizen. I support the idea of women and men being equally created by God, so the idea was interesting. The interviews and blogs seemed to highlight a theme of oppression encouraged by religion or spirituality. It was proposed by many a spiritual and non-spiritual person that Christianity was a major factor in the thought women were inferior to men. However, I would suggest just the opposite is true. It was the world's assertion that women were inferior to men and Christianity's role to foster the acceptance of equality of women and men.

Islam's founder: Muhammad and his Quran, in contrast, attack the nature of womankind, universally. Says the Quran: "Men are a degree above [women] in status" (Sura 2:228); and, "Allah has made the one [mankind] superior to the other [womankind]" (Sura 4:34). Allah himself made men superior to women, so asserts Muhammad. He also says in the hadith: "This [diminishment of a woman's testimony] is because of the deficiency of a woman's mind." This insults the one quality in humans that exalts them and gives them dignity; their rational, thinking mind. (In no place does Jesus or a New Testament author say that a woman's mind is deficient.)[34]

Philosophy's father: Aristotle believed women were inferior and described them as "deformed males". For example, in his work Politics, Aristotle states 'as regards the sexes, the male is by nature superior and the female inferior, the male ruler and the female subject. Another example is Cynthia Freeland's catalog where she quotes: "Aristotle says that the courage of a man lies in commanding, a woman's lies in obeying; that 'matter yearns for form, as the female for the male and the ugly for the beautiful'; that women have fewer teeth than men; that a female is an incomplete male or 'as it were, a deformity'. Aristotle believed that men and women naturally differed both physically and mentally. He claimed that women are 'more mischievous, less simple, more impulsive ... more compassionate ... more easily moved to tears ... more jealous, more querulous, more apt to scold and to strike ... more prone to despondency and less hopeful ... more void of shame or self-respect, more false of speech, more deceptive, of more retentive memory [and] ... also more wakeful; more shrinking [and] more difficult to rouse to action' than men."[35]

---

34   http://www.answering-islam.org/Authors/Arlandson/women_inferior.htm

35   https://en.wikipedia.org/wiki/Aristotle's_views_on_women

Evolutionists: Including Charles Darwin, also taught that women are biologically inferior to men. Darwin's ideas, including his view of women, have had a major impact on society. ... Darwin concluded that adult females of most species resembled the young of both sexes and from this and the other evidence, "reasoned that males are more evolutionarily advanced than females" (Kevles, 1986:8). Many anthropologists' contemporary to Darwin concluded that "women's brains were analogous to those of animals," which had "overdeveloped" sense organs "to the detriment of the brain" (Fee, 1979:418). Carl Vogt, a University of Geneva natural history professor who accepted many of "the conclusions of England's great modern naturalist, Charles Darwin," argued that "the child, the female and the senile white" all had the intellect and nature of the "grown-up Negro" (1863:192). Many of Darwin's followers accepted this reasoning ... [36]

So, what does the founder of Christianity say and demonstrate about God's view of women?

God created man and woman to be co-equal, partners. Through women, God brought forth kings, leaders, prophets, pastors and even the Son of God. While some religions do teach that women are inferior, the Bible says that God made both of the same flesh. Both male and female reflect His image. Without either sex, we could not fully understand the nature of God.[37]

- Jesus talked with women even though the Jewish culture believed "it was better that the words of the law be burned than delivered to women."
- He made them his friends (Luke 10:38, John 11:5).

---

36   http://www.icr.org/article/darwins-teaching-womens-inferiority/

37   https://www.raptureready.com/faq/faq235.html

- He answered their questions (John 4:9-11)
- He heard their cries (Luke 11:27)
- He offered His sympathy (Luke 23:28)
- He healed women (Luke 8:2)
- He praised their faith (Matt. 15:28)
- He included them in his teaching and vision (Matt. 15:38)
- He cared for them (Luke 13:11)
- He spoke of their noble qualities (Luke 18:1-8)
- He commended a woman's loving service of God (Luke 21:1-4)

A former Jewish enemy named Saul, who became Paul, expressed a sentiment in a letter to the Galatians church that divisions of sex disappeared.

"There is neither Jew nor Gentile, neither slave nor free, nor is there male and female, for you are all one in Christ Jesus" (Gal 3:28 NIV).

"Jesus presented the gospel equally as masculine in its strength and just as feminine in its tenderness that the equality of the two sexes in the highest matters must be recognized at once..."[38] The reality is any of the Ten Commandments apply equally to all of humanity and, as such, assumed equality.

Jesus didn't regard women as under a different code of morals. Jesus condemned all sin equally. He did not show favor or a difference in His hatred of it. He also didn't show any difference

---

38 *The Principles of Jesus*, Robert E. Speer, The Westminster Press, 1902, p.85

in His forgiveness. His call was for holiness from all who call Him Lord (John 8:1-11). His was a justice of equality of promise, punishment and forgiveness. There is no distinction between the salvation of men and women.

Leadership or headship does not assume superiority. It is just a role. God is the head of Christ, yet the two are the same. A husband and wife team are simply that: a team. They are both vital to the health of the family, but one must take the lead. Scripture leans toward the male being the provider and protector and the woman to be the comforter and nurturer. However, God is sovereign and always beyond our limited understanding.

It is so unfortunate that modern thought has tried to make these absolutes for the faith so as to get modern society to be at odds with them. The result has been division among non-Christians and Christians alike. It's a division which fails to allow people to discover a God who calls certain individuals to certain roles in uncertain times. God is bigger than our analysis of how the world works. I believe on occasion He uses the opposite of what we consider the standard to get our attention, then demonstrate our fallibility, His power and our need to rely on Him in all situations.

Jesus often confronted the spiritually elite to help them see the world in a different way. The Beatitudes are a great example of this. The beatitudes fit both sexes (all who claim Him as lord and Savior) to be under the law of service to God and others.

Jesus never recognized inferiority of women and his actions demonstrated equality between the sexes. If we are going to discover a life worth living, we must renew our understanding by His example.

The group discussion guide for this topic is in Appendix A on page 367.

RENEW

CHAPTER 19

WRATH

God's wrath is understood as justice based on our choices on earth determining our eternal placement in the life to come.

I grew up in a stable home with dad going to work and mom staying home with the kids. Dad came home every night at 5:30 and we had dinner together. Mom really ran the home. When dad came home from corporate America he was exhausted. He would have his water glass full of vodka and then we would eat. If something needed to be discussed, it was handled at the table or right after. I can remember a couple of times that when mom said, "This will have to wait until your father comes home," that I was scared. My parents believed in corporal punishment. My mom had a paint stick or a spoon. Dad had his hands. Neither was pleasant and rarely was there a lot of discussion or justification. Mom passed judgement and dad executed the wrath. To this day, I am afraid of wrath when I mess up. What about you?

This idea of wrath has shaped my understanding of God and it needs to be reviewed and then renewed in my soul. Let's start first with the definition of the word, then the cultural misunderstanding and then the spiritual applications.

The definition of wrath is:
- "Wrath" is a 12th century word that is defined by Merriam Webster as: strong vengeful anger or indignation. Or it is a retributory punishment for an offense or a crime.
- A synonym would be "indignation," which means anger aroused by something unjust, unworthy or mean.
- Type the word "wrath" into Google and get a definition of divine retribution. It is defined as a supernatural punishment of a person, a group of people or everyone by a deity, in response to some action.
- Both humans and God express wrath. God's wrath is perfect and always justified; man's is never holy and rarely justified.

When I say the words, "God's wrath," what do you think of? Floods, fire, smiting people, others turning to stone, death, genocide or natural disasters? Or do you think of God as a hater or God being harsh or a God who used to be angry at humans?

These perceptions are unhelpful to establishing a relationship with God or exploring the faith I espouse. I have some friends who really can't believe I would take this concept seriously because to them, it seems uneducated and antiquated.

I get their point: How can a God of love ever allow or even endorse actions which seem so contrary to the idea of love? It sounds disjointed, hypocritical, irrational and even cruel. David

Lamb wrote a wonderful book on this called, *God Behaving Badly*. I recommend it if you want to dig into specific events. However, I believe the greatest challenge we face with the wrath of God in our culture is a lack of reading and studying the Bible as the whole story of God's nature. If we read only certain parts and not others, we have an incomplete picture of God.

Think of moment in your life where you did something you knew was right at the time, but had it been taken out of context, you might be labeled as a not-so-good person. However, if the whole story is understood, your actions become reasonable.

On a personal level, the most recent action I took which some deem as unreasonable was the move from Oswego. Many people don't know the anguish and heartache that comes from leading. They also will never understand the heart of an entrepreneur who wrestles every day with corporate decision-making. Needless to say, I left Oswego broken and hurt. For a while, I believed God's wrath was upon me. However, God allows our hurt and then renews our hearts.

Theologian, scholar and pastor J.I. Packer from his book *Knowing God*, summarizes on page 151: "God's wrath in the Bible is never the capricious, self-indulgent, irritable, morally ignoble thing that human anger so often is. It is, instead, a right and necessary reaction to objective moral evil."[39]

The last sentence in that quote provides us a clear picture of the misunderstanding of culture. We want justice but are not capable of seeing all the factors needed to offer justice. Only God stands beyond our limitations of time and space, fully understanding all

---

39   *Knowing God*, JI Packer, IVP, Downers Grove, Il, 1973. P.151

the connected and intermingled aspects of the entirety of life. I believe it why scripture in Joel 2:13 and elsewhere that:

> "Rend your heart and not your garments. Return to the Lord your God, for he is gracious and compassionate, slow to anger and abounding in love, and he relents from sending calamity" (NIV).

God so wants His creation to come to Him; He keeps himself from reacting and coming in the day in which judgement will take place. He does so because He desires all to know Him forever.

God rules the world in such a way that brings Himself maximum exposure (glory) to His creation. When we realize this life is not about us or our way but His. Our finiteness comes into full contrast with His infinite being. It also means we come to understand God *always* acts justly and judges sin (i.e., respond with wrath), otherwise God would not be God. God's love for His glory motivates His wrath against sin.

God must hate and judge sin because its presence taints the mystery of His perfection. Herein lies the ultimate good news: "Christ Jesus came into the world to save sinners" (1 Timothy 1:15 NIV).

I like how Pastor Colin Smith of the Orchard Church in Arlington Heights, Illinois puts this in a recent blog:

> The Bible speaks about God's wrath being poured out at the cross: "I will soon pour out my wrath upon you and spend my anger against you" (Ezekiel 7:8). This takes us to the heart of what happened there: The divine wrath toward sin was poured out on Jesus. He became the "propitiation" for our sins (Romans 3:25), which means

that the payment for our sins was poured out on Jesus at Calvary. Don't ever get the idea that God loves you because Christ died for you. No, it's the other way around. Christ died for you because God loved you! He loved you even when you were the object of His wrath! God so loved the objects of His wrath that He spent the wrath on Himself at slow the cross.

The outpouring of God's wrath on Jesus was the greatest act of love this world has ever seen.

As such, because of Christ's action on our behalf, God can rightly call sinners justified (Rom. 3:26). God has done what we could not do. God no longer needs to bring wrath until the final day when Judgement of all takes place.

Charles Wesley rightly exalted this good news in a classic hymn "Can it Be"

And can it be that I should gain
An interest in the Saviour's blood?
Died He for me, who caused His pain!
For me, who Him to death pursued?
Amazing love! How can it be
That thou, my God, shouldst die for me?

So, what does a recognition of Christ's enduring our wrath (or judgement) mean? How do we respond to those who have not acquiesced to Jesus? Are we to let them continue their eternal path?

First, we are never to take matters into our hands. Wrath or judgment is the Lord's. God alone can avenge because His vengeance is perfect, and He restrains himself, whereas man's wrath is sinful, opening him up to demonic influence. For the Christian, anger and wrath are inconsistent with our new nature, which is the nature of Christ Himself (2 Cor. 5:17). To realize the freedom of our new nature, the believer needs the Holy Spirit to continually cleanse his heart of feelings. Romans 8 shows victory over sin in the life of one who is living in the Spirit (Rom. 8:5-8). Paul tells us in Philippians 4:4-7 tells us that the mind controlled by the Spirit is filled with peace.

Second, the truth about the wrath of God is a fearsome and terrifying thing. We only need to share our belief it is real. The Holy Spirit does the rest. We are not to generate a fire and brimstone moment for people. We only need to express the reality: Only those who have been covered by the blood of Christ, shed for us on the cross, can be assured that God's wrath will never fall on them. "Since we have now been justified by His blood, how much more shall we be saved from God's wrath through Him" (Romans 5:9).[40]

This understanding should call us and everyone we know to a renewed relationship by emulating Christ by loving those whom we struggle with or who seem opposed to our way of life.

The group discussion guide for this topic is in Appendix A on page 368.

---

40   https://www.gotquestions.org/wrath-of-God.html

CHAPTER 20

RICHES

Spiritual wealth is more important than material wealth because spiritual wealth is eternal.

I think I'm becoming more abstract in my thinking because I have wondered about the idea and meaning of the word 'poverty' and its antonym 'prosperity'?

Did you know the United Nations teaches that poverty is defined in either relative or absolute terms? Absolute poverty measures poverty in relation to the amount of money necessary to meet basic needs such as food clothing, and shelter. The concept of absolute poverty is not concerned with broader quality of life issues or with the overall level of inequality in society. The concept, therefore, fails to recognize that individuals have important social and cultural needs. This, and similar criticisms, led to the development of the concept of relative poverty. Relative poverty defines poverty in relation to the economic status of other members of the society: people are poor if they fall below prevailing standards of living in a given societal context. An important criticism of both concepts is that they are largely concerned with income and consumption.[41]

So, can prosperity be defined in similar terms of income and consumption? Can someone have relative prosperity, and another have absolute?

Prosperity, according to dictionary.com, means "a successful, flourishing, or thriving condition, especially in financial respects; good fortune."

Webster's 1828 Dictionary defines it as: "advance or gain in anything good or desirable; successful progress in any business or enterprise; success; attainment of a desired objective."

With these definitions, I believe we can have both a relative and an absolute level of prosperity. It can be relative when compared with others of the same area, region, nation or even world. It is absolute when all would agree the advance is good for all. However, is there a single idea or action which is good for all concerned? We could spend the whole rest of our time together discussing what could be considered good for all and my biggest concern would be that we would end up with criteria that gauges prosperity in the same way we gauge poverty: consumption and income. In a simpler term: riches, morula, denarii, drachma, pounds, marks, rubles, dollars or just plain money.

The danger of the power of money is its ability to gather affection, absorb trust and warp perceptions of the world around us. A man with riches must be on guard because riches alter perceptions. As such, an ailing man can never diagnose himself because the personal perception of the world defines under

---

41 http://www.unesco.org/new/en/social-and-human-sciences/themes/international-migration/glossary/poverty/

deludes. There is an absolute deceitfulness in every person's heart and as prosperity grows, delusion corresponds. Riches bring about a hardening influence. An influence which begins when a person believes good fortune comes more from one's efforts over God's or a higher power's grace.

In the Jewish understanding, the Old Testament Jews believed a person had a special blessing from God if they had riches. It was considered a sign of God's favor. In Islam, good fortune is considered a reward for faithful obedience. Is it true that God picks favorites (like a cosmic game of duck, duck, damned) or God loves those more who do what he says (like a wayward child is told to not question and do it will go okay for you)? I really shouldn't make light of these theological ideas, but they are still prevalent today and not just in Judaism and Islam, but also Christianity.

Jesus declared the rich of His day were woeful (Luke 6:24) and a lot of the poor were blessed (Luke 6:20). Jesus continued with this vein of thought when He clearly spoke against this idea (Luke 16:19-31), warned men against looking at riches as qualifier of God's hand and even went so far as to remind those around Him of the dangers of man's restless desire to have more (Luke 12:13-15). It is this desire which needs to be redirected to live less for oneself and more for the workers and the servants and the disenfranchised.

Our real possessions are what goes into our character or being. Many believe these are possessions we will carry into the next life. Therefore, the love of riches (money), or a more biblical term, "covetousness," becomes a major stumbling block. Jesus even places it with theft, wickedness and deceit (Mark 7:22; Rom. 1:29; 1 Cor. 6:10; Eph. 5:3-5; Col. 3:5; 1 Thess. 2:5). Jesus tried to convey the effects of the love of money. However, He never denounced money. He spoke of money and possessions as a sacred trust from God (Matt. 25:14-30; Luke 19:11-27). A trust based on an understanding of God's wishes or the riches provided. I personally love that Jesus never had any money of His own (Matt. 22:19; 12:24-27). His only retirement plan was to return to the place from which he came. He didn't need a 401K or a pension. He didn't need money to live or advance the Kingdom. He lived a faithful life and so when I hear people tell me what they will do when they retire, get a certain amount of money or win the lottery, I begin to wonder about their spiritual wealth?

I'll never forget when I heard a wealthy, middle-aged man tell another person in the church, he would help more when he retired and had time. This was his time to make money and he look forward to the day when work was not such a priority. In the moment, I wanted to correct him and ask him about his understanding of the scriptures. A servant doesn't choose when they serve or how they serve. They serve out of the overflow of God's grace, not their own hands.

Therein lies the problem with material riches:
1. There is never enough to satisfy.
2. It tends to enforce a misguided trust in things over God (Matt. 6:19-34; Rev. 3:17-18)
3. It deprives the possessor of the privilege of sacrifice (Luke 21:1-4; Mark 12:41-44)

Spiritual wealth is more important than material wealth of any kind (Luke 16:11). It is the greater of the two because it deals with today and eternity.

Proverbs 30:8 (NIV) states, "Give me neither poverty nor riches, give me my daily bread"

A few hundred years ago, the great preacher and evangelist John Wesley showed us another way. Wesley lived in economically uncertain times, yet from humble beginnings he became so well-known that his income eventually reached £1,400 per year. In 2001, this would be the equivalent of earning around $300,000.

So, what did he do with all this wealth? Did he tithe it? No. Wesley went way beyond tithing. He disciplined himself to live on just 30 pounds of the 1400 pounds he earned every year. He gave away 98 percent of all he earned and lived on just 2 percent!

Wesley once preached a sermon on Luke 16.9. In it, he spelled out his philosophy: Money is a tool that can be used for great good or great ill. "It is an excellent gift of God, answering the noblest ends," he claimed. "In the hands of his children, it is food for the hungry, drink for the thirsty, raiment for the naked: It gives to the traveler and the stranger where to lay his head. By it we may supply the place of a husband to the widow, and of a father to the fatherless. We may be a defense for the oppressed, a means of health to the sick, of ease to them that are in pain; it may be as eyes to the blind, as feet to the lame; yea, a lifter up from the gates of death! It is therefore of the highest concern that all who fear God know how to employ this valuable talent; that they be instructed how it may answer these glorious ends, and in the highest degree."

He went on to spell out three simple rules which can guide us: Gain all you can; save all you can; give all you can.

Wesley lived out these principles, on another occasion remarking: "If I leave behind me ten pounds ... you and all mankind [can] bear witness against me, that I have lived and died a thief and a robber."[42]

---

42   http://gbgm-umc.org/umhistory/wesley/sermons/serm-050.stm

Jesus clearly wanted us all to use both faithfully so that we could be trusted with even more (Luke 16:11). Are you faithful with the resources placed in your hands? How will you renew your life by looking at your riches as blessing to be a blessing to advance the rule and reign of Jesus?

The group discussion guide for this topic is in Appendix A on page 370.

CHAPTER 21

POVERTY

*Rarely will a human truly rely on God
until God is all he has.*

What is more physically or spiritually dangerous, wealth or poverty?

If we were to look solely at the environmental statistics, many would say being poor is more physically taxing because the pursuit of food, shelter, clothing, education, safe communities and healthcare takes its toll on people. However, statistics don't often tell the whole story.

In full disclosure, when I was growing up my dad used to say, "You can be happy whether you are rich or poor, it's just easier to be happy when you're rich." He also lived with a fear from his Great Depression childhood of going without. Being poor was associated with being both lazy and failure in his mind. He believed in the Protestant work ethic and often joked when the markets would dip, "At least we will be going to the poor house in a Cadillac." He believed status and having resources proved something to the world about your life.

I often wondered about my dad's drive to succeed and provide. I would question why work was so important and why anyone would allow himself to be less at work just to make sure his boss liked him. I've come to realize that my dad was like so many others in the neighborhoods in which we lived, middle managers who believed the greatest value in life was to sacrifice one's time and effort for a higher status in the world for his family and coming generations.

But not all families had the same opportunities my World War II father had. In a recent blog, a woman commented:

> My grandmother had my mother at sixteen. Two more daughters by the age of twenty. When my mom died, my sister was going through her stuff and found the note below written by my grandmother. I'm guessing it was when my mother was four years old. Beverly was the youngest, an infant at the time.
>
> "My daughters are hungry, and we have nowhere we can go to get help. Beverly has not eaten in ten days except for water and sugar in her bottle and I have stolen the sugar. If God will only find someone who will feed my daughters, I make a solemn vow unless they want to find me, I will never interfere in their lives in any way. I swear by every breath in my body. God help me — for they are my life."
>
> My grandmother gave up all three daughters to foster care and spent the next several years prostituting to survive. Along came the guy I grew up knowing as my

grandpa. Pulled her out of that life, married her and they lived a prosperous life.

To this day, I don't know how my mother and her two sisters reconnected with my grandmother.
The grandparents I grew up knowing were happy, loving, joyful to be around. I didn't know until much, much later from what depths she had risen.[43]

Can you imagine being so poor you had to give up your kids? I've seen it in Haiti. A working mom came to the gate and asked us to take her child. If we didn't, the mother claimed she would have to send the child to a distant relative who would feed the child in exchange for slave labor. The word for this type of slavery is "restiveks" and there are an estimated 300,000 in Haiti. It breaks my heart to think of this, but what other option does a semi-working-class person have? The choices are often less than ideal.

It's helpful in my pursuit of hope and renewal and as a self-avowed Christ follower to remember that Jesus' life began as a poor, working-class tradesman. He knew the daily grind of the poor and even though he was God with skin on (or the Christian term, incarnate), he chose to remain poor and homeless. His entire ministry was a witness to God's love, grace and mercy. It wasn't about possessions, or even promises of a life with more possessions. It was to show us that the only possession that really matters is one's life and what one chooses to do with it.

---

43 *Self.Reddit.com comment (2014) from the question: what is the most pathetic thing you had to do to survive?*

There were times when Jesus was hungry, but He and His companions seemed to not be in any need. While Jesus would teach voluntary sacrifice and even abstemiousness, He did not require his companions to be poor. If fact, some were not (Mark 1:20; 14:3; Luke 14:13).[44]

Jesus was a friend to the poor. He preached to them. He gave them hope through a vision of a heavenly mansion in the next realm and an incredible banquet table filled with food. He was concerned about the poor and proceeded to give them alms (gifts) when waiting for the next excursion. He was never concerned about his resources or those of His disciples. He knew their suffering and wants. He was focused on what was noble in them (Luke 21:3).

In the same way, he also refused to demonize the rich or the ruling class. He did not come to create strata or class division. Jesus steadfastly refused to allow class hatred or political rebellion (John 6:15). He encouraged those with power and money to experience a life without burden or guilt (Luke 19:8). He encouraged using God's generosity with others knowing this would be hard for the immature leaders.

In many ways, the story highlights the truth. Poverty is not the greatest spiritual peril, wealth is. *In wealth there is a capacity for great human service, but it is not greater than personal service in the poor).*[45] Jesus was trying to show that life is independent of possessions and one's faith and character are not dependent upon the stuff our lives.

---

44 *The Principles of Jesus*, Robert E. Speers, The Westminster Press, 1902, p.101

45 Ibid p.102

It makes sense when you think about it. Any wise man will give all that he has for his life (Matt. 16:26; 10:28). Possessions can't add to this life. Time can't be added either. Beyond the basics (food, water, clothes and shelter), the most valuable of all our possession remains the relationship with God. Any other possessions are not condemned, but He would commend the service developing character. Possessions are not about personal pleasure or amusement or diversion. They are about their use or distribution to grow the Kingdom. I love the story of Chuck Feeney.

Most people have heard of Warren Buffett and Bill Gates, but only a few may have heard of Chuck Feeney. *That is because the Irish-American billionaire has always insisted on doing philanthropy as discreetly as he can. For the past thirty years, Feeney has quietly given as much as $6.2 billion from his financial empire to charities and causes worldwide.*

It is estimated that the $1.3 billion he has left will be used up by 2016, with his foundation closing by 2020. Feeney, who made his vast fortune in duty-free shops, made no secret of his desire to be penniless before he dies. He hopes that his example will serve as a guide to his fellow wealthy philanthropists not to wait before their deaths before sharing their wealth. In fact, Feeney's life served to inspire both Gates and Buffett to start their own foundations.[46]

And if that didn't hit you, how about the story of Zell Kravinsky? Zell Kravinsky *knew he wasn't cut out for the wealthy way of living. Sure, he had made millions investing in real estate in his native Pennsylvania, but Kravinsky decided his dollars had*

---

46   https://www.forbes.com/forbes/welcome/?toURL=https://www.forbes.com/sites/danalexander/2014/06/18/warren-buffett-honors-his-hero-the-billionaire-who-secretly-gave-it-all-away/

a grander purpose than just fattening his bank account. In 2001, he began donating money and land to various charities until his contributions reached $45 million dollars. By then, his family and friends thought that he was being too impulsive, but Kravinsky brushed their reservations aside and said that he could always earn more money — though he'd likely give it away as well.

However, Kravinsky still felt that donating money and land wasn't enough. He decided to up the ante and gave his kidney to a total stranger. His move was met with mixed views, ranging from praise to disbelief. Even his wife threatened to leave him, although that was later defused thanks to famous singer Pat Boone, who knew what Kravinsky did and urged her to forgive him for being too generous. As for Kravinsky, he said that he would readily give any of his body parts again for any who needed it.[47]

Jesus shared the fact that the poor will always be among us (Mark 14:7; John 12:8). It was not a condemnation or an approval to ignore their plight. We are to accept the fact without further judgement by understanding the future Kingdom is theirs and their lot is blessed. I believe there are many who don't believe this idea. However, a person in poverty rarely wonders about the need for God or His provision because every day he or she has to practice complete trust in God. A position we can encourage with those who have resources to live but who often don't practice because their security in their physical abilities, skills or talents over-rides their realization of God's help.

---

47   https://listverse.com/2013/12/24/10-refreshing-stories-rich-people-who-gave-their-fortunes-away/

Herein lies the reason wealth is more spiritually dangerous than poverty. *Rarely will a human truly rely on God until God is all he has.* Comfort in one's own ability to provide is *the* pride that comes before the greatest fall of all, one's soul!

The group discussion guide for this topic is in Appendix A on page 370.

RENEW

CHAPTER 22

GIVING TO MAN

*Charity in giving means giving to another man,
not just to lighten his burden or support poor lifestyle
choices, but to leave a lasting piece of the best of one's self
in the hope it changes the recipient forever.*

Early one evening, a successful young man took his new Nissan Maxima to the mall to buy his girlfriend a Christmas present. He had heard on the radio that his usual route was closed off, so he decided to chance it, and go through the crazy-dangerous area of Chicago to get there. He figured it was a better choice than having to go all the way around the city, thus adding two hours to his journey.

Well, the area he had to cut through was in the southwest side of the city, known for its gang warfare and biker bars, and he had chosen the completely wrong time to go through, too, as young punks started to gather for their nightly escapades and certain young ladies went outside to claim their piece of the sidewalk for their nightly business of selling themselves.

At a red light, the young man stopped, and found himself in the middle of a gang war. The gang member from one group took a shot at his enemy, across the street, and the young man in the Maxima was the unfortunate barrier between them. The bullet barely grazed his shoulder, and he cried out in sharp pain, managing to pull over and stop the car.

He got out of the car, intending to go get help, but in his weakened state attracted the wrong kind of attention. A couple of kids looking for some quick drug money noticed his stupor and decided it would be easier to give him a couple of punches, than try to break into a store. They also noticed his car running close by, and put they put two and two together. Soon, he was out of a car, a cell phone and a wallet.

By the time they were gone, he was in rough shape and lay smashed and dirty on the sidewalk. He lay there for what seemed like hours, but what was only a few minutes. He was thrilled when he looked up and saw a pastor from a local church walk by. "Help!" he cried out feebly, but the leader crossed over the other side of the sidewalk and did not even look his way.

The Minister

The minister did not usually walk this way, but he was on his way to a board meeting for all the churches in his district. Unfortunately, it was in one of the rougher areas of town, and John really wasn't used to this environment. He wished he had been able to find parking closer, but he had been forced to walk several blocks to his destination.

He saw the man lying down from a few feet away and felt nervous. Who knows what that man had been imbibing in order to be that intoxicated? Often, these people were dangerous and unpredictable. Just for security's sake, he crossed over to the other side of the street. He was already late for the meeting, and he didn't want any complications. "I'm sure the police will deal with him," he thought. "I need to get going."

A faint wave of guilt washed over him, hoping the man would be okay, but he quickly told himself that he wasn't responsible for saving the world. "They have people for that," he thought. "It's not my calling."

The Church Lady

About a half hour later, a very frequent church-going lady walked by in a rush. She was carrying a Bible, and the injured young man thought for sure she would help him. He tried to call out to her, but she did not help. Instead, she put her nose in the air and quickly walked away in horror and disgust.

The woman had lived on that street for years and had seen everything decline in the last decade. What had once been a hard-working population had been overrun by hookers, pimps and drug addicts. Every day, she heard of more horrors on the nightly news, and it made her sick. She had once been proud to live here, but now she lived in fear. When she heard the young man call out to her, she was sure he would be begging for money to buy some more booze. She was tired of being lambasted by these welfare-dependent bums. She looked at him in disgust, angry at the way the country was going, and hurried home to her little apartment, safe with bars on the windows and a good security system. She knew she shouldn't have gone out so late in the afternoon.

The Christian Biker

Just as he was almost passing into unconsciousness, the young man caught a glimpse of a man in a jean vest covered with decals, and tight pants. He would have been afraid of this biker-looking man under different circumstance, but he had no fear left, only vacuous curiosity. "I wonder what kind of bike he drives," he pondered.

The man, who was dressed like a biker, parked his Harley-Davidson, and decided to hoof it to the bar where he was going to relax for a few hours. He had had a hard week at the mill and was looking forward to a few pops with some good friends. Later, he would grab a cab and pick up his bike in the morning. No one on the street would dare to touch it with his connections.

Just as he neared his destination, he noticed a young man who looked like he'd been beat up pretty badly. Feeling sorry for him, he went over and gently felt his wrist. Yes, he was still breathing. "Are you okay," he whispered, not wanting to startle him. "Not really," the young man replied. "Let me call you an ambulance," the biker said. "You look like you're in pretty bad shape." He used his cell phone to call 911, waited with the young man until they arrived, and paid the ambulance driver the $500 fee. "Take my cell," he told the young man. "Use it to call your Mom and Dad and girlfriend and tell them where you are. And here's a couple hundred to tide you over until you get all your I.D. straightened out. Sorry for what happened to you, man. Those guys were jerks."

The young man left in the ambulance and went to the hospital, used the cell phone to call his family and friends, and afterwards called the biker to leave a message about returning the cell phone. "How can I repay you," he asked. "Don't worry about it," the biker told him. "There are still a few of us Christ followers left in this world."[48]

---

[48] https://owlcation.com/humanities/The-Unscrupulous-Lawyer

We all have read the world has changed and technology advancements are the easiest proof of this. However, mankind and our proclivity to want it our way has not changed. We continue to marvel at stories like this one. Why? Because we are appalled by those who pass by and grateful for the person who stops. We all want to believe we would stop but many of us don't. Maybe the story gives us the average — two-thirds don't stop and one-third do. I can't prove it, but I know we all don't stop every time we see someone in need. Maybe it's because the media has told us horror stories, maybe it's our grade-school teachings of "stranger danger," or maybe it's just our preoccupation with our own lives and problems that we selfishly don't want to add another.

However, I do know those who stop or see a person in need and stop are people of virtue. The current virtue definition from Merriam-Webster defines virtue as:[49]

- *conformity to a standard of right: morality*
- *a particular moral excellence*
- *a beneficial quality or power of a thing*
- *manly strength or courage: valor*
- *a commendable quality or trait: merit*
- *a capacity to act: potency*
- *chastity, especially in a woman*

The Christian biker in our story gave to another out of a sense of virtue but also out of charity. There is a difference. I have had this conversation with many a short-term missionary. The act of giving to another person is exhilarating. We all love to serve. You don't have to be religious to serve to get a feel-good moment. But, just like a

---

49   https://www.merriam-webster.com/dictionary/virtue

quick "high," the feeling dissipates fast and you are left yearning for more. Some get addicted and others acknowledge the good feeling as an experience and go on in search of something else. In many ways, this type of giving is self-centered and no better than a roller coaster ride at the carnival. This is not Christian giving.

As many a scholar has noted, including Robert Spears, the leader of the Christian faith warns of this type of giving because there is a possibility for abuse, pretension, commercialism, spinelessness, laziness and selfishness (Matt. 6:1-4).

As a self-avowed Christ-follower, when a Christian decides to give, they are supposed to do so out of respect for Christ, His teaching and to leave a little of Him with those served. Irish priest, scholar and world acclaimed author from the turn of the last century, William Edward Hartpole Lecky, wrote in *History of European Morals from Augustus to Charlemagne*, "Christianity for the first time made charity a rudimentary virtue."[50]

The word "charity" here, according to the definition from Webster's dictionary of 1828 (Walking Lion Press, 2010) means, "A disposition of heart which inclines men to think favorably of their fellow men and do good. In a theological sense, it includes supreme love to God and universal good will to men."

No other figure in history commanded such giving. Charity in giving means giving to another man, not just to lighten his burden or support poor lifestyle choices, but to leave a lasting piece of the best of oneself that changes the recipient forever. Charity means more than just giving arbitrarily.

---

50   *History of European Morals from Augustus to Charlemagne*, William Edward Hartpole Lecky, D. Appleton and Company, 1869

Our initial story is a contemporary parable of the parable called the Good Samaritan. It highlights a giving that represents personal attention, service rendered, personal concern and intelligent use of resources. The use of a detested figure in both stories is to emphasize the larger point through surprising those who were listening. Jesus rebuked oppression of the poor, the abuse of the weak and powerless like widows and children and any type of exploitation. He also rebuked openly the spirit of externalism — outward signs instead of internal change (Luke 11:39-42). He urged any of his followers to give freely and generously just as they had received freely and generously (Matt. 10:8). In many ways, it is through giving our hearts are brought to a spiritual moment where we recognize giving costs us a bit of ourselves to be truly Christ-honoring.[51]

Now, let me be clear, Jesus didn't say, "Give money." He said, "Give to every man." We never should confine those words to money alone. Jesus did not always give alms (John 9: 1-12) or out of mere pity when asked (Matt. 9:27). He came to seek and save those who were without a faith, done with faith or undone by life. He did not come to give material help. He came to create followers of the Father and he gave accordingly. We must emulate this. When money will help remedy a situation, we must do it. When our discernment tells us giving to the man will cause him harm, we must withhold it. We must always ask ourselves, "Will my giving help the person come to a greater appreciation of the one true leader or detract from their ability to know Him?"

---

51   *The Principles of Jesus*, Robert E. Speer, The Westminster Press, 1902, p.106-108

The best example is the money given to the street drug addict or alcoholic. Money may not help. Food might not help. A ride to the hospital or the mission or the rehab center might be better. Or perhaps a conversation contacting the person's family to deliver a message life, or spending a lunch hour listening to the person over a cup of coffee.

The point is this: The virtue of a Christian giving to another person includes giving of oneself. As good friend once said, charity begins when we give from within to recognize the greater value of the person before us.

The group discussion guide for this topic is in Appendix A on page 372.

CHAPTER 23

GIVING TO GOD

Giving is the most genuine way to show one's trust in God.

Recently, I came out of a grocery store and there were a couple of scouts selling popcorn or cookies. I have nothing against popcorn or the scouts. I hate having people use their kids to beg for money to fund programs I don't have a vested interested in. I hate the cheerleaders on the corners begging for cash for the trip downstate. The football players selling discount coupon books. I dislike child car washes for new uniforms. I'd shake my head at Tootsie Roll vendors for Knights of Columbus. I know I'm getting to be a curmudgeon. I know stuff costs more these days and parents have less to go around. However, why don't we just say no to the cost increases or the trips or new uniforms. Why don't we ask why our schools don't have competitive enough athletic programs, since we already pay to support these? We should never have to raise money or funds for these "good" causes. Whew... I'm glad I got that off my chest.

Now, let's talk about giving from a different angle.

Donations from America's individuals, estates, foundations and corporations reached an estimated $373.25 billion in 2015, setting a record for the second year in a row, reports "Giving USA 2016: The Annual Report on Philanthropy for the Year 2015," released today. Amir Pasic, Ph.D., the Eugene R. Tempel Dean of the Indiana University Lilly Family School of Philanthropy added that, "The share of total giving going to each type of recipient was virtually the same in 2015 as it was in 2014 ... " Patrick M. Rooney, Ph.D., associate dean for academic affairs and research at the school says, "Each year, gifts of $100 million or more play a significant role for some individual donors and many different types of charities, and they do affect the numbers. However, Americans' collective generosity would still be enormous even without those jaw-dropping gifts. Philanthropy is quite democratic and always has been — more people give than vote in the U.S. — and $20, $10 and $1 gifts do make a cumulative difference."

Not only did individuals give the most, in 2015 they were responsible for two-thirds of the year's overall increase in total giving. All but one of nine categories that Giving USA's research covers saw increased giving in 2015; donations to foundations was the exception.

- *Religion — at $119.30 billion, 2015 giving increased 2.7 percent in current dollars, and 2.6 percent when adjusted for inflation.*
- *Education — giving increased to $57.48 billion, 8.9 percent more in current dollars than the 2014 total. The inflation-adjusted increase was 8.8 percent.*
- *Human Services — its $45.21 billion total was 4.2 percent higher, in current dollars, than in 2014. The inflation-adjusted increase was 4.1 percent.*

- *Foundations — at an estimated $42.26 billion in 2015, giving declined 3.8 percent in current dollars and decreased 4 percent when adjusted for inflation.*
- *Health — the $29.81 billion estimated for 2015 giving to this category was 1.3 percent higher, in current dollars, more than the 2014 estimate. When adjusted for inflation, the increase was 1.2 percent.*
- *Public/Society Benefit — the $26.95 billion estimate for 2015 increased 6 percent in current dollars over 2014. When adjusted for inflation, the increase was 5.9 percent.*
- *Arts/Culture/Humanities — at an estimated $17.07 billion, growth in current dollars was 7.0 percent in 2015. When adjusted for inflation, the increase was 6.8 percent.*
- *International Affairs — the $15.75 billion estimate for 2015 increased 17.5 percent, in current dollars, from 2014. The increase was 17.4 percent when adjusted for inflation.*
- *Environment/Animals — the $10.68 billion estimate for 2015 was up 6.2 percent in current dollars, and 6.1 percent when adjusted for inflation, over 2014 giving.*
- *Individuals — $6.56 billion estimate for 2015 was up 2 percent in current dollars. These contributions were largely in-kind donations of medicine contributed via pharmaceutical foundation's' patient assistance programs.*[52]

---

52   https://givingusa.org/giving-usa-2016/

All these stats are simply inspiring. However, as a percentage of GDP, these numbers on Americans' average giving represents only 2-3 percent depending on the news organization reporting. In addition, the numbers are skewed by those in lower- and middle-income categories. The working-class poor and middle class give more on a percentage basis than their wealthier counterparts.

We can find some sort of answer to these questions with the National Center for Charitable Statistics (NCCS), which describes the "U-shape" in charitable donations (as a percentage of income), with tax filers in the $45,000 to $50,000 range giving 4 percent of income, compared to only 2.4 percent for people in the bracket between $200,000 and $250,000. This is in keeping with the Chronicle of Philanthropy's map of charitable giving, in that low- to middle-income Americans give a bigger share of their income. Interestingly, in surveys of the wealthy, people with deep pockets report that they give in droves (95 percent of households) and give 9 percent of their income. Even if some rough household division puts the rate at about 25 percent per person, this number is still very much at odds with the 2.8 percent to 5.9 percent reported by the NCCS, which bases its analysis on the IRS's Statistics of Income (SOI) file. Ken Stern from the Atlantic Monthly found (although does not cite) statistics that the rich only gave 1.3 percent of their income to charity in 2011.[53]

No one is absolutely positive why this phenomenon occurs. In a recent article in *Psychology Today*, a Ph.D. candidate at Berkeley, Paul Piff, repeated the finding — and more: "Lower-income people were more generous, charitable, trusting and helpful to others

---

53 http://philanthropyoutlook.com/wp-content/uploads/2016/01/Philanthropy_Outlook_2016_2017.pdf

than were those with more wealth." The reason? "They were more attuned to the needs of others and more committed generally to the values of egalitarianism."

While stating an age-old axiom, Mr. Piff decided to test the hypothesis that:

> "... The rich are richer because they are more selfish or single-mindedly focused on their own advancement, but Piff's research suggests otherwise. His experiment primed subjects by showing sympathy inducing videos and encouraging them to imagine themselves in different financial circumstances. That changed their reactions — for both sets of subjects. In other words, the poor, imagining themselves rich, became less altruistic. The rich, imagining themselves poor, became more generous to the destitute and ill. Piff concluded: "Empathy and compassion appeared to be the key ingredients in the generosity of the poor."
>
> If we think of this in group terms, it makes perfect sense. Members of each group will identify with other members of the group to which they belong. Their issues will resonate more deeply. The rich will find it easier to give to the cultural institutions they and their friends patronize as well as the colleges and universities they attended. The poor will give to the neighbors suffering from the same problems they are struggling with or to the causes closer to home."[54]

---

54   *https://www.psychologytoday.com/blog/hidden-motives/201008/why-are-the-poor-more-generous*

I like this conclusion, but it's *not* the only deciding factor in a person's willingness to give.

Chronicle editor Stacy Palmer points out in her article about giving that church attendance also factored into people's likeliness to donate. She stated in an article that when you look at the statistics of giving by state and region you can see a pattern. One of the existing patterns has to do with religion: "Utah, for example, residents donated $65.60 to charity for every $1,000 they earned. Utah has a Mormon population of 62.2 percent, according to 2012 Census data. The Mormon church requires members to give at least 10 percent of their annual income to charity. Low levels of charitable giving in some states — New Hampshire having the lowest rate at 1.7 percent — could be attributed to low levels of church attendance," Ms. Palmer adds. The report did not examine giving rates for religious groups other than Christian denominations. "Religion has always played an important role in giving," she says. "People who are religious have always had a very strong tradition of charitable giving ... both to the church and to other solicitations." She was also quick to note that giving in "Bible belt" states has increased among religious as well as secular people. But the jury is out on this because the giving portion of a nominal believer's faith might be in rooted with other earlier teachings.[55]

Many religious faiths espouse giving to those in need. However, there is so much more.

The founder of Christianity never commanded or stated a rule of giving. Some scholars claim Jesus didn't articulate on percentage or endorse the Jewish concept of the tithe because it was an accepted part of their culture and not disputed like of the livelier

---

55   http://www.csmonitor.com/USA/USA-Update/2014/1006/US-poor-and-middle-class-give-more-to-charity-but-wealthy-pull-back

topics — for example, stealing or murder or sexuality. He didn't have to talk about murder or stealing. After all, Jesus didn't come to re-establish a second law but to supplant the law by fulfilling the original and providing his Spirit in each of us so that we could further these principles throughout the community and world.

A good Jew and (now) Christians were to give, but not just money. It says nothing about the tithe, *but* emphasizes the gift of one's whole life to God. Jesus claimed the teachings from God to Moses and those within the rest of Old Testament were more expansive than men had been content to acknowledge. He didn't want His followers to retreat back into the bondage of requirements but to assess one's own connection to God and give in a way that reflects it.

- Percentages don't reflect a person's heart
- Specific amounts are sources of pride or anguish
- Time at church doesn't bring about salvation
- Levels of Christian service don't get you a better seat in heaven
- It's about your heart and how your actions reflect it.

Giving is the most genuine way to show a trust in God. Giving of oneself for the community and furthering of the mission is a statement of belief.

There is a troubling story from the first generations of Christians. In the beginning, the Christians all banded together the way the early Jewish culture did, to help one another. They were taught to share everything. And then, one day, a wealthier gentleman and his wife who go by the names of Ananias and Sapphira sold a piece of their property. They agreed to give the proceeds to the movement, but they decided to keep a little for themselves. I'm sure the two had a good amount of discussion about it. Afterward,

Ananias went along with most of the proceeds being given to the leaders of the church, so the other Christians could be helped. Now, when we say most, we don't know the amount he and his wife held back, but let's just say it was significant. When he went to give the money to the elders, Peter, a disciple of Jesus, called him out on the amount he shorted the movement. This is where the story gets troublesome. The man dropped dead after Peter told him he lied to the Holy Spirit by keeping some of the money. After, they rolled him up in some carpet and buried him. His wife walked in three hours later with no knowledge of what had happened to her husband. Peter asks her if her husband told the truth about the amount. She said yes and was rebuked by Peter. She also dropped dead on the spot. Scriptures say, *"fear crept over the rest of the people"* who knew the whole story (Acts 5:1-11).

In the words of a seventh grader, that seems harsh. So, what do we make of this?

First, if you don't give to God, you are not going to drop dead tonight.

Second, the point Luke is making is God doesn't care what you give but what you hold back and why.

Third, God believes in the gathering of those who call Jesus Lord and Savior and that it is supposed to be a representative of Him in the present.

If you expect to discover a life worth living, renewing our ideas on what it means to give to God must be part of our growing spiritual maturity.

The group discussion guide for this topic is in Appendix A on page 373.

CHAPTER 24

WAR

The church has never been called to go to war.

The topic of war has come up regularly over the last 100 years. It especially heats up when war or the possibility of war seems imminent. The base question from Christians and non-Christians is the same: "Is it morally acceptable to go to war?"

At any given time in the world, there are military conflicts taking place. According to reference.com, as of September 2014 there are ten official wars and eight active military conflicts recognized by the United States. There are also other violent conflicts involving sixty-four countries and 576 militias and separatist groups.[56]

America is involved in some overtly and others covertly. Should we be involved in these — why or why not? It's an age-old question because human life is involved, and war can be construed as a violation of the scriptures. Thankfully, many philosophers and theologians have weighed in. The primary contemporary thought for war was developed long ago and was called the Just War Theory.

---

56   https://www.reference.com/government-politics/many-wars-going-world-right-now-ffd6236450ccb7ae

Just War Theory (Latin: jus bellum iustum) is a doctrine, also referred to as a tradition, of military ethics studied by theologians, ethicists, policy makers and military leaders.[57]

The history of Just War Theory begins in the works of some important philosophers. Augustine (354-430) provides a foundation for Just War Theory in Western literature. Thomas Aquinas (1225-1274) codified Augustine's reflections into the distinct criteria that remain the basis of Just War Theory as it is used today.[58]

Just War theorists argue that any war must be thought about systematically, in advance of any particular war, so that we can do the right thing when the circumstances arise. These are not questions to be answered by the seat of our president's pants, in response to the international or domestic whim of the moment. To act in such a way, they say, would be an injustice to all those who are sent to war, and especially to those whose lives are ended because of it.

All of these arguments against pacifism and "realism"— and for systematic analysis of the morality of war — are valid. They lend credence to the claim that Just War Theory is a practical and moral theory of war.

The tendency for the pacifist is to side with conscientious objectors, like the one portrayed in the true-life story of the movie of *Hacksaw Ridge*. It's the story of a conscientious objector who serves his country as a medic who saves lives only after being an outcast among his own. The realists want to point to the tragedy of the world and the state of human nature along with the seeming

---

57   https://en.wikipedia.org/wiki/Just_war_theory

58   https:// oregonstate.edu/instruct/phl201/modules/just_war_theory/criteria_intro.html

endless war present in the Old Testament. A fact, but one that fails to accept the idea of a theocracy versus a democracy. A difference between man's will and God's.

All forms of Just War Theory provide guidelines that fall into two categories: justice in entering a war, and justice in waging a war. (These two categories are known as jus ad bellum and jus in bello, respectively.) Broadly speaking, Just War Theory holds that a nation can go to war only in response to the impetus of a "just cause," with force as a "last resort" after all other non-military options have been considered and tried — with its decision to go to war motivated by "good intentions," with the aim of bringing about a "good outcome." And it holds that a nation must wage war only by means that are "proportional" to the ends it seeks, and while practicing "discrimination" between combatants and noncombatants. Finally, in a requirement that applies to both categories, Just War Theory holds that the decision-making power for when, why and how to wage war—including the declaration of war—must rest with a "legitimate authority."

By themselves, these guidelines — good intentions, just cause, last resort, proportionality, discrimination, and legitimate authority — are highly ambiguous. Their meaning and interpretation depend on the view of the just, the good and the legitimate presupposed by Just War Theory — that is, the theory's basic view of morality. Although advocates of Just War Theory differ on many specifics about the nature of morality, they all hold one fundamental idea in common. To zero in on this idea, let us turn to the origins of Just War Theory: the writings of the Christian theologian Saint Augustine on the proper use of violence by individuals.

In his work, Augustine asked whether a Christian can ever justify killing another, given the Biblical imperative to "turn the other cheek." Augustine's answer was this: One can use force, not to protect oneself, but to protect one's neighbor.

As the scholar Jean Elshtain, author of the highly regarded book Just War Against Terror, explains:

"For early Christians like Augustine, killing to defend oneself alone was not enjoined: It is better to suffer harm than to inflict it. But the obligation of charity obliges one to move in another direction: To save the lives of others, it may be necessary to imperil and even take the lives of their tormenter." [59]

Thus, according to Augustine, if only you are attacked, you are obligated to turn the other cheek and die, because personal self-defense is immoral; only if someone attacks your neighbor's cheek are you permitted to retaliate.

Augustine's theory is not about justice in the sense of the innocent defending their lives against the guilty. In Augustine's view, the guiding purpose and standard for the just use of force by individuals — trumping guilt or innocence — is that it must be an act of selfless service to others.

All of these boils down to this: One's life is not an end in itself, to be defended righteously for its own sake — but a means to some higher end, to be sacrificed or preserved as is required by one's moral duty to serve others. This is a perfectly consistent expression of the present-day morality of altruism.[60]

Altruism is defined as the belief in or practice of disinterested and selfless concern for the well-being of others.[61]

---

59   *Just War Against Terror*, Jean Bethke Elshtain, (New York: Basic Books, 2003), p. 57.

60   https://www.theobjectivestandard.com/issues/2006-spring/just-war-theory/#_edn6

61   https://www.merriam-webster.com/dictionary/altruism

WAR

The other side of the pendulum believes Jesus came to "inculcate such principles of conduct and to establish relations between God and Man that any unbrotherly conduct should cease." They often cite Matthew 5:38-48 as the cornerstone principle to love all regardless of race or creed so as there is no place for war.[62]

Alfred Thayer Mahan was a United States Naval officer and well-respected historian, whom some have called "the most important American strategist of the nineteenth century." He proposed that war is the employment of force for the attainment of an objective or for the prevention of injury. However, we must ask, can man determine God's right objective or His larger will for the world? After all, God has managed force for thousands of years. God Himself is constantly in the process of taking human life and has authorized man to be His agent in many cases. For this fact alone, war cannot be wrong just because it results in death. However, war as war is not justifiable. It requires an understanding that the possession of power is a talent committed in a sacred trust, for which an account will be exacted; and an obligation to resist external evil to be evaluated to protect the poor and powerless.[63]

Jesus' voice in the reading of Isaiah at the temple comes to mind. He said he had come: "To proclaim good news to the poor, to proclaim freedom to the prisoners, recovery of sight to the blind, to set the oppressed free and proclaim the year of the Lord's favor." We as Christians who claim allegiance to Him must continue to act in ways which honor this reading.

---

62 *The Principles of Jesus*, Robert E. Speer, 1902, p. 119-120

63 *The Principles of Jesus*, Robert E. Speer, The Westminster Press, 1902, p.121

It is true that Jesus spoke in the garden when Peter acted hastily to his unlawful arrest: "Put your sword back in its place," Jesus said to him, "for all who draw the sword will die by the sword (Matt. 26:52 NIV)." But he also said, "My Kingdom is not of this world. If it were, my servants would fight to prevent my arrest by the Jewish leaders. But now my Kingdom is from another place (John 18:36 NIV)." In stating this, He was submitting Himself to a death for the good of all men and the salvation of the world. We, in turn, must be willing to do the same when our death secures glory for Him.

The church has never been called to go to war. Governments have and have invoked God's name in the process. However, God calls His person to involve themselves only when evil is to be thwarted or justice for the powerless is the aim. Like the church, renewing our understanding of war helps us to develop our relationship with both God and others through our appropriate response to the ills of this world.

The group discussion guide for this topic is in Appendix A on page 374.

CHAPTER 25

NON-RESISTANCE/BOUNDARIES

"The everlasting rule is, that thou render good for thy brother's evil; the shape in which thou shalt render it, love shall prescribe."

When I was growing up, my mom told me never to fight. It wasn't Christian. We were told to turn the other cheek. I was also a middle kid, which means I really didn't like conflict anyway. I wanted everybody just to get along. However, let's just admit the world does not operate in this manner. The problem was, my mom and my upbringing led me to be an easy target as a kid. It was Jeff and Casey who did it the most. The two hoodlums from the neighborhood. Picked on, intimidated and bullied was my lot in life until my cousins showed up one Thanksgiving. You see, my cousins got the growth gene. They were both over six feet tall, with a father who made sure they knew how to fight; but they also were wise enough to know they couldn't fight for me. So, we started a backyard football game that almost always turned into someone fighting or me getting bullied. This time, my cousins kept the other neighborhood kids from jumping in on the fight and I stood toe-to-toe with the bully. They wouldn't let me back down or quit. It wasn't until the bully stopped that my cousins decided it was time for us all to go home. I was bruised and scraped, but I was sure if I ever had to defend myself again, I'd be ok. My Mom still overreacted when I came home, and my uncle smiled knowingly. It was an interesting moment in my life because I wondered: Did my mom and the priests all get the "turn the other cheek" idea wrong?

When in doubt about what it means to be a Christian, check the book right? So, I looked for Jesus' actions when conflict arose during His time on earth:

- When people threatened to stone Him, he made no resistance and simply walked away (Luke 4:29-30, John 8:59, 10:39)
- He disapproved of His disciples' use of violence when he was arrested (Matt. 26:52)
- He refrained from use of His power to get rid of his enemies (Matt. 26:53-54)
- When unjustly accused and tried, He endured insult without a word. (Matt. 26:67, Mark 14:65, Matt. 27:30)
- When confronted with torture and death, He did not resist (John 19:17)
- He told his disciples to act in a similar fashion when both were rejected from a village (Luke 9:54-55) and welcomed negatively (Matt. 10:23)

The greatest reference comes from a moment when Jesus was teaching some 2,000 years ago on the side of a hill. The people had come to hear what he had to say, and he was giving them a great deal to think about. Most of which was a correction of what the Jewish leadership had been teaching. In this case (Matt. 5:38-39), Jesus was addressing the idea of being personally insulted and the best course of action. He preferred that a person try to reconcile over retribution.

Jesus was teaching us principles to direct us in ways that will draw attention and glory to His name.

Henry Hart Milman, who wrote several acclaimed theological writings in the middle of the nineteenth century (best-known for his eight-volume *History of Latin Christianity*), believed the latter to be true. Jesus was not formulating a fixed rule of law, but a way of life. Milman stated, "It is an establishment of certain principles, the enforcement of certain definitions, the cultivation of a certain temper of mind, which the conscious (i.e. the moral judgement) is to apply to the ever-varying (demand) of time and place."[64] The point being, Jesus had the advantage of knowing that no person could take His life from him but that he would decide when He would lay it down. He (because He was God) knew when it would be best to submit and die without resistance. He measured all situations for the impact it would have on the furthering of the expanse of the Kingdom. He was not a law giver. He was the Lord of life (Luke 12:14) inspiring only the inward spirit of any man.

Jesus came to defeat the work of Satan. He gave his followers authority ... to overcome all the power of the enemy (Luke 10:19) and the forces of evil in society (Eph. 6:13). James and Peter tell us to resist the devil (James 4:7; 1 Peter 5:9), yet Jesus also wants to conquer our desire to retaliate and avenge. God's people must work for justice but not take personal revenge. Jesus stood silent before his accusers, allowing himself to be crucified, thereby winning the ultimate battle over the enemy (Col 2:15). Similarly, you and I can win the battles of the heart by learning to turn the other cheek so that others will come to be inspired to know Jesus.[65]

---

64   Ibid. p.125

65   Quest Bible p.1418 commentary

This is where the idea of boundaries comes into play. After all, there are many evil forces being generated by other entities (human, institution or spirit) which cripple our ability to become what God has created us for, that Jesus came to redeem and that the Holy Spirit has come to be present to guide. How is a Christian to respond to these debilitating obstacles?

Woodrow Wilson once said, "The only use of an obstacle is to be overcome. All that an obstacle does with brave men is, not to frighten them, but to challenge them."[66] I believe this is true for us when confronted with the evil forces of the world. We are "called" to overcome and this will look different in every situation, as well as in every person.

I've found it helpful to refer to what Dr. Townsend, the author of the best seller *Boundaries,* has said on many occasions about managing the unwanted aspects of life. He said:

> "Boundaries limit the effect of evil. Remember, because God does not control people, they are, in a certain way, free to be evil. He does not make them be good. He limits His sovereignty and control in some ways that we do not totally understand. But, even though He allows them to be evil, He limits the effects of their choices. He exercises limits on the effect that their choices will have on Him, His church, the world, etc."

He has also given us this (opportunity) to limit the effect that evil choices that people make can have on life. One of the best examples of that is in Matthew 18:15-18. It is

---

66   https://www.brainyquote.com/quotes/woodrow_wilson_403848

the role of us to take a stand and "bind" evil as it presents itself. Read Psalms 101 for a great description of how David thought about the things that must be bound so that the evil of others would not "cling" to him.

Additionally, God wants us to limit the effect that the evil is having on their lives as well. He wants us to restore those who get "caught up," by evil. We are to put boundaries on the cancer that is destroying them and be redemptive in their lives (Gal. 6:1).

> God is about life. He is about restoring good things. And to do that, evil things must be held in check and transformed. He has given us many tools to perform this function of the salt that seasons the earth:
> - Truth and Commands
> - Confrontation
> - Rebuke
> - Exhortation
> - Forgiveness
> - Group Intervention
> - Consequences
> - Discipline
> - Restoration
> - Limit Setting
> - Separation
>
> These are some of the processes that God has (given) us to limit and restore (that which is inherently) evil. And, they work. The problem is that we do not exercise our control and responsibility to do these things in our significant relationships, the church,

and the world at large. As has been the story since the garden of Eden, the mess is largely of our own making. If we would use our self-control to do these things, then we would not have the messes in various aspects of life in which we find ourselves. We have misused our freedom. But, the good news about boundaries is that you can take control back in your own areas of influence and begin to limit evil and restore life."[67]

Christian love and prudence are used in each case to decide the outward conduct needed as we are confronted with the question, what is the best course of action for this situation? What will bring the other person into a new relationship with Christ? If the answer is patience, then wait. If the answer is forbearance, continue to walk beside. If forgiveness, then ignore the offense. If separation, then leave or force the other out of your sphere of relevance. The deepest question revolves around what loving action will produce a recognition of God's presence in the world and of His love of you? Therein lies the answer to what type of non-resistance is God's way. As Robert Speer quotes, "The everlasting rule is, that thou render good for thy brother's evil; the shape in which thou shalt render it, love shall prescribe."[68]

The group discussion guide for this topic is in Appendix A on page 376.

---

67 http://www.cloudtownsend.com/scoop-on-boundaries/

68 *The Principles of Jesus*, Robert E. Speer, The Westminster Press, 1902, p.127

CHAPTER 26

RIGHTS

*Duty is always greater than a right for a Christian
because in foregoing our human/natural rights,
we show our trust in the Lord's love
to the surrounding culture.
This gives our lives eternal meaning.*

Have you ever heard the saying all you have to do in this life is die and pay taxes? I have to say I disagree. I think the statement fails to take into account the larger scope of what is taking place around us.

I believe we have all been put here on earth by a power greater than us to live a life worthy of our creator's ingenuity in crafting us. Let's face it, the human form is still as complex as ever, with new discoveries happening every day. It is as complicated as the galaxies and just as hard to recreate without divine spark.

I like George Washington Carver's quote: "No individual has any right to come into the world and go out of it without leaving behind him distinct and legitimate reasons for having passed through it."[69]

We can never claim to have the answers to what makes a life. However, we can realize all life has inherent value because it was made by a greater power and comes with inherent rights as well as duty.

A right, according to the dictionary, is:
1. That which is morally correct, just, or honorable.
2. A moral or legal entitlement to have or obtain something or to act in a certain way.[70]

These rights are often categorized as both *natural and legal rights.* Legal are bestowed upon an individual or a society by the system that monitors justice for the society. The second type of right is called natural or human rights. They are the universal rights of human beings that cannot be repealed or restrained because they are present in each person.

I love how a 16-year-old girl at the 1997 World Summit of Children put it:

> He prayed — it wasn't my religion.
>
> He ate — it wasn't my food.
>
> He spoke — it wasn't my language.
>
> He dressed — it wasn't what I wore.
>
> He took my hand — it wasn't the color of mine.
>
> But when he laughed — it was how I laughed.
>
> And when he cried — it was how I cried.

---

69   https://www.brainyquote.com/quotes/george_washington_carver_386067

70   https://en.oxforddictionaries.com/definition/right

The United Nations agreed to the definition of Human Rights in 1948 in a thirty-article document.[71] The first article of the Human Rights appeal outlines the intent of the rest of the articles. It states: "All human beings are born free and equal in dignity and rights. They are endowed with reason and conscience and should act towards one another in a spirit of brotherhood."

I find it interesting that the organization in charge of bringing countries together to avoid the worst possible outcomes of conflict needed to define what basic human rights were. The U.N. Human Rights document gives individuals "rights and/or authority" establishing the dignity of human existence with a multinational power to enforce them should they be violated. The United Nations established The Commission on Human Rights: "To examine, monitor and publicly report on human rights situations in specific countries or territories (known as country mechanisms or mandates,) as well as on major phenomena of human rights violations worldwide."[72]

The U.N. understood better than any other organization that there were differing opinions on the rights of humans in different cultures. Some cultures are okay with slavery, others with cultural class systems and still others with the advantage of certain sexes. With each difference comes a hurdle to be overcome, so the greater issue of de-humanizing individuals or whole classes of people can be reversed.

The U.N. document attempts to establish two types of rights: legal and natural. Legal rights are bestowed by a legal system and natural or human rights are universal and cannot be repealed or

---

71   http://www.un.org/en/universal-declaration-human-rights/

72   https://en.wikipedia.org/wiki/United_Nations_Commission_on_Human_Rights

lessened. By the U.N. adopting the commission's documentation and definition of legal and natural, rights were established. A significant achievement in and of itself because the establishment allows for: enforcement, violation, surrender or sacrifice of a person's rights.

"There can be no sacrifice of rights when there are no rights. The greatest sacrifice is the self — abasement of those who have the most rights. If one has no rights, we have no authority. If we have no authority, we don't have the power to waive them. And likewise, the possession of rights is no evidence that we are to use them. They may have been given to us, not to use, but to waive."[73]

In fact, I would side with the theologians who teach the decision to or *not* to exercise a right demonstrates a "duty or responsibility is higher than freedom; that when a man has a power, the first question to ask is, 'how and in what spirit is it my duty to use my power of privilege?'"

The definition of duty is:
1. Ethical, legal, or moral accountability, owed always or for a certain period, especially to someone who has a corresponding right to demand satisfaction of an obligation.
2. Responsibility of conduct, function, or performance that arises from an express or implied contract, or from the fact of holding an office or position.[74]

---

73 *The Principles of Jesus*, Robert E. Speers, The Westminster Press, 1902. P. 130

74 http://www.businessdictionary.com/definition/duty.html

There is no greater example of this then Jesus Christ's action on behalf of all creation. His entire life on earth was about surrendering His rights for the benefit of others (John 5:41-44). As Christians, we have a duty to follow in Christ's example and abandon our rights for the betterment of the rest of society. His example gave people pause to take notice of the one true God. The greatest human example of this was the Apostle Paul. Paul's writings make up 23 percent of the New Testament. They are divided in pastoral letters and general letters. I would categorize his writing as that of a father wondering what's going to happen to the next generation if they don't get this news. He lived his life for the cause and wrote about it often. His treatise to this topic of human rights as a Christian is spelled out in 1 Cor. 9:4-27. The point being, a duty is always greater than a right for a Christian because in the foregoing of our human /natural rights, we show our trust in the Lord's love to the surrounding culture. This gives our lives eternal meaning.

The group discussion guide for this topic is in Appendix A on page 377.

RENEW

CHAPTER 27

CHARACTER

All people who have asked to follow a spiritual path agree that it takes making uncomfortable decisions, determined effort, unceasing commitment and everyday obedience.

A wealthy sultan of the Muslim faith, Saladin, once approached Nathan the Wise, a Jewish scholar, with a question: "Your reputation for wisdom is great," said the Sultan. "You must have studied the great religions. Tell me, which is the best, Judaism, Islam or Christianity?"

Nathan the Wise found himself in a predicament. If he answered "Judaism," his Islamic friend would be insulted, but if he answered "Islam," he would lose his own integrity. Nathan the Wise thought for a moment then responded with a parable.

"Once upon a time, there was a king who possessed a magnificent opal ring. It glowed with thousands of colors, but its true power lay in the fact that it made a person beloved of God and others. For many generations, the ring was passed down from parent to favorite child, until finally it came to a king who had three children all equally favored. What was the king to do? He decided to fashion two more rings, each identical in appearance to the original. He then gave one to each child, with each believing they had the original ring.

But instead of harmony, the three rings brought conflict. Each child believed they possessed the true ring and therefore the right to inherit the throne. The tension was escalated when the rings were examined, but differences between them could not be determined."

At this point Saladin interrupts. "But surely my friend you are not suggesting that Christianity, Islam and Judaism are the same? Surely there are great differences between them?" "You are right Saladin" replied Nathan, "but each of these religions is based on faith and belief, and who can prove that one is superior to the other? But let me continue with my tale, for it is nearly at an end."

"The quarrel among the three children became so great it was brought before a judge. The judge listened as each child explained their case. When the time for judgment came all listened with great interest. 'I have been asked to decide which of these rings is the original,' began the judge. 'As the original ring made its wearer beloved of God and people, I can only conclude that none of you have the original ring, for your rings have brought hatred and strife between you. None of you is loved by the other, so I must conclude that the original ring perished with your father and that all three you possess counterfeits. Or it may be that your father was weary of the tyranny of a single ring, and made duplicates which he gave you. So let each of you prove his belief in his ring by conducting yourselves in a manner that befits those beloved of God and people." Source: Adapted from Gotthold Ephraim Lessing, Nathan der Weise (1779).

The story makes a few interesting points. The greatest of which is a person with character lives as an example of what he/she believes and values most.

As a self-avowed Christ-follower, I know Jesus hated religiosity (formerly known as externalism): an outward concern for the appearance of religion. He denounced it in the Pharisees and others. He went so far as to point the ridiculousness of the established rules (Matt. 15:18-20). He openly debated their error when they pointed it out. He tried to bring attention to the inner life over and above the outer rule based "law."

Now, Jesus never denied that our actions can and do influence our thoughts and thereby our character. He regularly established the will of man falls short of God's desire. However, if we are willing to surrender our will and connect to His, we will be influenced to follow through on actions which will ultimately result in more love, grace, mercy, hope and service in the world. This is true Christian character.

Jesus fixed his gaze on our inner life. Dwight Moody once said, "Character is what man is in the dark." Or from the motivational poster, "Character is what you do when no else is looking." Jesus made this clear in His Sermon from the Mount. A man's actions (good and bad) begin inside his thoughts.

I often joke that I'm grateful there is not a bubble above my head playing my every thought. I am just too human sometimes. I also know these thoughts can be held in check when I follow Christ's example to keep my life focused on the eternal — big picture (Matt. 5:45; Matt. 24:44; John 12:36). In fact, all people who have asked to follow a spiritual path agree that it takes making uncomfortable decisions, determined effort, unceasing commitment and everyday obedience. Being a Christian requires these aspects for spiritual development.

When I think of these requirements, I think of so many of the saints outlined in the Hall of fame of faith in Hebrews 11. However, I also think of people like Sister Teresa and Dietrich Bonhoeffer.

Dietrich Bonhoeffer was Professor of theology at the University of Berlin in Germany in the 1930s. At this time, German Christians were divided over Hitler. One group allied themselves with Hitler; they wanted a "pure" German nation. They formed an official German church which supported Hitler and banned Jews from holding official positions in the church. Bonhoeffer was among those who could not go along with Hitler's anti-Jewish, radically German vision. With others, he set up an underground church which explicitly refused to ally itself to Hitler's Third Reich vision. It was dangerous. In 1937, Bonhoeffer was fired. He fled to London.

Two years later Bonhoeffer was faced with a choice. He'd been offered one of the most prestigious theology appointments in the world — lecturing at Union Seminary in New York. Or, he could return to Germany to head up an illegal, underground seminary for the churches that refused to go along with Hitler. He decided his faith would be meaningless if he took the easy option. He headed back to Germany and found Hitler so evil that he abandoned his commitment to nonviolence and got involved in a plot to assassinate Hitler. The plot failed and, in 1943, Bonhoeffer was arrested. In prison, he led worship services for his fellow prisoners until the fateful day — April 9, 1945 — when he was executed by the Nazis. Through all this, what distressed Bonhoeffer was the way that so many Christians could sell out to Hitler's evil vision. How could people who owned the name of Christ so betray

Christ? How could they pray in a church which banned Jews from holding office? It convinced Bonhoeffer that religiosity in and of itself was worthless. It didn't matter how fervently a person believed in Jesus, how many times each day they prayed, how earnestly and sincerely they sang hymns on Sundays."[75]

Christian character is best defined by our willingness to speak and live the truth in both the easy and hard times of life. It's the reason RENEW includes regular serving components so as not to lose sight that Christian character requires more than listening and talking.

The group discussion guide for this topic is in Appendix A on page 378.

---

[75] https://storiesforpreaching.com/category/sermonillustrations/hypocricy/

RENEW

CHAPTER 28

DEATH

Death is the gateway to what is greater and to the creator.

Death and dying are always some of the most interesting topics of our faith journey.

It's one of the easiest topics to begin a conversation with but one of the hardest to finish because not many have gone into the afterlife for more than a few minutes outside of Jesus. But the topic of death and dying is so important to us because it helps define what we live for and what life's all about.

I had an interesting moment with a student this week where I substitute. The conversation started with what are you living your life for and quickly evolved into what do you believe happens when you die. He said, "I just mash all the major religions together and take the best from all of them and try to live for today." I asked about what happens after you die. He said, "I don't care. I'll figure that out when I get there." We may gasp at his answer, but this way of thinking is the same for many adults today. They don't want to think about death because it leads to change in one's actions now.

What happens when we die? Where do we go? Do we just stop existing? These are age-old questions that we all have.

The largest religions and worldviews all provide an answer for what happens after our hearts stop beating.

- Muslims believe that the present life is only a preparation for the next realm of existence. Muslims believe the soul remains in a kind of "soul sleep" until Judgment Day. When the Day of Judgment arrives, everyone is judged according to their deeds in life.
- Death in Hinduism is very spiritual, and it strongly believes in the rebirth and reincarnation of souls. So, according to Hinduism, death is regarded as a natural process in the existence of soul as a separate entity. When a person dies, the soul travels for some time to another world and finally returns to the earth to continue its journey.
- Buddhists look at death as taking a break from this materialistic world. Buddhist people do not think of death as a continuation of the soul, but consider it an awakening. They believe in reincarnation: Once a person dies on this earth, he will be reborn to a new life here and the status of that life depends on the work he did before his previous death.[76]
- Post-biblical Judaism offers a range of beliefs about life after death. Resurrection is by no means the only option; and, when it is specified, it is not a general

---

76   http://www.religiousmovements.org/views-on-death-according-to-different-religions/

word for life after death, but a term for one particular belief. In fact, resurrection is not simply a form of life after death; resurrection hasn't happened yet. People do not pass directly from death to resurrection, but go through an interim period, after which the death of the body will be reversed in resurrection. Resurrection does not, then, mean survival; it is not a way of describing the kind of life one might have immediately following physical death. It is not a description of death and/or the state which results from death. In both paganism and Judaism, it refers to the reversal, the undoing, the conquest of death and its effects. That is its whole point. That is what Homer, Plato, Aeschylus and the others denied; and it is what some Jews, and all early Christians, affirmed.[77]

No matter the worldview, physical death is an unavoidable fact. The physical realm ends for everyone on earth. While I find it comforting all the major religions believe life continues after our hearts stop beating, I also love what those who believe in what only can be proven empirically have discovered. A famous scientist once said, "Science, for instance, tells us that nothing in nature, not even the tiniest particle, can disappear without a trace. Nature does not know extinction. All it knows is transformation! Now, if God applies this fundamental principle to the most minute and insignificant parts of His universe, doesn't it make sense to assume

---

[77] http://ntwrightpage.com/2016/07/12/jesus-resurrection-and-christian-origins/

that He applies it also to the masterpiece of His creation — the human soul?"[78]

Did you hear that? Nothing disappears without a trace. Jesus knew this long before man was created. As followers of Jesus, we know this and so did Jesus when he faced death.

Jesus shared our mortality, but he knew the power of His Father, the place of heaven and the nature of His mission. He knew the outcome of His life was fait accompli, so he prepared those closest to Himself for His death (John 2:22). They were aware of it and some might say they expected it (Luke 9:22; 17:25; John 12:33; 18:32; Luke 24:21). He was not afraid. He stood calmly before the crowds, understanding the pain which would soon overtake him and deciding to move ahead anyhow. I respect how Robert Speer, in his acclaimed writing of *The Principles of Jesus* written in 1902, describes the moment:

> "But Jesus in the garden was shrinking from the thought, not of death on the cross, but of death before the cross. The strain through which was so great the He almost feared he would break under it, and He cried to God to save Him from death and was heard (Heb. 5:7)."[79]

When death came, Jesus met it, comforted others through it and even asked those who loved Him not to mourn (Luke 23:28,43,46; John 19:27). He was, after all, the Lord of death. He raised the dead — a daughter of a synagogue ruler, the son of a

---

[78] "Why I Believe in Immortality" and "What Do You Believe About Eternal Life" by James W. Moore, sermons.com

[79] *The Principles of Jesus*, Robert E. Speer, The Westminster Press, 1902,

Nain widow and even His friend Lazarus (Luke 8: 46-56; 7:14-15; John 11).
- He stood against death.
- The grave could not hold Him.
- Sheol couldn't contain Him.
- The devil couldn't stop him.

He would deliver us all from its bondage (Heb. 2:14-15) so that the wages of sin would no longer be death for those who make the decision to believe and repent. Therefore, resurrection defines the conqueror, the conquering of the sin of this life as well as the lives of those who strive for the same holiness.

The season of Lent is about recognizing all three of these facts and changing our lives accordingly. *Death is the gateway to what is greater and to the creator.* Therefore, death is not something to mourn and wail or allow to fester in our minds but a fact to accept and celebrate as a benefit for a life surrendered to the will of the creator. Hence the reason we should not fear death. *Death and death to oneself is not an outcome but a transfer station.* In life, it is a transfer of our old selves to new self. In death, it's a transfer of the physical for the immortal. It's a transfer of the finite to the eternal.

For the Christ-follower, Paul puts it best in his letter to the Corinthians:

> Where, O death, is your victory? Where, O death, is your sting? The sting of death is sin, and the power of sin is the law. But thanks be to God! He gives us the victory through our Lord Jesus Christ. Therefore, my dear brothers and sisters, stand firm. Let nothing move you. Always give yourselves fully to the work of the Lord, because you know

that your labor in the Lord is not in vain. 1 Cor. 15 55:58 (NIV)

Renewing one's view of death helps one to value and discover a life worth living by placing an increased importance on our interactions with God and others in the present.

The group discussion guide for this topic is in Appendix A on page 379.

CHAPTER 29

LOVE

*Loving one another is the ability to love
in a way that changes their circumstances or the world's
because of your word or deed.*

Is commanding another person to love even possible? Can someone be forced to love?

It's been stated before: For many people, the first experience of love helps them recognize the spiritual. Maybe it's the newfound sense of the unseen and unknown or it could be the greater meaning it provides in a life without much other. The experience of love has been analyzed a thousand different ways from just as many cultures. There are people who have offered to define the stages of love and others who want to show it's purely biological. Some religions even want to claim "love" as the greatest asset to knowing oneself.

Buddhism declares there are four elements of love. The first is maitra, which can be translated as loving kindness or benevolence. It is the ability to bring joy through fully understanding the person. Without understanding, love is an impossible thing. The second element of true love is compassion, karuna. This is not only the desire to *ease the pain of another* person, but the ability to do so. The third element of true love is joy, mudita. If there is no joy in love, it is not true love. The fourth element is upeksha, equanimity or freedom. In true love, you attain freedom. You must love in such a way that the person you love feels free, not only outside but also inside.[80]

Now, there is some interesting truth in these categories; however, awareness is never the answer. It is only the first step in recovery and in living a life filled with love.

Do you remember the first time you were really in love? The first hand-holding, deep discussion, hug, kiss, fight, separation and breakup? It was intense. From that moment on, many of us hoped to find it just as intense. Unfortunately, even if we did, we learned love had more than four elements, or seven stages or even renewed actions or inactions. The truth is, all love simmers and heats up over time only to become a comfortable relationship of shared values and customs. A place many would rally against, but in which others find deep peace, joy and yes, a true spiritual parallel to our relationship with God himself.

As a result, how we have experienced and understand love informs our expectations for being in relationship with both God and others. Unfortunately, many, if not all of us, have warped understandings of love. Thankfully, God demonstrates love to us in many ways. There is a witness to love in creation. In the expanse of the universe. In the beauty of nature. In the touch of someone you care for. In the kind words of an authentic relationship. In the provision of our every physical need. In all knowledge and wisdom, God's love is revealed.

---

80 http://spiritualityhealth.com/articles/four-aspects-love

Hence, the reason we say God's love for us is revealed in His coming as Jesus. The entire plan for our ability to spend the rest of our lives with God is born out of love (John 3:16). Jesus' own love for humanity was born out of His willingness to give His life out of love for us (John 15:13). Love is the cornerstone of our ability to be in a personal relationship with God (John 13:35; 14:15, 21 and 23). Loving others is the greatest spiritual act: selfless service to others in both our words and actions.

God helps us understand the interconnectedness of love through His intimate relationship with Jesus and Jesus' relationship with Him. Jesus lived this understanding by:

1. Keeping His commands
2. Living "in love" with the world
3. Staying obedient
4. Remaining aware of His role in the physical and spiritual worlds
5. Being aware of God's presence in all activities and outcomes

This is the divine love that is so expansive it lives on in and through humanity. In John 15, Jesus shares the secret to "real" love is the interconnection available to us all if we accept His love. He prays for this to happen in John 17:26. A prayer that leads to one of the greatest promises of love, God with us. Emmanuel. God with us.

I once heard a preacher say when we get to heaven we shouldn't be surprised when the saints of yesteryear coming running up to us to ask, "How was it to have God's spirit with you always? What was it like to have the power of the world available and abiding in you? How was it to love in the way God loves?"

As I reflect on the question, I wonder if I have lived, accessed or believed I had His power within me. *I wonder if I have ever taken the command to love my neighbor seriously and/or can anyone be ordered to love? Can someone be forced to love?*

I have tried to love my neighbor. I have done the local and international mission trips. I have given away stuff and simplified my life. I have even helped those who were helpless. I must admit as good of an effort as I have put forth, I'm not sure if it ever eclipsed the emotional vein of "love" with all its perception changing interactions. Love as a command will always be matter of will. As Robert Speer said in his writings in the early 1900s: "Love is the habit of unselfishness, of tenderness, of ministry rooted in the will and resting there on the solidarity of duty (responsibility)."[81] It is this type of love by which the power of Christianity is best lived.

There is a great story from World War Two that illustrates this.

During the Second World War, German paratroopers invaded the island of Crete. When they landed at Maleme, the islanders met them, bearing nothing other than kitchen knives and hay scythes. The consequences of resistance were devastating. The residents of entire villages were lined up and shot.

Overlooking the airstrip today is an institute for peace and understanding founded by a Greek man named Alexander Papaderous. Alexander was just six years old when the war started. His home village was destroyed, and he was imprisoned in a concentration camp. When the war ended, he became

---

81 *The Principles of Christianity*, Robert E. Speer, The Westminster Press, 1902, p.147

convinced his people needed to let go of the hatred the war had unleashed. To help the process, he founded his institute at this place that embodied the horrors and hatreds unleashed by the war.

One day, while taking questions at the end of a lecture, Alexander was asked, "What's the meaning of life?" There was nervous laughter in the room. It was such a weighty question. But Alexander answered it.

He opened his wallet, took out a small, round mirror and held it up for everyone to see. During the war, he was just a small boy when he came across a motorcycle wreck. The motorcycle had belonged to German soldiers. Alexander saw pieces of broken mirrors from the motorcycle lying on the ground. He tried to put them together but couldn't, so he took the largest piece and scratched it against a stone until its edges were smooth and it was round. He used it as a toy, fascinated by the way he could use it to shine light into holes and crevices.

He kept that mirror with him as he grew up, and over time it came to symbolize something very important. It became a metaphor for what he might do with his life.

I am a fragment of a mirror whose whole design and shape I do not know. Nevertheless, with what I have I can reflect light into the dark places of this world — into the black places in the hearts of men — and change some things in some people. Perhaps others may see and do likewise. This is what I am about. This is the meaning of my life.[82]

---

82 It Was on Fire When I Laid Down On It, Robert Fulghum, Random House Press, New York, 1988

Renewing love is the ability to love in a way that changes their circumstances — or the world's — as a result. Are you loving those around you so that they discover a life worth living?

The group discussion guide for this topic is in Appendix A on page 380.

CHAPTER 30

WORK

"Whatever you do, work at it with all your heart, as working for the Lord, not for men, since you know that you will receive an inheritance from the Lord as a reward. It is the Lord you are serving"
(Col 3:23-24 NIV).

Have you ever wondered if God cares about what we do for a living?

I can remember wondering what I was going to be when I grew up. I took the interests test in high school only to have it tell me, the highly allergic asthmatic, to be a forest ranger. I can remember telling my father when he asked the question after my first year of college that I was going to be a graphic artist, to which he responded, "Well, you'll never get a job doing that." I then remember taking a similar test later in life as an unhappy national sales manager only to discover I should be an entrepreneur or women's clothing designer. Needless to say, I followed the former only to discover it, too, was unfulfilling. God had called me to a different role.

It's been written that the average person graduating from college will have seven different careers in their lifetime and hold ten different jobs by the age of forty-two. The department of labor statistics also claims one-third of the workforce will turn over every year. The person behind the desk at the company you worked for will not be there in 4.2 years, down from 4.6 four years ago.[83] Technology and its advancement will require a life of continual learning and the days of learning a skill, getting a job and being in the same field for a lifetime are over!

Obviously in America, the social contract whereby the company took care of its employees and they stayed for a lifetime is over. Work is becoming less and less about a career and more about provision or self-fulfillment. So, does God care about what we do for a living? I would have to say definitely — yes and no. No, God doesn't care what you do for a living. However, he does what happens in our work lives. The scriptures in Genesis 2 make it clear. Work is a spiritual activity.

The Persian poet Gibran writes, *"Work is love made visible."*

Jesus worked. His first career was as a carpenter. His second was a rabbi/teacher and His third was Messiah and Savior. Through his life of work, he clearly shows us the value of job well done.

In the final sentences of his encyclical *On Human Work*, Pope John Paul II wrote: "Let the Christian who listens to the living word of God, uniting work with prayer, know the place work has not only in earthly progress but also in the development of the Kingdom of God, to which we are called through the power of the Holy Spirit and through the word of the gospel."[84]

---

83   https://www.bls.gov/news.release/pdf/tenure.pdf

84   *Laborem Exercens: On Human Work*, Pope John Paul II, Boston: Daughters of St. Paul, 1981, pp.63-64

There are two important scriptural ideas in the pope's teaching on work:

First, work and prayer are key in connecting the temporal world and the Kingdom of God. Work is not mere anguish. It is not the punishment for Adam and Eve's sin, but rather an essential element of discovering a life worth living. Work contributes not only to material well-being but also serves to advance the Kingdom of God

Second, since we are all called to work in the process of building the Kingdom, then work cannot be limited merely to paid employment. All activity which helps build the Kingdom is work: on the job, in our volunteer activities, with our family, and in the community in which we live. And the value of all work is to be judged not by the compensation we receive but by its contribution to building the Kingdom.[85]

All of which reminds me of a story from Bob Perks entitled, "I Love My Garbage Man." He states, "*I had been working much too long on this job. I guess things could have been worse. I certainly wasn't doing hard labor. But going door to door asking questions as a representative of the federal government wasn't the most satisfying position either. It was August. It was hot. I had to wear a tie.*

"Hello. My name is Bob Perks and we are doing a survey in this neighborhood ..."

"I'm not interested! Good bye!" Slam, lock. You can't imagine how many times I heard that. I finally caught on and began with "Before you slam the door, I am not selling anything, and I just

---

85 *Confident and Competent — A Challenge for the Lay Church*, William L. Droel and Gregory F. Augustine Pierce, Chicago, 1987

need to ask a few questions about yourself and the community." The young woman inside the doorway, paused for a moment, raised her eyebrows as she shrugged her shoulders, confused by my rude introduction. "Sure. Come on in. Don't mind the mess. It's tough keeping up with my kids." It was an older home in a section of the valley where people with meager income found affordable shelter. With the little they had, the home looked comfortable and welcoming. "I just need to ask a few questions about yourself and family. Although this may sound personal I won't need to use your names. This information will be used … " She interrupted me. "Would you like a glass of cold water? You look like you've had a rough day." "Why yes!" I said eagerly. Just as she returned with the water, a man came walking in the front door. It was her husband. "Joe, this man is here to do a survey." I stood and politely introduced myself. Joe was tall and lean. His face was rough and aged looking, although I figured he was in his early twenties. His hands were like leather. The kind of hands you get from working hard, not pushing pencils. She leaned toward him and kissed him gently on the cheek. As they looked at each other you could see the love that held them together. She smiled and tilted her head, laying it on his shoulder. He touched her face with his hands and softly said "I love you!" They may not have had material wealth, but these two were richer than most people I know. They had a powerful love. The kind of love that keeps your head up when things are looking down. "Joe works for the borough." she said. "What do you do?" I asked. She jumped right in not letting him answer. "Joe collects garbage. You know I'm so proud of him. " Honey, I'm sure the man doesn't want to hear this." said Joe. "No, really I do." I said. "You see Bob, Joe is the best garbage man in the borough. He can stack more garbage on the truck than anyone else. He gets so much in one truck that they don't have to make as many runs," she said with such passion. "In the long run," Joe continues, "I save the borough money. Man, hours are down and the cost per truck is less." There was silence. I didn't know what to say. I shook my head searching for the right words. "That's incredible! Most people would gripe about a job like that. It certainly is a difficult one. But your attitude about it is amazing," I said. She walked over to the shelf next to the couch. As she turned she held in her hand a small framed paper. "When we had our third child, Joe lost his job. We were on unemployment for a time and then eventually welfare. He couldn't find work anywhere. Then, one day, he was sent on an interview here in this community. They offered him the job he now holds. He came home depressed and ashamed. Telling me this was the best he could do. It actually paid less than we got on welfare."

She paused for a moment and walked toward Joe, "I have always been proud of him and always will be. You see I don't think the job makes the man. I believe the man makes the job!" "We needed to live in the borough in order to work here. So, we rented this home." Joe said. "When we moved in, this quote was hanging on the wall just inside the front door. It has made all the difference to us, Bob. I knew that Joe was doing the right thing," she said as she handed me the frame. It said:

> If a man is called to be a street sweeper, he should sweep the streets even as Michelangelo painted or Beethoven composed music, or Shakespeare wrote poetry. He should sweep streets so well that all the hosts of heaven and earth will pause to say, "Here lived a great street sweeper who did his job well." — Martin Luther King

"I love him for who he is. But what he does he does the best. I love my garbage man!"[86]

All of this falls in line with a piece a scripture that is easy to overlook. It comes from John 6 in which Jesus is asked what a person is required to do as a work for the Lord. Jesus responds, "The work of the God is this: to believe in the one He has sent." Our primary work is to first to believe and then to follow this up with doing the work of the Lord. The Greek word for "doer" is the one which our word "poet" is derived. It means a maker, a performer, a man who accomplishes things. That is what a Christian is to do says Robert Spears.[87]

Interestingly, this is a work we will never be able to fully accomplish. Unlike Jesus, who completed His work (John 17:4), we will not finish because we are imperfect beings striving towards perfection. However, it's in our imperfection humanity can identify when our toil is as Paul recommends in his letter to the Colossians 3:23-24 when he states, "Whatever you do, work at it with all your heart, as working for the Lord, not for men, since you know that you will receive an inheritance from the Lord as a reward. It is the Lord you are serving" (NIV).

The group discussion guide for this topic is in Appendix A on page 382.

---

86   Bob Perks Copyright 2001

87   *The Principles of Christianity*, Robert E. Speer, The Westminster Press, Chicago, 1902. P.151

CHAPTER 31

TEACHING

*Jesus' relational connection to those He taught
increased their connection to Him, the content
and the goal of His appearance.*

Who is your favorite teacher? No. It's not a security question. Who was your favorite teacher and why? Mine was Mr. Wells at Carmel Junior High in Carmel, Indiana. He made history come alive. He would read from historical documents in a way that made the tales of crossing the ocean in the Santa Maria come alive. He would stand on his desk and shout. He didn't care about the grades as much as he cared if we understood the concepts he was teaching.

It would be another twenty-five years before I would find another teacher with the ability to make the abstract come alive. It happened over the radio. I would be traveling around Chicago trying to sell office equipment and listening to the radio. It was pre-podcast and digital radio, so I would flip radio stations at every commercial. I stumbled upon Dr. Tony Evans. An African-American preacher who made the stories of the Bible come alive. He could keep my interest by passionately telling stories to prove a larger life point. His voice would lead me to want to know more.

Both teachers awakened my spirit to want to know more. The former made it hip to learn and visualize while I read. The later helped me see a worldview I would have never considered without his passionate dissertation of the facts.

As a self-avowed Christ-follower, I'm grateful Jesus had this same type of effect on his immediate followers and then on the generations that followed. He began his ministry as a teacher and His life would become the ultimate learning example. The Bible is full of examples of Jesus being called a teacher. In each case the Greek word for "master" means teacher and his students were called disciples or translated slightly more clearly as "learners." His opponents may have had a problem calling Him the Messiah, but they recognized his incredible qualities as a teacher (John 3:2; Mark 12:14) The interesting point is Jesus was never referred to as a preacher. Four different words are used in the New Testament for the word "preaching." In Luke 9:60, the word translated as preaching has the meaning "to tell thoroughly." The uniqueness should not be lost on us. Jesus was a teacher who preferred to teach through discourse and use real-life examples.

Certainly, Jesus spoke to his followers and disciples in connected discourses, but His preaching was in the mainly academic or applied stream of teaching. He was regularly interrupted to be questioned by both verbal as well as non-verbal means. This is particularly evident in exchanges in John 14:5-18, John 6:28-60 and John 8. Jesus used common language, themes, objects and speech to ensure the greatest number of followers would be able to discover the spiritual truths being offered by Him (Matt. 5:14; John 3:8, 4:34-35, 6:35, 7:37-38, 8:12, 15:1-7).

Robert Speers wrote in 1902 of Jesus' methods of teachings, "There is a place for formal, connected, uninterrupted statement of Christian truth; but it is a small place in comparison with that for colloquial teaching, where a teacher asks questions to make sure the pupil will understand, and the teacher understood. Of course, the set and uninterrupted discourse is easier, but it's less valuable. Most is forgotten. The average hearer cannot take it in or carry it away."[88]

What an excellent observation and it's even more relevant today than when it was written. I was taught the average public speaker should have only twenty minutes of continuous content and a single overarching point if you are going to keep your audience's concentration.[89] The most recent reports are showing that attention span is shortening due to use of electronics (phones, tablets and video games). It's now suggested that if a person is going to speak more than a few minutes, the speaker needs to have above average oratory skills as well as visual aids to keep the audience engaged.

The point being, attention and engagement require a relational connection to the speaker, the content and the goal. In a recent article on the five best ways to teach any subject, the author shared the importance of:

---

88 *The Principles of Jesus,* Robert E. Speers, The Westminster Press, Chicago, 1902, p.155

89 https://medium.com/the-art-of-keynoting/the-20-minute-rule-for-great-public-speaking-on-attention-spans-and-keeping-focus-7370cf06b636#.y2gajitdb

1. Teacher Clarity

When a teacher begins a new unit of study or project with students, she clarifies the purpose and learning goals, and provides explicit criteria on how students can be successful. It's ideal to also present models or examples to students so they can see what the end product looks like.

2. Classroom Discussion

Teachers need to frequently step offstage and facilitate entire class discussion. This allows students to learn from each other. It's also a great opportunity for teachers to formatively assess (through observation) how well students are grasping new content and concepts.

3. Feedback

How do learners know they are moving forward without steady, consistent feedback? They often won't. Along with individual feedback (written or verbal), teachers need to provide whole-group feedback on patterns they see in the collective class' growth and areas of need. Students also need to be given opportunities to provide feedback to the teacher so that she can adjust the learning process, materials and instruction accordingly.

4. Formative Assessments

In order to provide students with effective and accurate feedback, teachers need to assess frequently and routinely where students are in relation to the unit of study's learning goals or product (summative assessment). Hattie recommends that teachers spend the same amount of time on formative evaluation as they do on summative assessment.

5. Metacognitive Strategies

Students are given opportunities to plan and organize, monitor their own work, direct their own learning, and to self-reflect along the way. When we provide students with time and space to be aware of their own knowledge and their own thinking, student ownership increases. And research shows that metacognition can be taught. [90]

Jesus used all these strategies in one form or another. As such, he was able to make our common, daily conversation a platform for a presentation that helps the average person discover a life worth living, even today. It's the reason at RENEW we believe in facilitating our relationships with God and others through intentional time of sharing informally and formally.

The group discussion guide for this topic is in Appendix A on page 383.

---

90   www.edutopia.org/5highlyeffectiveteachingpractices/

RENEW

CHAPTER 32

DISEASE

*It is a distortion of the gospel to make it
a magical panacea for disease.*

Do you ever wonder about why God chooses to heal some sick people and not others?

The question really created a crisis of faith for me in my faith journey. I was serving at a local hospital and a Christian woman who had five boys was dying from an inoperable stomach tumor. Her pastor, saints of the church and yours truly would wander into her room and pray with all the fervor we could muster. I can remember thinking God was going to heal her. The God I knew would never subject this woman and her husband to the process of dying. She was a Christian. God is our great protector and healer. She was a good woman. Her husband was faithful to Christ. A good churchgoer and even a believer in prayer. However, in the end, I would come into the hospital and go up to her room one day to discover she had passed the evening before. The cancer killed her. I remember the feeling of disbelief, the anger and even the pain of thinking of her children growing up without her.

Why didn't God heal her? The answers I had formulated didn't seem adequate. Why would God allow it? Why would God allow the world to be corrupted so beyond repair?

These questions are not unique to me or this experience. The answers have created and destroyed people's faith. However, maybe we are looking at the situation with the wrong perspective. We are asking: Why God doesn't do what we think is right, versus wondering what He might be doing despite the brokenness of the person, place, situation or world in which we live.

After all, Jesus healed a lot of sickness and disease as a part of his ministry. He did it out of love and it validated the prophecies. As a result, many friends of friends would come to know Him for generations.

Jesus recognized the reality of disease. He never said their sickness was imaginary or sin-based. He spoke of disease in the same way He spoke of the seas, the synagogue, food, flocks of sheep or any other truth. Disease is a fact of life and death (John 11:4). He sent his disciples to preach, heal and cleanse those seriously ill (Matt. 10:7-8). He equated service to those ill as service to Him. *He sympathized deeply with the sufferings of His people* (Matt. 8:17). Yet, He did not abolish disease. He never promised too. He did deliver some from it. His disciples healed others as well. However, He never made a universal promise of physical healing for anyone afflicted (Phil 2:26-27, 3:21; 2 Tim 4:20). He can and does heal today. Sometimes He heals sometimes physically, often mentally, and in all ways spiritually.

In fact, some of the greatest stories of God's healing grace come from those not fully physically healed but spiritually. Take, for an example the story of Joni Erickson.

In the summer of 1967, Joni Erickson and her sister rode their horses to the Chesapeake Bay to go for a swim. The result was tragic. Joni dived into shallow water, struck her head on a rock and became a quadriplegic. She was paralyzed from the neck down.

During two years of often painful rehabilitation Joni learned how to paint with her mouth, and what this disability meant for her faith. At times Joni was angry with God, demanding to know why He let this happen, even at times wishing she hadn't survived. But in the years since, Joni has learned that it is in her weakness that God's strength can shine through. She has been a source of enormous blessing to people all over the world as she shares the faith that sustains her.

At first Joni found it impossible to reconcile her condition with her belief in a loving God. But one night, Joni became convinced God did understand. The catalyst was a good friend who said to her, "Joni, Jesus knows how you feel. He was paralyzed. He couldn't move or change position on the cross. He was paralyzed by the nails." The realization was profoundly comforting. "God became incredibly close to me and eventually I understood that He loves me. I had no other identity but God, and gradually He became enough," stated Joni. "I prayed for healing and truly believed it would come. The Bible speaks of our bodies 'being glorified'. Now I realize I will be healed; I'm just going through a forty- or fifty-year delay, and God stays with me even through that."[91]

We are prone to make too much of our bodies and draw too sharp a line between God's activity and the orderly process

---

91   Source: Joni and friends website, Joni's books

of nature, as well as His special intervention. It is a distortion of the gospel to make it a magical panacea for disease. It is misleading to regard a miraculous healing as any more the work of God than the slow and regular knitting of a broken bone. It is God at work in each case. He makes the sun come and go with every rotation of our planet in demonstration of His power.

We do not honor God when we insist upon His working for us in some special way that we define. We honor him best when we do all we can by use of means and using faith to accomplish the ends that we believe will be pleasing to Him and the growth of His Kingdom.[92]

The group discussion guide for this topic is in Appendix A on page 384.

---

[92] *The Principles of Jesus*, Robert E. Speer, The Westminster Press, Chicago, 1902, p.164

CHAPTER 33

KINGDOM OF HEAVEN

*The Kingdom of heaven is both
in the future and the present.*

There's an interesting phenomenon that takes place during funeral services. Those who get up to speak on behalf of the newly departed color the person's life in platitudes. They normally try to make the person out to be a good person whether they were or not and then they talk about seeing them in heaven or what St. Peter will be saying to them when they reach the mythical pearly gates. I think this type of conversation is comforting to some because they don't want to address the deeper issue: What happens after we die?

I spoke a little bit about this when I spoke about death. I reviewed what the five major religions believe about death and the afterlife. You can read or listen to that discussion later.

Unfortunately, I have never been to the next realm, but I remember speaking to my mother about it. My mom had an aneurysm at the base of the brain burst when she was packing for my father's first retirement trip. It killed her for a few minutes and if it weren't for a great medical staff at the hospital she would have departed for good. She ended up having brain surgery and being in a coma for a while. However, she eventually came to and described floating above the operating table, hearing all the voices, seeing all the people and then feeling pulled higher towards a very bright light. She said she probably wouldn't have come back had she not heard my sister's voice calling to her. She was never quite the same afterward, but she was my mom. She has gone on now and so has my dad, but their memory lives with me.

As a Christ-follower, my understanding of heaven is informed by the teachings of Jesus. The New Testament speaks of heaven some 276 times. Jesus spoke of heaven on a regular basis. He did not speak of it as a state of mind but as a real place where God is present along with His followers (children) who have accepted His principles. "Your Father in heaven," Jesus was fond of saying (Matt. 5:16, 45; 6:1,8; 7:11, 21; 10:32-33; 12:50; 16:17; 18:10, 14, 19).

One of the greatest descriptions of heaven comes from the apostle John. He had the privilege to see and report on the heavenly city (Rev. 21:10-27). John witnessed that heaven (the new earth) possesses the "glory of God" (Rev. 21:11), the very presence of God. Because heaven has no night and the Lord Himself is the light, the sun and moon are no longer needed (Rev. 22:5).

The city is filled with the brilliance of costly stones and crystal-clear jasper. Heaven has twelve gates (Rev. 21:12) and twelve foundations (Rev. 21:14). The paradise of the Garden of Eden is restored: The river of the water of life flows freely and the tree of life is available once again, fruit grows monthly with leaves that "heal the nations" (Rev. 22:1-2). John's description of heaven is beyond the ability of man to describe (1 Cor. 2:9) so we know even his descriptions of what he saw and experienced are limited. Heaven is greater than even our imagination.

I remember listening to a preacher on the radio a number years ago share that heaven for most men and women who don't sing sounded like torture - unlimited days of singing the same hymn verses repeatedly while listening to harps play. He went on to describe a belief that heaven will be an extended version of the perfect moment on earth. For him, it was the perfect golf shot just as you see it takeoff and before it lands. It's the moment you fall in love. It's the great conversation in which you feel a connection. It's the realization of the plan going off without a hitch. It's the smile and belly laugh of a small child. It's the perfect sense that all is right in the world. It's the gently warm breeze on your face after a long winter. It's all these moments for eternity, forever and then more.

The scriptures describe Heaven as a place where there will be no more tears, no more pain and no more sorrow (Rev. 21:4). There will be no more separation, because death will be conquered (Rev. 20:6). The best thing about heaven is the presence of our Lord and Savior (1 John 3:2). We will be face-to-face with Him who loved us and sacrificed Himself so that we can enjoy His presence.

Jesus knew this place well for it is where he came from. He didn't have to speculate about it. He had come from it and spoke with firsthand knowledge about it, the plan to bring it to earth and even His eventual return to it all had a sense of urgency because of His love for us. His desire is all would come to know Him before he reappears (Luke 24:51; Acts 1:9-11). The end of times imagery of the Kingdom of heaven descending, and all of earth being made new, offers many a believer hope in times of distress in this life.

The Kingdom Jesus was striving to establish among men was referred to by Him as the Kingdom of heaven or the Kingdom of God. It's phrase with a lot of scholarly debate, but the words reveal the idea that He longed for the day when the principles of heaven would prevail on earth. A principle so important that when the disciples asked how they should pray, he responded with "thy Kingdom come on earth as it is in heaven" (Matt. 6:10). Did you know the words "Kingdom of heaven" and "Kingdom of God" are considered mostly synonymous in the reading of the parceled scriptures today?[93] While there are debatable differences in the use of the terms, for our topic they're similar enough for us to claim those entering will be:

- Believers in Jesus and His work on our behalf (John 3:16)
- Poor in spirit
- Persecuted for righteous sake
- Obedient to living for Him and His will
- Humble in serving others especially those for whom compassion is hard
- Selfless

Jesus was fond of speaking in parables about the Kingdom of Heaven. There are seven in Matthew 13. The lessons reveal forgiveness, impartial love, unmerited grace and mercy as the normal aspects of heaven and therefore important to be practiced and experienced now. In fact, they are part of our role in our prayer to bring the Kingdom of Heaven to earth (Matt. 18:23-25, 20:1-14, 22:2-14; 25:1-13).

---

93   https://Bible.org/the Kingdom of heaven/

RENEW is our attempt to live this idea. A place where we celebrate, enjoy and grow in ways that help us be assistants to God in bringing the Kingdom down from heaven and into the present day.

The group discussion guide for this topic is in Appendix A on page 384.

RENEW

CHAPTER 34

HELL

*Ignoring sin against God
doesn't mean the consequences disappear.*

I can remember a few years ago having a discussion with a professing Christian. We were talking about the idea of who goes to heaven and who doesn't. At one point, I brought up the report that Jeffrey Dahmer, the rapist and mass murdering Milwaukee cannibal, professed his faith in Jesus before dying.[94] To which my Christian, friend said, "Too bad for him that he wouldn't get to go." I couldn't let the error in theology stand. I spoke of death bed confessions, the unmerited grace and mercy of God and the major reason for Jesus' coming. I might as well have been talking to a wall. The person said, "God would never forgive His hideous actions." Stunned, I ended the conversation with the comment, "I don't think we get to judge a person's heart so I'm glad my eternal fate isn't in your hands." We laughed nervously and backed away from each other.

---

94 http://www.christianitytoday.com/ct/2006/september/34.125.html

Heaven and hell are interesting topics for Christians and non-Christians.

In a recent "2014 Pew Religious Landscape Study", it was found that the public believes more in heaven than they do in hell. Roughly seven in ten (72 percent) Americans say they believe in heaven — defined as a place: "where people who have led good lives are eternally rewarded," according to the "Pew Research Center's 2014 Religious Landscape Study". But, at the same time, 58 percent of U.S. adults also believe in hell — a place :"where people who have led bad lives and die without being sorry are eternally punished."

It's interesting to note that Muslims are similar to Christians in views of an afterlife, with 89 percent saying they believe in heaven and 76 percent believing in hell. Among other non-Christians, however, beliefs that there are places of eternal reward and punishment after death are not as widely held. Roughly half of Hindus, Buddhists and Jews believe in heaven. And roughly a third or less of Buddhists, Hindus, and Jews believe in the concept of hell. Not surprisingly, far fewer religious "nones" — a group that includes atheists, agnostics and people who say their religion is "nothing in particular" — say they believe in the existence of heaven and hell. Fewer than four in ten (37 percent) "nones" say they believe in heaven, while 27 percent believe in hell.[95]

The reality is, Jesus talked more about hell than heaven. Unfortunately, it's a place for people we've known close and from a distance. Many don't want to believe in it because basically they believe all of the human race has some good in it. But how

---

95   http://www.pewresearch.org/fact-tank/2015/11/10/most-americans-believe-in-heaven-and-hell

good is good enough and how bad do you have to be to go to hell? Napoleon, Hitler, Stalin bad? Or serial killers Speck, Gacy or Dahmer bad? Or just a child molester? A wife beater? Where is the line? Who gets to make the call? The problem is, we all have hearts and a nature which cries for what we want over and above other people's needs or wants. Let's just be honest for a second, we point at others who act worse than us so we can justify our own defects or minimize our sins, so we can believe we are good enough to be in God's presence. We all do it. We all fall short of the glory of God (Romans 3:23 NIV).

The mainstream media leads us astray by asserting that if God is about love, then he could never condemn anyone to hell and therefore, hell must not exist. However, the fatal flaw in this thinking is that God determines your place in eternity when, in effect, we do. We have a choice to believe and repent (to change) or ignore the teaching of the ages and continue in our own power. A way of living many have chosen to the gates of insanity and eternal death. As C.S. Lewis said, there are, in the end, only two groups of people in the world—those who say to God, "Your will be done," and those to whom God says, "Your will be done." Hell is a door locked from the inside.

God's love is just. It offers mercy and grace for all willing to recognize the problem in the mirror, admit it and ask for some help. Hence the reason God broke through the veil of the spiritual in the form of Jesus. He came to make sure we understood his love was about justice. All actions have a consequence, but Christ has come out of love to minimize the eternal effects through His own sacrifice.

Preacher/theologian J.D. Greer says it this way: "People often feel that hell is some great blemish on God's love, [but] the Bible presents it as the opposite. Hell magnifies for us the love of God by showing us how far God went, and how much he went through, to save us."[96]

There are two different words translated as hell in the New Testament. The first literally means "the unseen world," or the place of departed spirits. Jesus uses it three times, but each time with more significance including Matt. 11:23 where it means complete degradation. The other word translated as hell is "Gehenna." Gehenna was the valley of Hinnom, a gully in which the trash of Jerusalem, including enemies of the state, were burned. It's a meaningful term to the people Jesus was speaking to. He was making sure they understood some sins are to be feared and shunned because they led to that place (Matt. 5:22).

The predominant image of hell in the Bible is that of fire. Fire represents insatiable desire. Leave a fire unchecked, and it continues to grow. Nurse a sin — jealousy, lust, racism, pride — and that fire will eventually consume you, burning brighter and brighter until you are indistinguishable from it.[97]

Jesus was clear that the inner life must be purged from all hellish tastes and dispositions (Mark 9:43, 45, 47) (POJ p.175).

God created us for heaven, but the rebellion of the human race, in which we are all participating, has destined us for hell. Hell, not heaven, is our default destination. Notice the breadth of who is described as going to hell in Revelation 21:8:

"But as for the cowardly, the faithless, the detestable, as for murderers, the sexually immoral, sorcerers, idolaters and all liars,

---

96 http://www.jdgreear.com/my_weblog/2017/03/hell-is-the-default-destination.html#more-20622

97 Ibid.

their portion will be in the lake that burns with fire and sulfur, which is the second death" [98]

The scripture equalizes cowardly, faithless, idolaters and liars with those we all might say deserve eternal struggle. In other words, those who don't stand for God, who deny his existence, who claim another God and who are believers in name only (the cultural Christian) are destined for a place where God allows us to let go of His hand and become our sin. Some might claim this is unjust, but all sin is magnified by who it is committed against. If you punch your brother, it's less severe than punching a police officer or a judge. Sin against an everlasting, all-powerful God is infinitely more scandalous and ignoring it doesn't mean the consequence for it disappears.

The physical aspects of life have consequences. What you do has consequences. The mental aspects of what we think have consequences. What you think has consequences. The spiritual aspects of life have consequences. What you believe, and worship, has consequences. Be careful what you choose.

The group discussion guide for this topic is in Appendix A on page 386.

---

98   Ibid.

RENEW

CHAPTER 35

FALSEHOOD

The greatest lie of our time is the acceptance and justification of lying.

Is it ever okay to lie? A little white lie? What about if your life depended on it? What about if your family or friend's life depended on it?

Merriam Webster definition: To lie is to do or say anything untrue with the intention to deceive; to create a false or misleading impression

Most major religions recognize lying as wrong and a separation from God. An interesting exception comes from Islam. Muslims can lie to unbelievers in order to defeat them. There are several forms:

- Taqiyya - Saying something that isn't true as it relates to the Muslim identity.
- Kitman - Lying by omission. An example would be when Muslim apologists quote only a fragment of verse 5:32 (that if anyone kills "it shall be as if he had killed all mankind"), while neglecting to mention that

the rest of the verse (and the next) mandate murder in undefined cases of corruption and mischief.
- Tawriya - Intentionally creating a false impression.
- Muruna - Blending in by setting aside some practices of Islam or Sharia in order to advance others.

Like Islam, our culture has also defended the practice of lying as a necessity in certain circumstances, as well as justifying it as defense mechanism; it's also a coping mechanism and a survival technique.[99]

Lying or self-deception is a part of everyday human interactions. In many cases, lying can be beneficial for those who lie and those who are being lied to. Most of this type of lying with positive consequences occurs in a controlled way, thoughtfully, with careful weighing of beneficial consequences.[100]

M. Scott Peck devoted his career to psychiatry and psychotherapy in prison cells, and throughout his career, he made conclusions on lies and truth. He also believed lying was a defense mechanism and used as an ego defense depending on circumstances. He also classified lying into two types; the black ones of which we know is not true and the white ones which is also false but still leaves a significant part of the truth. In everyday language, a white lie is acceptable because it does not destroy someone else's dignity or hurt somebody's feelings. However, he concluded that as much as white lies on the surface are no less than a lie, or are excusable, they are but as deadly and destructive as black lies. White lies further create superficial interactions, because they are bounded by the opposite of what is truth — a lie.

---

99   https://www.brainyquote.com/quotes/quotes/m/monicaraym572079.html

100   http://depressiond.com/pathological-liar/

Perhaps, lying is the basest of all types of ego defenses. Denying to one's self what is truth is lying, as well as repressing unconscious thoughts and feelings not only to one's self but also to the outside world.

Denial, repression, suppression, regression, sublimation and other defenses are associated with withholding of the truth. To withhold truth is to suppress information, which is common to all types of lies according to Peck. Withholding of truth may be a white lie, because on the surface, it is difficult to detect and confront. Withholding of truth as a white lie is more destructive than black ones, because black lies are obvious while white ones require contemplation and discussion.

So, from a societal perspective, is it permissible to lie or not?

Withholding of truth, as much as it is dangerous, is also necessary in society, and especially in politics. Selective withholding of one's opinion is a necessity, otherwise, society would be in total turmoil if everyone expressed their anger, hostility, aggression and antagonism to anyone of authority. There is a saying that goes: "There are words better left unsaid" and "things better left unknown." Hence, even social institutions — not only familial, but also political and religious — lie. People lie and so does society. No one is an exception.[101]

So, the cultural experts agree lying is a part of the world in which we live, but what would be best for the Kingdom — to lie or not lie? If we look to Jesus example, he never lied. As Robert Speer shares, "If it is impossible or wrong for God to lie, it is impossible and wrong for us to ever lie as well." He also asserted the devil was the

---

101   http://theaspirantonline.blogspot.com/2009/12/lying-as-defense-mechanism_3114.html

father of lies and He did not make room for some lies that did not bear the stamp of the devil's paternity.

I was in for the third or fourth time when a missionary and a trusted Haitian shared a Haitian saying, "Milk the white cow dry." The meaning of which is take as much as you can from the white people by any means. Take it from the tourist, the short-term missionaries, the aid workers, the long-term missionaries, the foreign businesses, anyone. The two individuals began to share the history of Haiti, the defeat of the French, the overthrow of puppet governments, the spiritual mix of Catholicism and voodoo, the psyche of many Haitians that God understood their deception and lying because of their physical desperation. Does the phrase by any means necessary ring true here? Lying had become culturally and spiritually justified. The evil one reigned.

The one aspect the Haitians had trouble with was pointing to scriptures which justify lying. Some studied enough to go to John 7:8-10 and others would go to Luke 24:28. The former was Jesus' contradiction about attending the Passover in Jerusalem and the latter was when His Holy Spirit suggested to the fellow travelers on the road to Emmaus that he was going on further than their home. The John passage in context is Jesus refusing to go with his brothers because they didn't understand the timing of God's will and therefore needed to protect everyone from the opposition. In Luke 24:28, Jesus continued the walk, knowing their custom and their teaching and wanting to test their sincerity of inviting someone to stay the night.

It is impossible and wrong for God ever lie, so it should be important for us to strive to never lie. Jesus held this view. He had justification to lie in many a situation while on earth, for there was trouble all around him. Surely, a white lie would have been acceptable right? Of course not! Even a small white lie not acceptable because a lie destroys trust in friends and foes alike. It affects a person's integrity like no other action.

As Nietzsche says, "The lie told from necessity or to serve another is always, even in the most favorable of circumstances, a sign of either truth, or of a love lacking wisdom." Or the person is full of selfishness and cowardice.[102] In the book, *A Lie Never Justifiable: A Study in Ethics* by Henry Clay Trumbull, the famous early nineteenth century Bishop and theologian Hans Lassen Martensen (1808-1884) says, "A lie of exigency (a state of affairs that makes urgent demands a leader must act in any sudden way) cannot occur with a personality that is found in possession of full courage, of perfect love and holiness, or of enlightened, all penetrating glance... It is this that we see in Christ, in whose mouth no guile was found in whom we find nothing that even remotely belongs to the category of the exigent lie (1 Peter 2:22, 3:10)."

In the book of Revelation, the complexity or simpleness of a lie or lies, regardless of argument or justification is still a lie and an affront to God. The greatest lie of our time is the acceptance and justification of lying. It is yet another reason we all need God's renewing grace, mercy and forgiveness. Without it, we are all apt to be disqualified for the prize of this life and the authenticity of the two most important relationships, a relationship with God and others.

The group discussion guide for this topic is in Appendix A on page 387.

---

[102] *The Principles of Jesus*, Robert E. Speer, The Westminster Press, Chicago, 1902, p.184

CHAPTER 36

JUDGEMENT

To discern and judge comes with responsibility. We must be in relationship with God through prayer, meditation, reading of the Word and the honest counsel of others with similar values.

I'll never forget the day I was introduced to an app called, Hot or Not. It was 2006 and the website had two million hits within the first couple of months. It was an instant success. It's a website where people post pictures of themselves or a friend and the post is judged if the person is good looking or not. The site was sold to Avid Media in 2008 for a rumored $20 million and has gross revenues of $7.5 million today. It has become more of a dating site, but the fact remains: people love to judge others. It's a guilty pleasure of America.

We are a society addicted to judgement. The whole idea of politically correct statements and actions is a reaction to our judging. We figure if we strive to accept everyone and everything as acceptable, the problem of judgement will disappear, right? Wrong. Even the idea of politically correct ideas or acceptance is in and of itself judgement. When something is not politically correct, we are judging it instead of discerning, is it truth? For example, the idea of recognizing someone by the color of their skin or their height or the type of clothes they wear is considered politically incorrect. Why? Because defining them by any of these characteristics might hurt their feelings. The fact is, I'm short. Just because you call me vertically challenged doesn't change the fact. "Just the facts" said Detective Friday.

We love to judge others based on our idea of how the world should be. We judge every day and in every way. You are judging this idea right now, so how can judgement be considered wrong? Therein lies the question: Is judging bad?

Biblical Judaism included laws and obligations that people judge one another fairly and with loving kindness. The Mishnah (a collection of Rabbinical writings dated back to 200 C.E.) has a quote that says: "Judge everyone favorably," because every person is believed to have some goodness in them and as we judge others we should keep this in mind.[103]

Muslims are asked not to judge one another unless they would have clear proof, to judge fairly when they do and to leave all final judgement to Allah. Man does not have the authority to judge another in matters of faith as he cannot see into the hearts of others; therefore, Allah enjoins that He be the Judge of such affairs.[104]

Gandhi believed in judging people of other faiths from *their* standpoint rather than his own. He expected religion to take into

---

[103] www.psychologytoday.com/blog/the-personality-analyst/201009/Jewish-teachings-about-judging-others/

[104] www.islam.stackexchange.com//what-does-Islam-say-about-judging-others/

account the practical life and always wanted to appeal to reason and morality. He said, "It has been my experience that I am always true from my point of view but am often wrong from the point of view of my critics. I know we are both right from our respective viewpoints of view. ... Gandhi shares a story in which he justifies this practice. It is the story of six blind men and a seventh who can see. The name of the story is "Blind Men and the Elephant" and was originally written as a poem by John Godfrey Saxe (1816-1887).

It was six men of Indostan, To learning much inclined, Who went to see the Elephant (Though all of them were blind), That each by observation Might satisfy his mind.

The First approached the Elephant And happening to fall Against his broad and sturdy side, At once began to bawl: "God bless me! but the Elephant Is very like a wall!"

The Second, feeling of the tusk, Cried, -"Ho! what have we here So very round and smooth and sharp? To me 'tis mighty clear, this wonder of an Elephant Is very like a spear!"

The Third approached the animal And happening to take The squirming trunk within his hands, Thus boldly up and spoke: "I see," — quoth he — "the Elephant Is very like a snake!"

The Fourth reached out an eager hand, And felt about the knee: "What most this wondrous beast is like a mighty plain," — quoth he — "Tis clear enough the Elephant Is very like a tree!"

The Fifth, who chanced to touch the ear, Said- "E'en the blindest man Can tell what this resembles most; Deny the fact who can, this marvel of an Elephant Is very like a fan!"

The Sixth no sooner had begun About the beast to grope, Then, seizing on the swinging tail That fell within his scope, "I see," -quoth he,- "the Elephant Is very like a rope!"

And so these men of Indostan Disputed loud and long, Each in his own opinion Exceeding stiff and strong, Though each was partly in the right, And all were in the wrong!

The seven blind men who gave seven different descriptions of the elephant were all right from their respective points of view and wrong the viewpoint of one another and right and wrong from the point of the view of the man who knew the elephant."[105]

What a wonderful perspective on judgement because the final point defines that a single truth exists — the elephant exists. Jesus spoke of this truth while He was standing on hill a few thousand years ago. He said, "Judge not, that you will not be judged, for with what you judge, you will be judged" (Matt. 7:1-2). What a condemning thought when taken without context or investigation. It is probably the most misquoted saying of Jesus. The formerly Christian or the secular all know this verse and like to use it when a Christian points out an err in life. As if to say, "Don't judge me, you hypocrite."

However, this is an uninformed viewpoint.

Yes. Jesus said not to judge. He said, "I judge no man" (John 8:15, John 12:47, Luke 12:14). However, He, John the Baptist, apostle Paul and other disciples did judge.

- Jesus judges the multitudes (Luke 12:57 and John 7:24)
- Jesus curses the Pharisees (Luke 11:42, Matt. 23:27, 33)
- Jesus claims he came to judge the world (John 9:39)
- Jesus claims his judgement is right (John 5:30)
- Jesus approves of certain behaviors (Luke 21:3-4 "the widow")

---

105   www.ncbi.nlm.nih.gov/pic/articles/pmc3400300

JUDGEMENT

- Jesus disapproves of a disciple's behavior (Matt. 16:23)

Judgement is unavoidable. Everything we do or say, don't do or don't say, involves a judgement. We must discern our words, actions and thoughts in response to our interpretation of the world around us. It would simply be unwise not to. So, what did Jesus mean then by the words "judge not"?

I like how Robert Speer, in his book *Principles of Jesus,* put this in 1902:

"(Judgement) ... Jesus did not mean to forbid formation of those necessary judgements which determine our entire course of action in life and all our deeds and words and our choices."[106]

He did teach and God's word teaches:
- Superficial judgement is wrong (Prov. 18:13; Luke 7:36-50)
- Hypercritical judgement is wrong (Matt. 6:2; 5, 16)
- Harsh and unforgiving judgement is wrong (Titus 3:2)
- Self-righteous judgement is wrong (James 4:6; Luke 18:9-14)
- False judgement is wrong (Prov. 19:5, Titus 3:2)

If we are to live by God's will, we must be willing to investigate and formulate appropriate judgements and speak truth. Unfortunately, many no longer think in such a critical manner. We prefer to drift with the latest cultural bias. Living by truth requires us to renew, define, become resolute and bring our conduct in line with the larger Christian philosophy of life. We must:

---

[106] *The Principles of Jesus,* Robert E. Speer, The Westminster Press, Chicago, 1902, p.188

- Pursue God's ideal (his will - Matt. 7:24)
- Discern the right course (Col 1:9; 1 Thess. 5:21)
- Gently confront ourselves and others (Gal 6:1)
- Speak truth (Eph. 4:15).

Finally, Jesus' warning about judgement must be heeded. To discern and judge comes with responsibility. We must be in relationship with God through prayer, meditation, reading of the Word and the honest counsel of others with similar values. As Jesus said, "My judgement is righteous, because I seek not mine own will, but by the will of Him who sent me" (John 5:30). All judgement must pass through this lens.

We are to judge with Christian truth in the forefront and our instinctual nature in background.

The group discussion guide for this topic is in Appendix A on page 388.

CHAPTER 37

FAITH

*Faith, like trust, is prominent throughout the
New Testament and fosters all renewal.*

I heard a speaker recently ask the question, "Do you have faith, or do you have doubt in search of experience?" What a great question. Do I believe in a worldview or am I still in search of proof that what I believe is true in all circumstances?

What do you have faith in?

We all have faith in something because having faith is natural. If a person does not have faith in God, they will have faith in something else that takes the place of God. They may have faith in themselves and their abilities. They may have faith in their government. They may have faith in the economy. They may have faith in an industry. They may have faith in science and/or technology. They may have faith in certain individuals. They may have faith in nature. But whatever it is, they will have faith. To be without faith is to be without a philosophy of life. That is, who, what, how and why of our existence.

Faith is critical in every philosophy. When developing a philosophy, we must be extremely careful to base our case on the most truthful assumptions — otherwise, should one of the assumptions prove to be untrue (as it appears the assumptions of the theory of evolution will be), the whole philosophy will crumble. If evolution crumbles, Marxism and Humanism are intellectually dead.

Christian philosophy: Many hold it to be the most rational of all worldviews, and it requires no more faith than any other philosophy. Indeed, we could argue that it takes a great deal more faith to believe in the spontaneous generation of Darwinian evolution or the randomness of all nature (i.e., that the universe happened by accident) than it does to accept the Christian doctrine of Creator.[107]

Giuseppe Mazzini (1805-1872), who lived over 150 years ago, wrote in his book, *Faith and the Future* the following definition of faith:

> "Faith requires an aim capable of embracing life as a whole, of concentrating all its manifestations, of directing its various modes of activity, or of repressing them all in favor of one alone. It requires an earnest, unalterable conviction that that aim will be realized; a profound belief in a mission and the obligation to fulfill it; and the consciousness of a supreme power watching over the path of the faithful towards its accomplishment. These elements are indispensable to faith; and where any one of these is wanting, we shall have sects, schools, political

---

107   http://www.allaboutworldview.org/christian-philosophy.htm

parties, but no faith — no constant hourly sacrifice for the sake of a great religious idea."[108]

Giuseppe's definition has four indispensable elements of faith. They are:

1) An aim capable of embracing life as a whole — an all-consuming goal of life

We have come to understand our lives and the lives of those around us being interconnected by our relationship with the Creator as well as the creation. We have faith, because we have come to see our Lord in everything surrounding us. A good example of this comes from an often-circulated story from the U.S. Civil War. Abraham Lincoln was meeting with a group of ministers for a prayer breakfast. Lincoln was not a churchgoer but was a man of deep, if at times unorthodox, faith. At one point, one of the ministers said, "Mr. President, let us pray that God is on our side". Lincoln's response showed far greater insight, "No, gentlemen, let us pray that we are on God's side." Lincoln reminded those ministers that religion is not a tool by which we get God to do what we want but an invitation to open ourselves to being and doing what God wants.

Our role in this life is to embrace all of what God is doing among us and then get involved. Henry Blackaby coined the phrase, "Look for where God is at work and get involved." It should never be the other way around.

---

108 *Essays of Giuseppe Mazzini*, Joseph Mazzini and Thomas Okey, JM Dent Company, London, 1894

2) Conviction that the aim will be realized — certainty of the outcome

Faith requires a trust that our understanding of what is taking place in the world around us is in fact the one and only truth. When we understand this to be true, no amount of persuasion will create doubt in the outcome.

In the year 156, an 86-year-old man was brought before a Roman official and asked to renounce his atheism. He was no atheist by our standards. Rather, he was the devout Christian bishop Polycarp. To the Romans, however, he was an atheist, for he refused to worship the emperor as a god along with the other gods of Rome.

Polycarp knew denial would mean a painful death — either being thrown into the arena with a wild animal or burned alive on a pyre. Three times he was questioned, three times invited to renounce his "atheism", but no renunciation of Christ would he make. "Swear and I release; curse Christ", urged the Roman official, to which Polycarp replied, "Eighty-six years have I served him (Christ), and he has done me no wrong: how then can I blaspheme my King who saved me?" Polycarp was not spared. A pyre was built and he was burned alive, but his words echo down through time to us: "Eighty-six years have I served him (Christ), and he has done me no wrong: how then can I blaspheme my King who saved me?" [109]

3) Belief in the mission

Belief in the mission is critical to sustaining one's faith. We know Jesus has commanded us to love one another, to share the

---

[109] Based on a text from Lightfoot, Apostolic Fathers cited in A New Eusebius. Documents Illustrating the History of the Church to AD 337.

good news with the world and live in ways which help others come to recognize Him in this life. Our faith is strengthened when we recognize the paradox of faith that happens when we are willing to follow through and then take action. When we follow through in this manner, our faith builds as much as, if not more than, the person we share it with because it reinforces our convictions as others experience Christ for the first time.

John Burke offers the Good News in his book, *Unshockable Love*, in a way most in our society can hear. He says, "Love, adoption, security, stress-free living, burden-free responsibility, joy from within, soulful peace, worth, value and guidance from His ever-present Spirit leading us into overflowing Life, and forgiveness from all sin and freedom from all condemnation too! That's the life in God's Kingdom we invite people into! We're not selling fire insurance to keep people out of hell; we're inviting people into a life with God as his children, and of course none of his children will be cast out. You can't overcommunicate God's goodness."[110]

4) Consciousness of God's oversight — we understand the outcome is already determined by God for the furtherment of His Kingdom.

The final element of faith is being conscious of God's role in the process. Many times, people will speak of God's goodness and still worry or try to control the outcome by more and more activity. However, real faith culminates in a person's ability to rest in the Lord's goodness.

During the deepest, darkest days of apartheid when the government tried to shut down opposition by canceling a political rally, Archbishop Desmond Tutu declared that he would hold a

---

110   *Unshockable Love*, John Burke, Bakers Books, 2013, p.156

church service instead. St. George's Cathedral in Cape Town, South Africa was filled with worshippers. Outside the cathedral hundreds of police gathered, a show of force intended to intimidate. As Tutu was preaching they entered the Cathedral, armed, and lined the walls. They took out notebooks and recorded Tutu's words. But Tutu would not be intimidated. He preached against the evils of apartheid, declaring it could not endure. At one extraordinary point he addressed the police directly and said,

"You are powerful. You are very powerful, but you are not gods and I serve a God who cannot be mocked. So, since you've already lost, since you've already lost, I invite you today to come and join the winning side!"

With that the congregation erupted in dance and song. The police didn't know what to do. Their attempts at intimidation had failed, overcome by the archbishop's confidence that God and goodness would triumph over evil. It was but a matter of time.[111]

Many marvel at the archbishop's boldness, but he had faith. He knew the outcome was certain. He had known the history of God's movement in the world. He had read the hall of fame of faith in Hebrews 11. He didn't just read it passively, he read it assertively.

The writer of Hebrews uses the written queue "By Faith" to encourage the reader to live like those who have come before us. Just say the words, "BY FAITH!" and feel the power.

The scripture begins: "Now faith is the assurance of things hoped for, the conviction of things not seen. For by it, the people of Old received their commendation. By faith, we understand that the universe was created by the word of God, so that what is seen is not made out of things that are visible."

---

111   *God's Politics*, Jim Wallis, Harper One, 2015

FAITH

It is here that the author proceeds to summarize those who have had a persistent hope in the promises of God.

"BY FAITH!" Abe gave an acceptable sacrifice to the Lord.
"BY FAITH!" God lifted Enoch out of this life.
"BY FAITH!" Noah at the ripe old age of 600, built a boat in a desert, listened to his neighbor's scoff, his wife shrug, his son-in-law's doubt and the world cry out. He feared the Lord.
"BY FAITH!" Abram and Sarah were faithful. Abram saved a lot and tithed to the priest Melchizedek. He packed up his family and moved to where God said to go, he led his son to the altar of sacrifice, he became the first 100-year-old father of a newborn. He obeyed God.
"BY FAITH!" Sarah gave herself freely to another man to save her husband, gave him another wife when she thought she was infertile and bore him a son at the age of ninety to begin the process of fulfilling God's promise of descendants too numerous to count.
"BY FAITH!" Isaac invoked blessings on his Sons.
"BY FAITH!" Jacob, who on his deathbed blessed his grandsons.
"BY FAITH!" Joseph did not become bitter toward his brothers, resent his captors or give up on God's promise to return the people of Israel to Canaan.
"BY FAITH!" Moses stuttered his way to rescue a nation. He convinced a slave nation to put blood over their doors, to follow him into a parted Red Sea and stay

committed to follow a cloud for over forty years.

"BY FAITH!" Rahab, a prostitute, risked her life by housing spies, helping them to escape and overturning the power in Jericho to the God of Jehovah.

"BY FAITH!" Naaman was healed by jumping in a river of leprosy.

"BY FAITH!" Elijah, who took on the Baal priests and who would eventually be taken to heaven.

"BY FAITH!" All our Old Testament heroes declared their understanding of the life to come by their actions and pronouncements in the here and now. However, it didn't stop there.

"BY FAITH!" All but one of the original disciples said yes to Jesus and all but two died martyrs' deaths.

"BY FAITH!" The Widow gave out of her poverty or need.

"BY FAITH!" Zacchaeus went all in and gave away his fortune and was redeemed.

"BY FAITH!" the disciples had holed up in Jerusalem for almost fifty days waiting and praying on the Lord. Then one day, boom, the Holy Spirit comes in power and authority. The neighbors are drawn and the disciples all begin to speak in new languages.

"BY FAITH!" The Philippians church supported Paul in his efforts to evangelize the world.

"BY FAITH!" Paul, Silas, Timothy, Barnabas, and even Apollos lived in a way that the world took notice. They didn't have the scriptures we have or the biblical knowledge, but they had the experiential knowledge. They had the opportunity to test God and to experience God through Jesus Christ before having committed to the cause.

So where does that leave us? Do you wonder about your faith? Do you have a confidence in things unseen? Would you wait on the Lord an hour, a day, fifty days, a year or forty years for Him to come and bless you with His presence? Would you be so bold to test the Lord by committing to a one-year practice of being obediently generous?

Dr. Martin Luther King Jr once said, "Faith is taking the first step even when you don't see the whole staircase."

Faith, like trust, is prominent throughout the New Testament associated with renewal:

Faith is the substance of things hoped for (Heb. 11:1)
Faith is a sister to joy (1 Peter 1:8) and hope (1 Peter 1:21)
Faith is the secret to victory over the world (1 John 5:5)
Faith removes shame and failure our of life and fills us with confidence (1 Peter 2:6; Heb. 10:22; Rom 9:33)
Faith begets patience and content (2 Thess. 1:4; Rev. 2:19; 13:10)
Faith unlocks the future and us perfect assurance in it (2 Tim. 1:12)
Faith speaks of rest and removal of our burdens (Heb. 4:3; Matt. 11:28)

So, I'll ask you to reflect again, "What do you have faith in knowing the benefits of trusting God with your life?"

The group discussion guide for this topic is in Appendix A on page 390.

CHAPTER 38

SACRIFICE

*"Whatever you abandon here for Him would be given
back a hundredfold and will inherit eternal life
(Matt. 19:29 NIV).*

The Army made Desmond Doss' life hell during training. "It started out as harassment and then it became abusive," Benedict says. He interviewed several World War II veterans who were in Doss' battalion. They considered him a pest, questioned his sincerity and threw shoes at him while he prayed. "They just saw him as a slacker," the filmmaker says, "someone who shouldn't have been allowed in the Army, and somebody who was their weakest link in the chain." Doss' commanding officer, Capt. Jack Glover, tried to get him transferred. In the documentary, Glover says Doss told him," 'Don't ever doubt my courage because I will be right by your side saving life while you take life.'" Glover's response: " 'You're not going to be by my damn side if you don't have a gun.'"

But hard as they tried, the Army couldn't force Doss to use a weapon. A 1940 law allowed conscientious objectors to serve the war effort in "noncombatant" positions, so Doss went with his company as a medic to the Pacific theater. And at Okinawa in the spring of 1945, Doss' company faced a grueling task: Climb a steep, jagged cliff — sometimes called Hacksaw Ridge — to a plateau where thousands of heavily armed Japanese soldiers were waiting for them. The terrain was treacherous. "It was full of caves and holes and the Japanese were dug in underground," says Mel Gibson, who re-created the battle in Hacksaw Ridge. " ... The Japanese called it 'the rain of steel' because there was so much iron flying around."

Under a barrage of gunfire and explosions, Doss crawled on the ground from wounded soldier to wounded soldier. He dragged severely injured men to the edge of the ridge, tied a rope around their bodies and lowered them down to other medics below. In Benedict's documentary, Doss says: "I was praying the whole time. I just kept praying, 'Lord, please help me get one more.'" Veteran Carl Bentley, who was also at Hacksaw Ridge, says in the documentary, "It's as if God had his hand on [Doss'] shoulder. It's the only explanation I can give."

Doss saved 75 men — including his captain, Jack Glover — over a 12-hour period. The same soldiers who had shamed him now praised him. "He was one of the bravest persons alive," Glover says in the documentary. "And then to have him end up saving my life was the irony of the whole thing."

President Harry Truman awarded Doss the Medal of Honor in 1945. He died in 2006.[112]

The story demonstrates conviction, determination, nationalism and most of all sacrifice. The greatest of these is sacrifice.

---

112   http://www.npr.org/2016/11/04/500548745/the-real-hacksaw-ridge-soldier-saved-75-souls-without-ever-carrying-a-gun

The definition of sacrifice from *Merriam Webster Dictionary* is:
1. an act of offering to a deity something precious
2. destruction or surrender of something for the sake of something else

Desmond's great line in both the movie and in real life is: "Lord please help me get one more."

It's a power line in the movie. I found myself chanting it along with him. However, it also strengthens Robert Speer's suggestion that sacrifice really means: "Sacrifice is the rendering to God that which has never been consecrated to Him before."[113]

Desmond was offering the Lord his life for the sake of others. He was embodying the idea that we are to be living sacrifices for God to use as He sees fit. We all want to say we are committed to God or that we believe in God but very few believe they should be poured out for God to achieve His will. We prefer the kind of sacrifice that is only slightly inconvenient.

The customary use of the of the word sacrifice is either material offerings made to God by his followers in the Old Testament, or the loss and yielding of our personal interests as part of some offering to Him. The interesting point is the latter is almost never used in the New Testament scriptures but is often referenced in a similar fashion to the Old Testament (Mark 12:33; Luke 2:24; Acts 7:41-42; 1 Cor. 10:18; Heb. 9:9, 10:1).

The greatest example of sacrifice is Jesus Himself.

---

113 *The Principles of Jesus*, John E Speer, The Westminster Press, 1902, p.199

- He came to do God's will (John 6:38)
- He yielded himself to the Father and His purpose (John 7:29, 17:4)
- He surrendered what he might have accomplished on earth for what was accomplished for others (mark 15:31)
- He fulfilled the Old Testament requirements completely concluding with being the Passover lamb for our sin (1 Cor. 5:7; Heb. 10:12-18)
- He made the only true sacrifice of a humble and contrite spirit (Ps. 51:17)
- While Jesus was alive, he called men to set Himself and His service above their own lives (Luke 9:24):
- Homes (Luke 14:26)
- Occupations (Luke 5:10, 27)
- Possessions (Luke 14:33)
- Comfort and Ease (Luke 9:57-62)
- Jesus said, "If any man come after Me, let him deny himself and take up his cross daily and follow me" (Luke 9:23).

Sacrifice in the sense of self-denial lays the emphasis on what we leave behind. However, sacrifice in the sense of self-devotion is focused on what we move toward. Self-denial will always be hard because we are limiting our desires for a time when we will return to them. Like an addict, whose white knuckles are hanging on to thought that sobriety will somehow be better or greater than the memory of the high. Self-sacrifice is different. It's easier from the beginning and throughout because there is a permanence to the decision. It comes with an understanding the old has passed away and there is no turning back. We have taken out the trash and the garbage man has come and gone.

Jesus' call to his disciples was/is a call to come and die. To sacrifice the old. Not just deny the old for a period. It is the offer of a life many cannot imagine. Jesus told his disciples they would be fishers of men (Luke 5:10). A thought on the service which seems like a duty, but is really a statement of enduring relationship. When a man/woman decides to come to Jesus, a relationship is formed between the person and Christ, but also between the person who God used to reach them. It's an everlasting bond. Hence, the second promise from Christ when he says of those willing to sacrifice for him, "Whatever you abandon here for Him would be given back a hundredfold and will inherit eternal life (Matt. 19:29 NIV). The truth is that when we decided to devote our lives (read sacrifice our lives), He will devote himself to us. He will meet us in our life, here and now.

It's the reason He looks to see us make steps of surrender towards him and then renews us accordingly. Not to have us recognize his presence and become content but to increase our willingness to continue to pour out more and more of ourselves, our heart, our mind and our soul.

The group discussion guide for this topic is in Appendix A on page 391.

RENEW

CHAPTER 39

HOLY SPIRIT

*The Holy Spirit is the renewal power to use
our unique gifting and talents to bear witness of Jesus
and renew all mankind.*

Who remembers the cartoon *Casper the Friendly Ghost*? The character was cute, but did you ever consider he was a dead little boy who, according to the video, had died tragically after a sledding accident and catching pneumonia. The cartoon made the idea of ghosts not so scary for a whole generation of people. However, I would venture to say almost all humans have contemplated the prospect of ghosts of those from long ago.

It's with this knowledge many come to hear the story of God's spirit breaking onto the scene.

I can remember a small group experience from long ago where a person in the small group stormed after they read a section in Acts about the Pentecost because someone in the group shared what I lovingly call a "whack-a-doodle experience" and then stated if you have never received the Holy Spirit in a profound way then you can't claim to be a Christian. The person who stormed out said they never wanted to lose control "like that."

I could identify because I'll never forget an experience I had in college.

I had a roommate who had a grandmother who he would visit on occasion in Kentucky. On one occasion, he invited me to come along and so I did. I met his grandparents who lived off a two-lane blacktop road in the middle nowhere. On Sunday morning, his grandma arose before 5 a.m. and cooked us breakfast and informed us we were going to church at Fifth and Main. Now, I was brought up Catholic, had never been to another church and wasn't all too sure about who God was really was at that point. But I went because I wanted to be polite. We got in the car about 7 a.m. and began driving. We drove for a while on the blacktop, and then made a left onto a gravel road. We travelled quite aways and then turned right onto a couple of ruts in the woods and then we drove through a forest area. The ruts disappeared and we were four-wheel-driving in the Buick LeSabre until all of the sudden we reached a clearing. There were four to five shotgun shanties on stilts. One had a cross on the front. We pulled up to the sound of a generator running. I looked at Grandma and she said that the musicians were some real cute girls and she had one picked out for me. I really got nervous. We went inside this shanty to a room with thirty to forty chairs, people barefoot and a stage set up with three to four guitars. I settled in. After the girl band came onstage, three women all over 300 pounds, and sang four to five songs with perfect harmony, I knew something was up. The preacher stood up and then preached a hell-fire sermon to which several in the congregation stood up, *waved their hands and made confessions. Then the pastor laid his hands on them. Immediately, they fell to the ground and started flopping around on the floor like fish that just came off the line. It was quite an experience. On the way home, Grandma told us that was the most powerful Holy Ghost event they had been to in a while. I wondered, "How can this be?" A better question would have been who is this Holy Spirit?*

The Holy Spirit has been around since the beginning. We find the first mention of the Spirit in Genesis 1:1-2, "In the beginning God created the heavens and the earth. Now the earth was formless and empty, darkness was over the surface of the deep and the spirit of God was hovering over the waters." In Genesis 2, we find God's Spirit is breathed into the nostrils of man and he becomes a living being.

Throughout the Old Testament, we see how the Spirit of God was placed on people at particular times for particular purpose or task. The word Spirit is mentioned some 800 times in scripture. The Hebrew word is Rauch, "a violent exhalation, a blast of breath, a strong wind." The New Testament uses the Greek word "pneuma" which also conveys breath and wind. We cannot fully live with breath. We can feel the experience of the wind, but we cannot see it. We can see its impact and we do not have to see it to acknowledge its presence. These moments of infilling offered the world new insights and dimensions with a greater spiritual impact to what could have been otherwise considered ordinary. Bezalel was an artist who possessed incredible craftsmanship. Gideon was given leadership, Samson was given strength, Isaiah the ability to preach the good news. Even Ezekiel, Joel and Jeremiah were offered prophetic words of the future and a promise that this aspect of our relationship would change at some point for the better. This built the anticipation for the Messiah's appearance and when Jesus references this change and speaks of living water, He is foretelling the world we live in today.

You see, the Holy Spirit is a person. He has all the characteristics of personhood. He thinks (Acts 15:28), speaks (Acts 1:16), leads (Rom. 8:14) and be grieved (Eph. 4:30). He is sometimes described as the Spirit of Christ (Rom. 8:9) or the Spirit of Jesus (Acts 16:7).[114] He is the way in which Jesus remains present with His people. He is our counselor, comforter, encourager and sustainer.

A little while ago, a movie came out called *The Shack*, based on the book of the same name. I will never forget how upset some Christians were over the portrayal of God as a black female and then the way the relationship between the God, His son and His Spirit seemed almost hierarchal, as if to say there were three distinct Gods. I agree it's a problem in the story because it's untrue, but it is a fictional novel. Fiction is never to be confused with reality or a classroom for theological doctrines. Three in one is a tough concept.

I was in a men's bible study a few years ago. We were discussing the relationship between all three. We talked about the junior high classroom way of explaining it and even the way cults disavow scriptures about three in one. I mention the doctrine of Triune God. They all rolled their eyes and told me to speak English. We laughed, and the group moved into the scriptures. After a few cups of coffee and some more bacon, we concluded Jesus was both human and divine and we would never fully understand how the Holy Spirit guided him or when and where his divine nature or humanness would be revealed. We believed He was both and

---

114 *Questions of Life,* Nicky Gumbel, Kingsway publishing, 2003, p.120

HOLY SPIRIT

His Spirit is with us even today. That was enough for a Saturday morning. There were lawns to be cut and chores to be done.

As Christ-followers, we know from the scriptures the Spirit descended on Jesus at His baptism (Matt. 3:16), made Him unique to the Prophet John the Baptist (John 1:33-34), led Jesus in the wilderness (Luke 4:1), gave Him power in service (Luke 4:14) and moved Him through the rest of His ministry (Matt. 12:28; Luke 4:18).

It was this same Spirit that Jesus arranged to be given to all who are willing to follow in His footsteps (John 14:16, 26; 16:7-14). The thought of which almost overwhelms me; to think you and I have access to the same Spirit which used to guide only the prophets of old. The only condition is to believe and practice the disciplines they did to know God's ways in this life. The Spirit:

> Teaches us the ways of God (1 Cor. 2:13)
> Assists us in remembering Jesus words (Rom. 8:16)
> Directs our witness of Him in this life (Acts 5:32)
> Convicts the world of its error in His desires (1 Cor. 2:10)
> Guides us in the study of the truth (Rom. 8:14; Gal. 5:18)
> Hones our hearing, speech and declaration to others about Him (1 Tim. 4:1; Heb. 3:7; 10:15)
> Provide discernment and knowledge of things to come (1 Peter 1:11)
> Moves us to glorify Him in our fear, uncertainty and lack of knowledge (John 16:14; Acts 13:2)

I imagine, sometimes, getting to heaven and meeting the Old Testament prophets and having them excitedly asking what it is was like to have God's power and connection available all the time (John 3:34). I also think of their disappointment when they hear I often ignored the gift or only partially responded to the prompting.

Now, the reality is the power He promised is *not* the power to do whatever we want or imitate the life of another no matter how perfect. It's the renewal power to do our assigned part through our unique gifting and talents to bear witness to Jesus to all mankind. It's key to understand that the power, insight and courage given to us through the Holy Spirit is to complete His command to go to all nations and share the truth (Matt. 28:18-20).

The group discussion guide for this topic is in Appendix A on page 393.

CHAPTER 40

PLEASURE

Christ's message has the power to renew the moments of this life and transform them into pleasure.

When I say the word pleasure, what do you think of: time with a good book, a massage, a day at the beach, a motorcycle ride, a day off? All of these are pleasurable activities. Maybe you have said it after a hard week or after a particularly challenging event in life. But do we deserve to experience pleasure in this life? If so, to what extent?

For some, pleasure becomes a pursuit. Sigmund Freud was the first to coin the phrase the "pleasure principle" to characterize the tendency of people to seek pleasure and avoid pain. Freud argued that people will sometimes go to great lengths to avoid even momentary pain, particularly at times of psychological weakness or vulnerability. While modern psychologists typically do not follow traditional Freudian theory, they often use the "pleasure principle" and related concepts in therapy in the hope of breaking cycles that result in the pursuit of pleasure alone.

It's been said before, the greatest detriment to a life of peace and joy may be the human pursuit of comfort and ease. We often work hard and overly schedule our lives for years in the hopes of acquiring enough resources to live in comfort. In America, we have institutionalized this belief and called it retirement.

The great novelist Rudyard Kipling once gave a commencement address at McGill University in Montreal. He warned the graduates about making money, position or glory their life ambition. "Someday," he said, "you will meet a man who cares for none of these things. Then you will know how poor you are."

Are all pleasures of this life and time wrong? No. God created everything in this world and invited us to enjoy His creation. It all screams out his name — from the smallest particle to the expanse of the galaxy. However, when pleasure becomes the sole aim of our lives, our lives are now in conflict with God's purpose.

If you're a Christ-follower like me, Jesus did condemn all excessive thought and action about this side of life (Matt. 6:19-34). He condemned all waste, extravagance and vulgar displays. Selfishness, careless spending and exclusiveness, are all hostile to the Spirit of Jesus' life and His teaching. (Luke 12:19-21)

Jesus' constant emphasis was on what is enduring. "Jesus came to lift the whole set of life's tastes and desires to a new and higher plane of pleasure, to fill men with joy; but not through just through the tangible senses of our physical life, but of spirit, not of this world only, but of the world to come as well."[115]

---

115 *The Principles of Jesus*, Robert E Speer, The Westminster Press, 1902, p.217

Phil Jackson was coach of the Chicago Bulls basketball team during the days of Michael Jordan. Before turning his hand to coaching, Jackson played for the New York Knicks in the 1970s. During his time with the Knicks, the team won the championship. He had reached the goal, the dream he had been striving for since he was a child. A short time later, he was in New York and went out to celebrate with family and friends. The restaurant was crowded with famous people like Robert Redford and Dustin Hoffman. But instead of feeling joy, this is what Jackson wrote about his feelings: 'The intense feeling of connection with my teammates that I had experienced in Los Angeles seemed like a distant memory. Instead of being overwhelmed with joy, I felt empty and confused. 'Was this it,' I kept saying to myself. Is this what was supposed to bring me happiness? Clearly the answer lay somewhere else.' He later understood what was missing. He writes, "What I was missing was spiritual direction."[116]

Phil's story is not uncommon. Many a person has achieved great success only to stand alone and wonder if this is all there is. The hollowness of those moments stands as proof that the only true pleasures of this life are connected to those above and beyond this life. A concept many wrestle with because we are sold the idea in this culture that only the success and pleasure of this world will bring happiness. In the words of that famous philosopher from *Talladega Nights*, Ricky Bobby, "If you're not first, you're last."

If you have a problem with connecting this life to the next, I thought I'd help by reading a list from an unknown author clarifying what living with God's Kingdom in mind looks like:

---

116   *Sacred Hoops*, Phil Jackson, Perfection Pre-Bid, 2010

1. God won't ask what kind of fancy car you drove. He will ask how many people you took to church who didn't have transportation.
2. God won't ask the size of your house. He'll ask how many people you helped who didn't have a house.
3. God won't ask how many fancy clothes you had in your closet. He will ask how many of those clothes you gave away to those who didn't have any.
4. God won't ask what social class you were in. He will ask what kindness you displayed.
5. God won't ask about your material possessions. He'll ask whether those possessions dictated your life.
6. God won't ask what your highest salary was. He'll ask if you trampled over anybody to obtain that salary.
7. God won't ask how much overtime you worked. He will ask if you worked overtime for your family.
8. God won't ask how many promotions you received. He will ask what you did to promote others.
9. God won't ask what your job title was. He will ask if you performed your job to the best of your ability.
10. God won't ask how many promotions you took to chase a dollar bill. He will ask how many promotions you refused to advance your family's quality of life.
11. God won't ask how many times you didn't cheat on your spouse. He will ask how many times you lusted after another. Or slept with someone you weren't married to?

12. *God won't ask about your degrees. He'll ask how many people you thanked for helping you get those degrees.*
13. *God won't ask what your parents did to help you. He will ask what you did to help your parents.*
14. *God won't ask what you did to help yourself. He will ask what you did to help others.*
15. *God won't ask how many friends you had. He will ask how many people you were a friend to.*
16. *God won't ask what you did to protect your rights. He will ask what you did to protect the right of others.*
17. *God won't ask what neighborhood you lived in. He will ask what other neighborhoods you visited.*
18. *God won't ask how many times you told the truth. He will ask how many times you told a lie.*
19. *God won't ask about the color of your skin. He will ask about the color of your heart.*
20. *God won't ask how many times your deeds matched your words. He will ask how many times they didn't.*

Christ's message for us is profound because it has the power to take all the lasting moments of this life like love, sympathy, service, devotion, deep joy in assurance, elevation of the mind, pain and even hardship — and renew them into contentment or pleasure. The only commitment is to believe in an inclusive relationship with Jesus and then be guided by it (1 Tim. 4:8; 2 Tim 1:1;1 Cor. 3:21-23; Matt. 6:33).

The group discussion guide for this topic is in Appendix A on page 394.

CHAPTER 41

PURPOSE OF LIFE

"If we are willing to do the will of God, the secrets of the Highest and the Unseen will unfold for us and the true purpose of life will unveil for us it's hidden mystery"
(John 7:17).

Have you ever struggled with what your purpose is in life? I have. I know plenty of others who have and still do. If you haven't, you are an anomaly because eventually, we all wake up and wonder, "Is this as good as it gets?" It happened to me several years ago. I was a businessman in a warehouse with a growing staff and weekly profit report. I was alone in the office and was looking at a particularly good report when I wondered if this was all there is to life. Get up. Go to work. Make some money. Go home. Is this really it? Is this what God created me for? It would start a spiral of thought about the purpose of life.

I'd investigate the ideas of life being about enlightenment, morality, knowledge, energy, vibrations, virtue, happiness, suffering, psychology, philosophy, religion and even good orderly directions. The contemplation would take me to those revered as wise,

profound and even famous for an answer. However, the quotes often left me more confused and depressed. For example:
Was Eleanor Roosevelt, right?

"The purpose of life is to live it, to taste experience to the utmost, to reach out eagerly and without fear for newer and richer experience."
— Eleanor Roosevelt[117]

Did Johann Wolfgang von Goethe better illuminate our life?

"The human race is a monotonous affair. Most people spend the greatest part of their time working in order to live, and what little freedom remains so fills them with fear that they seek out any and every means to be rid of it."
— Johann Wolfgang von Goethe, *The Sorrows of Young Werther*[118]

Or was life just about making a mark to be remembered?

"The purpose of life is not to be happy. It is to be useful, to be honorable, to be compassionate, to have it make some difference that you have lived and lived well."
— Ralph Waldo Emerson[119]

---

117   https://www.goodreads.com/author/show/44566.Eleanor_Roosevelt

118   https://www.goodreads.com/work/quotes/746264

119   https://www.goodreads.com/author/show/12080.Ralph_Waldo_Emerson

As a recovering alcoholic, I can honestly admit I knew more about what my purpose was *not*, than what it is. I had to do some real soul searching because my heart was so unsettled. I can remember paying a counselor good money to take a 300-question personality and interest profile to help me discern what I'm supposed to do with my life. It came back that I should be an entrepreneur, a CEO or a fashion designer. Seriously?!

I can also remember taking a Christian gifts inventory as part of a church initiative to get volunteers at some point, only to discover I had the gift of speaking, teaching and leading. All of which were great validation of what I already knew, but which failed to help answer the question, what is the purpose of my life now? I would pray and plead with God for help. I'd ask for an email, a fax or a sign from God. I'd get discouraged. Friends would offer suggestions. I'd try a few of their ideas but nothing felt right. I know leading your life by how things feel is not appropriate but without a sincere connection, I knew I wouldn't stick with it.

My renewal came after months of praying when a friend asked me to serve at a community outreach event for some church. He didn't go there, but he liked the idea of helping others. I have to admit the day was long, but it was inspiring. The smiles of the children and the families was all I needed to want to do more. I also discovered the whole event challenged my idea about Christians. Prior to the event, I considered most of Christians hypocrites. However, the folks I hung out with were genuine people willing to offer themselves and their time to help people in need. They weren't condemning or judgmental. They just wanted to help as a way to be like their Savior.

As a result, the purpose of life was revealed as a two-fold mission. First, it's to be a service of God (Matt. 6:24); in love (Mark

12:30); and in holiness (Matt. 5:48). But it doesn't end there, as I thought when I immaturely judged those in a church. The second part of our purpose is to be of service to our fellow man (Matt. 10:28; Luke 22:26-27); in love (Mark 12:31); and in humility (Matt. 20:26). Herein lies the fundamental principle of a Christian life: One's life is not for one's own gain but to use it as a sacrifice for greater significance.

This significance is found in only one place: Jesus. It is in His companionship we find:

- Purity (Matt. 5:8; James 1:27; 2 Tim. 2:22)
- Freedom (John 8:31-32)
- Unconditional love (John 13:1, 15:13)
- Strength (Eph. 6:10; 2 Tim. 2:1; 1 John 2:14; 1 Cor. 1:25)
- Eternal life (1 John 2:17)
- Motivation (John 6:38; Heb. 10:7)
- Fulfilment (John 6:51; 4:34)

Just as Jesus came to serve God and others, we are to attempt the same. Our life's purpose is found in His companionship and the companionship of His followers. These two relationships create a willingness to strive to serve as He did. In striving/serving, we continue His work in the world. A quick review of Jesus' actions while physically present tell us to renew life through:

- Love
- Forgiveness of sins
- Offers of compassion
- Comforting the sick and mourning
- Being a peacemaker and joy giver
- Living unselfishly in all areas of life

- Staying focused on the spiritual
- Declaring the immortality of life
- Giving glory to God in all things

Metaphorically, we renew our lives to become the salt (Matt. 5:13), light (Matt. 5:14) and living water (John 4:14) to those around us.

Robert Speer says this well in *The Principles of Jesus*, "If we are willing to do the will of God, the secrets of the Highest and the Unseen will unfold for us and the true purpose of life will unveil for us its hidden mystery (John 7:17)."[120]

The group discussion guide for this topic is in Appendix A on page 341.

---

120 *The Principles of Jesus*, Robert E. Speers, The Westminster Press, Chicago, 1902.

RENEW

CHAPTER 42

JESUS

Jesus is God?

Several years ago I was on my way into a meeting when a friend I hadn't seen in a while asked, "How's life?" I proceeded to tell him about selling my business and deciding to enter seminary. He had a puzzled look on his face. After an awkward moment of silence, he asked, "Do you really believe in Jesus? Why?" Time stopped. My mind raced into panic mode as I considered all the possible ways to answer his second question. You would think I would have a great answer since I had just sold my business and dedicated everything to following Christ. But in that moment, I stammered, "I believe in Jesus because of the sense of peace that has come since I declared my faith in Him and committed my life." He smirked and then shared how he played guitar every fourth weekend at a large church in the area but really didn't understand what all the fuss was about. He then wandered away and left me standing there wondering.

The question has haunted me ever since. Who is Jesus? Who is He historically? Who is He to others? Why does His name cause some to weep, others to leap for joy and still others to immediately get angry?

Type the question into Google (the purveyor of all knowledge and no wisdom) and there will be thousands of answers. Wikipedia will tell you this: "Jesus (c. 4 BC – c. AD 30 / 33), also referred to as Jesus of Nazareth and Jesus Christ, was a first-century Jewish preacher and religious leader. He is the central figure of Christianity. Most Christians believe he is the incarnation of God the Son and the awaited Messiah (Christ) prophesied in the Old Testament." It goes on to provide basic ideas about the faith He founded and claim what other religions believe about Him. Wikipedia also offers this:

> Jesus also figures in non-Christian religions and new religious movements. In Islam, Jesus (commonly transliterated as Isa) is considered one of God's important prophets and the Messiah. Muslims believe Jesus was a bringer of scripture and was born of a virgin but was not the Son of God. The Quran states that Jesus Himself never claimed divinity. Most Muslims do not believe that he was crucified but believe that he was physically raised into Heaven by God. In contrast, Judaism rejects the belief that Jesus was the awaited Messiah, arguing that he did not fulfill Messianic prophecies, and was neither divine nor resurrected.[121]

The explanation is factual but falls short of the explanation as to why so many would literally and figuratively die because of His existence.

---

121 https://en.wikipedia.org/wiki/Jesus

JESUS

C.S. Lewis in his book *Mere Christianity* writes the following:

I am trying here to prevent anyone from saying the really foolish thing that people often say about Him: 'I'm ready to accept Jesus as a great moral teacher, but I don't accept his claim to be God.' That is the one thing we must not say. A man who was merely a man and said the sort of things Jesus said would not be a great moral teacher. He would either be a lunatic—on a level with a man who says he is a poached egg—or else he would be the Devil of hell. You must make your choice. Either this man was, and is, the Son of God, or else a madman or something worse. You can shut him up for fool, you can spit at him and kill him as a demon; or you can fall at his feet and call him Lord and God. But let us not come up with any patronizing nonsense about his being a great human teacher. He has not left that option open to us. He did not intend to.[122]

Jesus is God in human form. In saying this, we are claiming God is so powerful He stepped through the veil (or across the chasm) between the spiritual and physical world. In the acceptance of God who can do this and become human, we must then ask, why? Why would a creator become human? Why go from having and knowing all to come to a place so broken? The conventional answer is love. A love so deep and wide, we (all humanity) would struggle to accept this love or even believe it is possible. However, Jesus' birth, life, death and resurrection screams love. The birth shouts love of and for His creation. His life declares love through example and parental care. His gruesome death declares an unfathomable willingness to intervene in a world with a perfect justice only deep love can explain. It also gives us pause to reflect

---

122   *Mere Christianity*, CS Lewis.

on His death and the reasoning that He would allow Himself to be sacrificed for the penalty of whole world's sins. Jesus had to be God so that He could pay our debt. Jesus' deity is why He proclaimed, "I am the way and the truth and the life. No one comes to the Father except through me" (John 14:6). Hence, eternal life is available only through faith in Jesus Christ.

If my friend were to ask me today why I believe in Jesus, I believe I would answer like Vernon Grounds when he said:

Everything in Christ astonishes me. His spirit overawes me, and His will confounds me. Between Him and whoever else in the world, there is no possible term of comparison. He is truly a being by Himself. His ideas and sentiments, the truth which He announces, His manner of convincing, are not explained either by human organization or by the nature of things ... His religion is a revelation from an intelligence which certainly is not that of man ... one can find absolutely nowhere, but in Him alone, the imitation of the example of His life ... I search in vain in history to find the similar to Jesus Christ, or anything which can approach the gospel. Neither history, nor humanity, nor the ages, nor nature, offer me anything with which I am able to compare it or to explain it. Here everything is extraordinary.[123]

Jesus is God.

The group discussion guide for this topic is in Appendix A on page 398.

---

123 *The reason For Hope*, Vernon Grounds, Moody Press. 1945

CHAPTER 43

MORAL IDEAS

Jesus offered: "An illumination, a divine forth-setting of ultimate principles, stated in a way to eliminate any possibility of reinterpretation or compromise."

The definition of morality is: "A set of principles concerning the distinction between right and wrong or good and bad behavior. It is also considered a system of values and principles of conduct, especially one held by a specified person or society."

Simply: It's the determination of what is right and wrong.

But where do our society's values originate?

For most societies, the values originate from our understanding of God or some other spiritual entity. The principles of Christianity are based on the Word of God and teachings of Jesus. First and foremost, love (1 John 4:19) — both the love of God and others. However, other notable values include: reverence of God (Luke 12:5), responsibility/duty (John 14:15; 15:14), obedience and unity with God (John 5:19). These values drive our understanding of right and wrong. They are at the core of own actions and our judgement of the world around us.

Of all the aspects of the world in which we live, what is the one aspect you find most reprehensible? If you could change it, would you?

If you had the power to change it, would you end poverty or the systems which entrap others, feed everyone, offer clean water, end imprisonment, erase borders, redistribute wealth, create justice systems without influence? What would you change? I've decided I would end the declaring of a belief in anything I couldn't explain or defend.

Recently, I was in a recovery meeting. At the end, the group circles up to say the Lord's Prayer. I decided to listen instead of reciting. I was struck by the beauty of a chorus of voices and then a thought crossed my mind. There is an agnostic, a Jew, a Christian and a Hindu standing hand-in-hand praying the prayer Jesus gave us. It was beautiful until the group said, "Thy Kingdom come, thy will be done, on earth as it is in heaven" and a lightning bolt struck. I drifted into the thought: "Do they even know what they are praying? Do they understand? Is it even realistic to pray for this?"

When we are praying these words given by Jesus, we are asking for perfection in this world: personal, communal and national. We are praying for God's will and to use us in the process. It's a unified prayer of relationship with Him. We are praying for His return and His leadership. Simple words with profound implications. We are praying for Him to institute those aspects He finds objectionable or in opposition. We are praying for His standards. Standards we have been made aware of by His revelation. They define perfection or success for us as humans. We are praying for change.

On a personal level, perfection is a disciple who embodies the teacher (5:48, 6:40). It's the goal of all spiritual life: to attain a level of understanding and submission to a greater ideal. On the communal level, it's the idea of a community with the goal of an all-encompassing love being a singular focus (John 17:23). On a worldly level, it is the idea of a world remade complete (2 Cor. 7:1; James 2:22; 1 John 4:17-18; Heb. 2:10, 5:9). It's the idea of a world with no pain, no tears, no selfishness, perfect in all aspects (Rev. 21:1-4).

Many will say this idea of perfection is impossible. The founder of Methodism, John Wesley once wrote a sermon about this idea and the potential to be attained in this life. It would be a message he would be ridiculed for. He would clarify but the establishment would not relent. The idea was radical — "Thy Kingdom come."

The early writers of the Christian faith would also need to help the world understand the Kingdom being spoken of was as much a set of guiding values as a place of residence. The moral idea is Christian character being lived. It is the endless quest of perfection to be more and more like God (Luke 6:40). It's a belief that while we all fall short of the glory of God, the progress we make is counted as righteousness and should afford us peace and joy. A peace and joy only possible because of an assurance anything done in following His footsteps requires a reliance on the Holy Spirit power in our life (Phil. 3:12-13, 2 Cor. 13:11) and willingness to strive for justice (good) for the brotherhood of all humanity.

Are we our brother's keeper? The culture of the Middle East, especially during Jesus' time, *was not* centered on the individual but on the family and the community (extended community). The family unit was the physical, mental and spiritual center. It provided the social security of the day. The question of whether one is to be another's keeper is only a recent development due in part to advancements in the availability of basics (Food, Water, Shelter, Clothing).

Jesus was no social reformer. He offered *"An illumination, a divine forth-setting of ultimate principles, stated in a way to eliminate any possibility of re-interpretation or compromise."*[124] This illumination is best referenced in His Sermon on the Mount (Matt. 5-7). A set of timeless principles which crystallize God's values to be embodied practically today.

One of those principles is the idea of praying for certain ideas. One such idea is to pray for the Kingdom to come. In praying as Jesus instructed, we are calling for the body to act as His presence in this world. We are to continue the fulfillment He spoke of (Isaiah 61:1-2) in the synagogue and lived daily. It's simple but not easy. We are to: *"Preach the good new to the poor, to proclaim freedom for the prisoners, recovery of site for the blind, to release of the oppressed and proclaim the year of the Lord's favor."* This is both a temporal and spiritual declaration. Nowhere does it say as Christ's ambassadors should we stir up strife, take sides with the empowered (rich) over the less fortunate, add burdens to those uniformed or ignore the needy.

Jesus reveals through his teaching a renewed focus is to live with a single mission above our own wants and desires. We are to make disciples of all nations bringing them into the brotherhood, teaching them to obey everything commanded and understand it is by His power more come to know Him (Matt. 28:18-20).

The group discussion guide for this topic is in Appendix A on page 399.

---

[124] *The Principles of Jesus*, Robert E. Speers, The Westminster Press, Chicago, 1902, p.238

CHAPTER 44

GOOD NEWS

God did not send Jesus to control us but to free us and renew us to be more of what He designed us to be.

Has anybody ever been excited to share good news with you but they didn't make any sense? Sure, you nodded your head and acted like you understood. But after they walked away, you just shrugged your shoulders, shook your head and wondered, "what the heck was that?"

There is an Alcoholic Anonymous circuit speaker, Earl Hightower, who tells a story of first coming into recovery and being confused by some of the slogans of recovery. The one saying that caused him the most confusion was "let it go." He shares that when he was only a few weeks sober and still mad as hell at his circumstances, an AA old timer came up to him and told him to just "let it go" and others around the recovery table would nod their heads knowingly. Earl says, "I wondered what the hell they were talking about, so I asked. 'What does that mean?' To which the old timer said, "I don't know they said it to me when I first came around so I'm saying it to you. Why don't you stay around until you figure it out?"

I think we in Christendom have sayings like this. The most well-known is, "the gospel" or an offshoot of this is "Jesus saves." People use these words and have no clue what they are talking about. They heard them when they showed up at a store for religious goods called a church. Life had been pretty good since, so they share the words with others. They don't understand the claim they are making. They just feel like they should tell somebody because it's what western Christianity teaches. Unfortunately, this creates believers who can now be categorized as Moralistic Therapeutic Deism believers. An idea which has become extremely harmful because it gives off the aura of Christianity without the essence and often leads people down a path of giving up on God, His Son and oneself as an image bearer.

Moralistic Therapeutic Deism (MTD) is a term that was first introduced in the book *Soul Searching: The Religious and Spiritual Lives of American Teenagers* (2005) by sociologists Christian Smith and Melinda Lundquist Denton. The book is the result of the research project the "National Study of Youth and Religion" of 3,000 student-age participants. In short, a person is a Moralistic Therapeutic Deist if they believe: 1. "A god exists who created and ordered the world and watches over human life on earth." 2. "God wants people to be good, nice and fair to each other, as taught in the Bible and by most world religions." 3. "The central goal of life is to be happy and to feel good about oneself." 4. "Good people go to heaven when they die." 5. "God does not need to be particularly involved in one's life except when God is needed to resolve a problem."[125]

---

125   http://www.albertmohler.com/2005/04/11/moralistic-therapeutic-deism-the-new-american-religion-2/

In many ways, those afflicted with MTD have become fans of God. They like the idea of a powerful God for the problems they themselves cannot completely figure out. However, they are unwilling to fully engage Him in their life or seek out the deeper meaning of why He had to come to come to earth to save and what their relationship is called to be now. The MTD worshipper often ends up struggling when God doesn't rescue or act in accordance with their wishes.

So, what is the gospel?

There are long drawn out explanations from all kinds of scholars who love to use big words to sell books to academics who want to further pontificate on the idea. The result has been a complication of what God so wanted us to understand that He became man in Jesus. A story many can't fathom and yet, we recite historically as: "He came, He suffered, He died, He rose for the forgiveness of sins and life eternal." It's a simple statement (creed actually) with profound reverberations.

The creed is life-changing when people take the time to allow the implications to settle into the deepest regions of one's soul. The good news is not of God's existence but Jesus' interaction with us, for us and through us. As Robert Speer said in 1908, "All other religions are separable from their founders. ... To remove the Christological element is radically to alter its character, to destroy the class in which it stands by itself and to reduce its in kind to the level of other religions. It is to rob it of its power.... The human heart needs the personal experience of God and if it is denied the joy of merging itself in God in Christ and still preserving personality, it will seek the sense of divine unity and will secure it at the expense of the personality and responsibility, safeguarded to us by the historic doctrine of the Christian faith."[126]

I like how Hugh Halter says it in his book entitled *Flesh*:

"I think you missed the main message of Jesus amid all the religion and struggles of life. Jesus came to change everything you don't like. An everywhere he went, He talked about a Kingdom of God coming into the Kingdom of darkness and winning out. The Kingdom of heaven simply means that the way things are in heaven can begin to change the way things are on earth. You probably know that He died on a cross and that is a key part of the story, but the reason He did that was so that something incredible could happen to His people."[127]

Hugh expands ....
"Jesus' gospel includes salvation of our souls, but that's just the starting point. The Kingdom of God means that God is making things right: people get help; they have food on the table, protection from enemies, healing for diseases; and they will get a fresh start. The Kingdom means the abuses stop, the poor are cared for, and everyone can be accepted into a true community of meaning and substance."[128]

---

126 *The Principles of Jesus*, Robert E. Speers, The Westminster Press, Chicago, 1902, p.253-54

127 *Flesh*, Hugh Halter, David Cook Publishing, Colorado, Springs, CO, 2014, p.180-181

128 *Flesh*, Hugh Halter, David Cook Publishing, Colorado, Springs, CO, 2014 p.55

Many people can't fathom this idea of good happening because of the evil they see or have experienced in the world today. As a result, they wonder about the "love" of an all-loving and perfect God who allows such evil to exist. This is a short-sighted viewpoint because it fails to consider man's free will. Obviously, God designed us with this aspect of human nature to allow us to decide what we want to reign over our lives. It takes love to allow those you care about to choose not to stay in relationship with you. Herein lies the spiritual paradox of true love. It is only when one frees another of all constraint that they can give of themselves fully. It is not loving to make a person's every decision, it's control. God did not send Jesus to control us but to free us and renew us to be more of what He designed us to be: image bearers of Him. The gospel is unique in its offering because we get to decide what Kingdom we want to be associated with: the Jesus Kingdom or the individualist cultural Kingdom. Sadly, many choose the cultural above the spiritual. God will not force you to choose His Kingdom reign. But when we "let it go" or turn over our control, His Kingdom will win out.

The group discussion guide for this topic is in Appendix A on page 400.

RENEW

CHAPTER 45

THE SUPERNATURAL

A good friend stumbled upon a movie called the *Finger of God* a few years back. He bought it and lent it to me. I've watched it on several occasions wondering if it was a spoof on miracles. It has the feel of Spinal Tap for Christians. If you want to see a clip, go to YouTube and type in: https://youtu.be/bSiTnN3uU3g. The video clip is an extreme example of how many people get caught up in chasing the miracle, the experience or the feeling versus pursuing a relationship with God through Jesus. I have watched the whole movie a couple of times and it makes the idea of miracle which by definition is something out of the norm, become ordinary. As Theologian and author, RC Sproul says, "If you expect a miracle — if miracles are expectable — there's nothing miraculous about them. If they're ordinary, then they carry no certifiable weight. It's by their extraordinary character that they have sign power: significance."[129]

I believe miracles take place today. I believe the scriptures that describe miracles taking place after Jesus' resurrection have

---

129   http://www.ligonier.org/blog/does-rcsproul-believe-miracles/

continued. I also believe Jesus left behind His Spirit to connect with ours so through our faith we will continue His work in this realm. Faith requires trust in the unseen and I would add in the presently unknowable.

The known world in which we live is often considered the natural world. Natural refers to the laws of the physical plane in which we live. It is the laws of cause and effect, orderly succession, understandable by what we, as humans, know of the ways this world works. Supernatural implies the suspension of the laws of nature.[130]

Supernatural is the realm of activity of unseen agent's unknowable by science because it is "above" or transcending or going beyond nature. We often call events of the supernatural, "miracles." They are events are unable to be explained by science or predicted by the scientist, even one who has all the information possible about the context and applicable natural laws.

There was a story from a number of years ago from a woman in Arkansas. Her husband, Shane, who was a construction contractor and volunteer youth minister at Osage Baptist Church in rural Osage, Arkansas, called and said our little boy, Braedyn, had been in a wreck and was in terrible shape. I asked if Braedyn would be OK. My husband had no response, which alarmed me terribly. Waiting for my parents to drive me to the hospital, I felt so helpless. I dropped to my knees and began praying! Then I started phoning everyone I knew and asked for prayer and they called other people. When I arrived at the hospital, my husband was crying in a way I had never seen a man cry. He didn't want

---

130   *The Principles of Jesus*, Robert E. Speers, The Westminster Press, Chicago, 1902, p.255

me to see Braedyn. When I did, it was terrible. His head was caved in on the right side. He had blood coming from his ears, eyes, nose and mouth. His pelvis appeared to be completely crushed. His catheter was full of blood, which means internal bleeding. The doctor told us the prognosis looked "very grave" and he might not make the flight to a big hospital in Springfield, Missouri. The thought of placing my baby on a helicopter by himself was just more than I could handle. The pilot asked if I wanted to ride, which is not usually allowed. I held onto my little boy's arm and prayed during the whole flight that God would heal his broken little body. I told God I knew Braedyn was only on loan to me, but I wasn't ready to not be his mommy. I fully trusted God that He would take care of my baby boy. When we landed, everything was so fast-paced. I was placed in a little room all by myself. There, I just continued to pray. After an eternity — actually only about 40 minutes — the doctor came into the room. He seemed to be in shock! All of the x-rays and tests had been redone and my little boy didn't have a broken bone in his body. No internal bleeding. He was bruised and banged up very badly, but the doctor said "I can't explain what happened. I thought I was going to be telling you there was nothing we could do, but instead I get to tell you that you are very lucky." I said, "We are not lucky, we are blessed! Our God saved our little boy." When we finally got to see him, his head was no longer caved in. He did have to be bed-bound for two weeks, but it was nothing we couldn't handle. When we went for a check-up, our family doctor cried and hugged Braedyn. He said, "I prayed so hard but I never thought I would see this little guy again." God is so good! Braedyn is our little miracle boy![131]

---

131 http://www.beliefnet.com/faiths/galleries/12-absolutely-amazing-miracles.asp

Again, for our time together: Supernatural is the realm of activity of unseen agents unknowable by science because it is "above" or transcending or going beyond nature.

Colin Brown, a theology professor at Fuller Seminary, writes, "When I drive along the freeway and see a green sign that reads 'Pasadena: Next 11 Exits,' I am not being treated to a logical demonstration that each and all of the next 11 off ramps will lead me to Pasadena. I am being given a pointer. Only in following the directions of the sign do I discover whether the sign is telling the truth or not."

He goes on to say, "Miracles are like warning flags. They signal the presence of a different order of reality that is present during our everyday world."[132]

Signs are never ends in themselves. They do not point to themselves. They are not proof of anything in themselves. They exist not to make us think we have arrived, but to lead us somewhere new.

Under this definition, Jesus himself was supernatural. He did supernatural works. His teaching was supernatural. The greatest of which was the resurrection. It's the only action that needed to be validated because with it, all other aspects of Jesus life are confirmed.

The first supernatural moment (miracle) came through His entrance into the material by taking on human form (Luke 1:26-28; Matt. 1:18-25). The second miracle came through His continual connection with God (John 10:30) demonstrated by conversation with Him as well as other spiritual beings. The most important

---

132 http://www.christianitytoday.com/ct/2012/september/a-new-age-of-miracles.html?start=2

supernatural event came through His resurrection and ascension to heaven. An event witnessed, confirmed and unexplainable by the current understanding of the world in which we live.

Jesus' life, death, resurrection and ascension elevated all our lives to more than our physical experience. It expanded what the most intellectual suspected but could not prove. There is a supernatural side of our world. While unseen, it still is present.

Jesus understood the supernatural. He did not set to prove it. He came to renew our relationship with it by showing us the way to the heart of God.

The group discussion guide for this topic is in Appendix A on page 402.

RENEW

CHAPTER 46

TECHNOLOGY

When the technology begins to interfere with either your relationship with God or other people, the technology must be restricted.

Did you know nine out of ten Americans are online every day? Did you know eight out of ten have a smartphone? Did you know 62 percent get all their news from the Internet? Did you know the majority of usage of the web is for social media, gaming and pornography? Did you know 51 percent of households now own and use a tablet?[133]

Technology has been affecting our lives — public and private — with ever increasing regularity. Its effects have been researched and blogged about for some time now. Many would propose that technology is morally neutral. It is but a tool that can be used for evil or good. Technology is "amoral." However, that is a naive statement when we admit our motivations are never fully altruistic. As Christians, we admit since the days of Adam our hearts lean

---

133   http://www.pewresearch.org/fact-tank/2017/01/12/evolution-of-technology/

towards immoral. As Tim Challies states in his book *The Next Story*, "The things we create assist us in overcoming the consequences of the curse also seek to dominate us, drawing our hearts from away from God rather than drawing us toward Him in dependence and faith."[134] Technology changes how we think and know other human creation and poses a greater risk of increasing our thinking of being self-reliant, no longer in need of Savior.

It not only changes us individually, it redefines community.

An article by the Harvard political science department asked some questions regarding its effects on democracy, political culture and even government policy. The article did little to answer the question except to note the original hopes of greater engagement by more in people in the process has been altered significantly in recent years through the analysis of the public's habits, preferences and viewing habits. It went so far as to state the hope of more involvement has been dashed by a savvy few who have figured ways to affect the debate with sheer amounts of data (some true and some not so much).[135]

Wes Avram from Yale University also wrote a great piece in 2011 on the connecting of theology and technology. As a part of the article he talks of secular gathering in the tech capital of Silicon Valley where the young and the old gathered to discuss technology and career. He shares what he learned:

"Fail fast," we were told, "and move on." In the economy to come, we were told, we must all "make our own jobs" — maximizing impression, value, and the energy of others to create and leverage our own. It's what sociologist Zygmut Bowman calls

---

134   *The Next Story*, Tim Challies, Zondervan, 2011

135   https://ash.harvard.edu/promise-and-perils-digital-technology

"liquid capitalism" — electronic, mediated, short-term, with high production design and always catchy labels...."

He then asked the questions many of us are asking tonight as we look at the intersection of theology and technology.

" ... Do we resist it, with the hope of preserving an older memory? Do we harness it, with sure confidence that it is a gift from God? Or do we find ways to critically but realistically engage?"

He concluded that in a hypermediated world where everyone is connected at all times and much of the under thirty crowd is victim to FOMO — fear of missing out — we must begin to discuss the reality of missing the greatest of all announcements — life with purpose.

While FOMO has been a part of every new generation in the same way there is predictability in the stability of age, there is something different about this moment in history.

"FOMO is now supported technologically, mediated electronically and monetized for profit in ways we've never seen. It is becoming the signature reason for wiring in. And that might make it the great underestimated impulse behind social media — more powerful than the desire for association and friendship that we're told stands behind it all. FOMO rules. And when it seems like there is so much more to miss out on these days when we can capture the world on a tiny screen in our palms, FOMO also drives. The fear fuels itself ... The instant response becomes the most valuable response, and so information dissemination and those in charge of it have become choreographers of immediacy rather than midwives of a slower wisdom."

This new set of expectations has slid into place without much conversation, resistance, or even notice. Yet religious tradition has some questions to ask. For hasn't the religious vision of spiritual maturity always staked at least part of its claim on the value of "missing out"? Hasn't it cherished the experience of deep exploration, of closing off options, focusing attention, and accepting limits? Hasn't spiritual wisdom demanded patience, forgiveness, a grace that is shaped (not data-banked) by memory? And haven't the disciplines of restraint, choice, concentration, humility, and focus been essential to the work of prayer? Can these questions be asked today without appearing hopelessly naive?

"... We no longer use Google to search the internet. Instead, the internet now uses Google (and Facebook) to search us — our habits, beliefs, preferences, apparent worth, relationships, weaknesses, future actions, and more. What comes, then, of the theologically rich notion of the private, upon which all possibility of commitment and love through the course of suffering is based? Do not ethics require a healthy distinction between private and public, an orderly way of guarding the eye and deliberately missing out? And doesn't a healthy soteriology require the same, whereby we allow the One who searches us to be a Loving Other (Holy Spirit) and not a piece of impersonal software.

The Holy Spirit searches us, not to feed our FOMO, but to fill it and so quiet it. The Spirit searches us to know our innermost thoughts, to unearth and reveal to us our deeper, hidden desires, and to shape our desires in ways that might teach us to say "no" as well as "yes," and transform our fear of missing out into a desire for love. What becomes now of that possibility? It isn't gone, but is it changing?"[136]

---

136 http://reflections.yale.edu/article/ibelieve-facing-new-media-explosion/connecting-theology-technology

Technology offers five distinct benefits for the Kingdom: 1) It amplifies the voice of God's message through the preacher's ability to share the gospel to more individuals through presentation both in person as well as electronically. 2) It increases the availability of good teaching. 3) It shortens the discipleship cycle from immaturity to maturity due to the constant availability of teaching. 4) It offers multiple worship experiences. 5) It provides grace to those in the minority or with communication issues.

The issues technology creates for the Kingdom are: 1) The ability to distract from God's greater purpose and connection with Him. 2) The ability it provides for people to isolate. 3) Its failure to create Christian community. 4) Its ability to reduce worship to a theatrical event for the enjoyment of the followers, not God. 5) It advances the culture outside the doors of the church to redefine and reshape those inside the church. 6) It fosters complacency in the pursuit of a relationship with God and others.[137]

Technology bring consensus, coherence, convenience and conformity to culture. God's Word often brings singularity, divisiveness, obedience and discipline.

The contrast is striking; so how are we to view technology?

There is a great saying from the minimalists, "Love people, use things. Don't use people and love things." Technology is great when it is used to better the lives of those around us. When the technology begins to interfere with either your relationship with God or other people, the technology must be restricted.

The simplest answer to the question of whether a technology is a good use or not for us is to discern, "Knowing the nature of God,

---

[137] http://www3.dbu.edu/Naugle/pdf/The%20Effect%20of%20Technology%20on%20Christianity2.pdf

would this be honoring to Him and the message He wants for us to live and offer to others?"

Simple. Renewing. Loving.

The group discussion guide for this topic is in Appendix A on page 403.

CHAPTER 47

SEX

Jesus endorsed the sexual prohibitions in the Law still apply and challenged us to an even higher standard.

On July 20, 1969, as commander of the Apollo 11 Lunar Module, Neil Armstrong was the first person to set foot on the moon. His first words after stepping on the moon, "That's one small step for a man, one giant leap for mankind," were televised to earth and heard by millions. Urban legend has it that just before he re-entered the lander, he made the enigmatic remark: "Good luck, Mr. Gorsky." Many people at NASA thought it was a casual remark concerning some rival Soviet Cosmonaut. However, upon checking, there was no Gorsky in either the Russian or American space programs. Over the years many people questioned Armstrong as to what the "Good luck, Mr. Gorsky" statement meant, but Armstrong always just smiled. On July 5, 1995, in Tampa Bay, Florida, while answering questions following a speech, a reporter brought up the 26-year-old question to Armstrong. This time he finally responded. Mr. Gorsky had died and so Neil Armstrong felt he could answer the question. In 1938, when he was a kid in a small Midwest town, he was playing baseball with a friend in the backyard. His friend hit a fly ball, which landed in his neighbor's yard by the bedroom windows. His neighbors were Mr. and Mrs. Gorsky. As he leaned down to pick up the ball, young Armstrong heard Mrs. Gorsky shouting at Mr. Gorsky. "Sex! You want sex?! You'll get sex when the kid next door walks on the moon!"[138]

Why does the idea of sex get so much of our attention? Some want to say it's because as a culture we have repressed our feelings and have made it more interesting than it should be. Doug Whitmore wrote in the "Think Big blog" recently, "Sex is only controversial because it is intellectually ignored as a basic human instinct, during a human early development. ... early humans did not avoid the subject, as there is no sound "reason" for doing so. Yet somewhere in social evolution, concepts and groups made decisions about what was acceptable to be spoken about, taught and reflected upon. Only things that are not equally and/or properly understood are controversial. For lacking equal and proper understanding."

So, let's review some facts about sex in America as relayed by Carol M. Norün in her message to Morgan Park UMC back in 2009:

"Did you know, for example, that in 1960 there were about 439,000 unmarried couples living together in the United States, but by 1998 the number had risen to 4,200,000 couples? Couples who cohabit prior to marriage have a 46-50 percent higher divorce rate than the rest of the married population (whose divorce rate is 40-50 percent anyway). And yet the ministers I talk to acknowledge that most of the couples they marry are already living together;

---

138   *Jokes and Stories from a Salesman's Briefcase*, Kim Cooper, Xliberus Corporation, 2004, p.151

that's just the way things are today. They're consenting adults; it's no big deal. We Christians seem to have forgotten Hebrews 13:4, where it says, "Let marriage be held in honor among all, and let the marriage bed be undefiled; for God will judge the immoral and adulterous." Did you realize that the divorce rate among Christians is as high or higher than the general population? The church should do more than offer a safe place for those who are divorced, though that's important; it should also be ministering to strengthen and save marriages.

Are you aware that in 1960, single women accounted for just over 5 percent of the babies born in the United States, but by 1985 the rate had grown to 36.8 percent, and by 2005, 70 percent of African-American, 46 percent of Asian-American and 25 percent of white infants were born to single women? All the studies agree that single mothers are likely to have a lifetime of lower incomes and less education; that their children are more apt to live in poverty, have less education, become sexually active at a younger age, and are at risk for delinquency and gang involvement.

According to Planned Parenthood and the Guttmacher Institute, there are 1.37 million abortions in the United States every year. The typical woman seeking an abortion is 20-24 years old, never married, identifies herself as Protestant, and has a household income of $30,000-$60,000 per year. And 93 percent of all abortions occur not because of medical problems but for "social reasons," that is, the child is not wanted.

Still another sign of sexual brokenness is our culture's addiction to pornography, especially on the internet. Between 1998 and 2005 the number of porn websites grew 3,000 percent to 420 million. And of course, those statistics are eleven years old; who knows how many million more sites there are by now. This easily accessible pornography promotes sexual exploitation of and violence toward children, among other evils, and internet porn has enslaved the minds of people both inside and outside the church — clergy and laity alike.

The most scientifically rigorous study on the sexual habits of Americans shows that the typical homosexual lifestyle, especially among males, differs dramatically from American averages, and these differences are all critical risk factors for multiple medical problems. This study revealed that 2.8 percent of males and 1.4 percent of females identify themselves as homosexual. Less than 2 percent of these are monogamous, and the average number of lifetime sexual partners is fifty. 65 percent of the male homosexuals reported they had engaged in anal intercourse in the last twelve months. In clinical terms, they have a 25-30-year decrease in life expectancy, multiple bowel and other infectious diseases, a much higher incidence of suicide, and a tendency toward a chronic, potentially fatal liver disease — infectious hepatitis, which increases the risk of liver cancer. And then there's HIV-AIDS."

With the facts in hand, let's take a look at how the Judeo-Christian view of sex, as outlined in the Christian Scriptures, gives a warning about because of its effect on our spirituality or connection to God.

The Old Testament explicitly prohibits the following sexual activities:

- Adultery (Exod. 20:14, Lev. 18:20, Deut. 5:18).
- Bestiality (Lev. 18:23, Deut. 27:21).
- Homosexual acts (Lev. 18:22).
- Incest (Lev. 18:6–18; Deut. 22:30; 27:20, 22–23).
- Prostitution (Heb. zānāh; Lev. 19:29, Deut. 23:18).
- Rape (Deut. 22:25–29).

- Sex before marriage (Exod. 22:16–17).
- Shrine-prostitution (Heb. qādēš, qe dēšāh; Deut. 23:17).
- Transvestism (Deut. 22:5).
- Unclean acts (Lev. 18:19).
- Violation of betrothal (Deut. 22:23–27).

These restrictions have the effect of confining sexual activity to marriage and the protecting of married life. Although they are negative, their purpose is positive. Moses told the people, "YHWH commanded us to observe all these statutes ... for our good always" (Deut. 6:24).

In addition to the explicit prohibitions listed above, the Law implicitly outlaws a number of other activities associated with sex.

- Abortion. The Law laid down that, if a pregnant woman is accidentally struck when men are fighting and 'her children come out', any fatality should be recompensed 'life for life' (Exod. 21:22–25). This almost certainly applied to the fetus as well as the mother, showing the value placed on this. A man seducing or raping a woman had to take responsibility for her, not leave her to contemplate abortion (Exod. 22:16–17, Deut. 22:28–29).
- Contraception. God's disapproval of this is implied by his condemnation of Onan to death for regularly practicing coitus interruptus with his brother's widow (Gen 38:8–10). While his crime was partly that he failed to fulfil his duty by his brother of producing offspring for him (Deut. 25:5–6), this was not his whole crime, for, under the Law, failure to fulfil this duty, while

being regarded as a serious offense, did not carry the death penalty (Deut. 25:7–10).

- Nudity. Before the Fall, Adam and Eve were not ashamed of being naked (Gen. 2:25). After the Fall, they were, and used leaves to cover themselves (3:7). God subsequently provided them with garments of skin (3:21). From this point onward, exposure of nakedness is regarded as shameful (9:20-27; Exod. 20:26, 28:42-43).
- Pedophilia. The Law refers to the innocence of infants (Deut. 1:39). There was no explicit law against sexual abuse of children, presumably because the wrongness of this did not need to be spelled out.
- Polygamy. Though practiced in the Old Testament, this goes against the basis for marriage set out in Genesis 2:18–24. While Solomon had many wives and concubines (1 Kings 11:1-3), in the Song of Songs, he discovers the joy of having one lover (Song 6:8–9).
- Pornography. Pornographic plaques and figurines were a feature of pagan worship in the ancient Near East. The Law required the Israelites to destroy these (Exod. 34:13 etc.).
- Promiscuity. This is effectively outlawed by other prohibitions.
- Self-gratification. God's disapproval of this is implied by his condemnation of Onan (Gen. 38:8–10). He does not, however, condemn those who do this involuntarily (Lev. 15:16–18, Deut. 23:9–11).

Jesus' affirmation of the Old Testament Law applies to them. He himself outlawed promiscuity (under Mark 7:22), affirmed the basis for marriage (Matt. 19:4-6), spoke against harming children (Luke 17:1-2) and referred to the shame of nakedness (Rev. 3:17–18). Early Christians took abortion to be wrong (Didache 2.2).

The Didache, meaning "teaching," is the short name of a Christian manual compiled before 300 A.D. The full title is *The Teaching of the Twelve Apostles*. Some Christians thought Didache was inspired, but the church rejected it when making the final decision which books to include in the New Testament. Didache contained instructions for Christian groups and its statement of belief may be the first written catechism. It has four parts: The first is the "Two Ways, the Way of Life and the Way of Death;" the second explains how to perform rituals such as baptism, fasting and Communion; the third covers ministry and how to deal with traveling teachers; the fourth part is a reminder that Jesus is coming again, with quotations from several New Testament passages which exhort Christians to live godly lives and prepare for "that day."[139]

Having affirmed the Law to his disciples, Jesus continues, "For I say to you that, unless your righteousness surpasses that of the scribes and Pharisees, you will certainly not enter the Kingdom of heaven" (Matt. 5:20). What he means by surpassing he explains further in verses 21-48. He does this by means of a series of examples. In these, he raises the standard set by the Law.

Jesus is not condemning a momentary temptation, but the fostering of desire. Over-friendly looks and gestures, he says, are to be completely resisted (29-30). Jesus does not state how other sexual prohibitions in the Law are to be taken further. He presumably

---

139   https://www.christianhistoryinstitute.org/study/module/didache/

left this to his hearers to work out, by following the pattern of verses 27-28; i.e., "You have heard that it was said, 'Do not do X.' But I say to you that everyone who fosters a desire to do X has already done it in his heart." Gratefully, Jesus accompanied his call for high standards with the promise of help to keep them, in the person of the Holy Spirit (John 14:15–17, 15:1–8). As Paul testified to the Romans, the Spirit makes a critical difference in our fight against the flesh (Rom. 7:24–8:4). Jesus taught his disciples to love others (Matt. 22:34–40, John 13:34–35). Does this mean that sexual activities prohibited in the Law are permissible if they are carried out in love? The answer is no. Christian love thus involves seeking the good of another as specified by the Law.

The New Testament provides the following examples of how this balance should be struck and sexual sins dealt with.

- • Paul instructs the Galatians, "Brothers, if someone is overtaken in some misdeed, you who are spiritual should restore such a one in a spirit of meekness, watching yourself, lest you also be tempted" (Gal. 6:1). Jude writes, "… Have mercy on those who doubt, save others by snatching out of the fire; and have mercy on others with fear, hating even the undergarment (**chitōn**) stained by the flesh" (Jude 22–23).
- • Paul directs the Corinthians for tolerating a man who was committing incest with his father's wife (1 Cor. 5). In the Law, this was a capital offence (Lev. 20:11). He tells them to excommunicate (2b, 13b). His aim is both to remove from the bad influence (6-8) and help the man to appreciate the seriousness of his misconduct, to repent of it, and be saved (5b). In a subsequent letter, Paul tells the Corinthians to "forgive

and comfort" a member of the church whom they had disciplined, and for whom the discipline had had the desired effect (2 Cor. 2:5–11).

Jesus taught that the sexual prohibitions in the Law still apply, and then challenged us to an even higher standard. This means we are even more in need of His forgiveness, and the help of the Holy Spirit. The good news of this teaching comes with the understanding:

1. God created the avenue for procreation. It was HE who made it instinctual and enjoyable. It was God who created the institution of marriage.
2. Jesus came to validate and fulfill the teachings, as well as to offer forgiveness, mercy and grace when we fall short.
3. Finally, it was Jesus who provided His Holy Spirit to guide us in what is appropriate and to help us in our weakness. The beauty of which must not be overlooked.

NOTES: If you'd like more information, please read the following articles: https://theologicalstudies.org.uk/pdf/smorality_nelson.pdf, www.AmericanCatholic.org June 2003, www.smartmarriage.com, Barna Research Group 1999 —Dec 21, quoted in www.religioustolerance.org, www.childtrendsdatabank.org, www.agi-usa.org, David Hammer, Associated Press, in www.mlive.com, July 27, 2005., The Kinsey Report, *Sexual Behavior of the Human Male*, is of limited accuracy and usefulness, because he was working with a male prison population, i.e., men without access to female partners, and he included in his estimated 10 percent of the population anyone who had ever had even a *single* homosexual encounter., *The Social Organization of Sexuality: Sexual Practices in the United States*, quoting in Jeffrey

Satinover, M.D., *Homosexuality and the Politics of Truth.* Grand Rapids: Baker Books, 1996, pp 51, 55., Christopher Seitz, "Sexuality and Scripture's Plain Sense: The Christian Community and the Law of God," in David L. Balch, editor, *Homosexuality, Science, and The 'Plain Sense' of Scripture.* Grand Rapids: Eerdmans Publishing, 200, p. 179.

The group discussion guide for this topic is in Appendix A on page 405.

CHAPTER 48

IDOLS

As the living images of God, we are to represent Christ everywhere and to everyone.

Do you have any idols in your life? The greatest blessing to any group of believers is the person willing to ask the most basic of questions. A short time ago, a person asked, "If there is a prohibition against idols, why isn't the cross considered one?

Let's break this question into a few others and try to answer it thoughtfully.

First, What's an idol?

Merriam Webster says, "An idol is defined an image or representation of a god used as an object of worship. It can come in many tangible forms."

In her book *Finding Truth*, Nancy Pearcy said this: "An idol is anything we want more than God, anything we rely on more that God, anything we look to for greater fulfillment than God. Idolatry is thus the hidden sin driving all other sins."

Idols are usually a focus of worship or a tool used to direct veneration or worship to what it represents. In the Bible, the Old

Testament speaks of idols that Israel sometimes worshipped in hopes of having good crops, wealth, blessings upon children or defense. In modern times, many people worship idols of money, possessions or reputation. Some people venerate historic figures that are important to them. These may include religious figures in history, ancient ancestors, philosophers, or even political or national leaders. Essentially, an idol is anything real or imagined that takes a person's focus off of the one true God and gives dedication, veneration or worship to something or someone other than the one true God.

Idols are bad because no idol represents a true deity or true reality. Idols take our attention away from the reality of Jesus and put it squarely on something that is evil or that does not exist. In Isaiah 45:7 God declares that He is: "the One forming light and creating darkness, causing well-being and creating calamity; I am the LORD who does all these". Idols pull us away from reality and from the God who created all reality. We might call idol worship, "spiritual adultery." Just as a person is jealous for his or her spouse if they are with another person, so too, God is jealous that our expressions of spiritual worship should be reserved only for him and not for the false idols of other religious systems. It may seem counter-intuitive, but a physical representation of something takes the focus off of the actual thing it represents.

Second, yes there a prohibition against idols and idol worship in the Bible. In the original Hebrew language when two clauses are paired together as in the commandment, "Thou shalt not make ... Thou shalt not bow down ... ," it does not mean two ideas but one. In most other languages the meaning would be conveyed, "Thou shalt not make ... in order to bow down to." A single idea which expresses the root is the problem. John Calvin, the theologian, once commented: "There is no necessity to refute what some have foolishly imagined, that sculpture and painting of every kind are condemned here." He said this because the culture of his day was trying to demonize artistic expression as idol making and therefore worship.

Back in the day, the temple (and the tabernacle) had objects inside them — none of which were to be worshiped. These items included the altar of incense, the ark of the covenant, the golden lampstand, etc. Each of these had a noble purpose, but none of them were worshiped.

I think we can admit that it would seem the Cross is in fact being used as an idol in some places. I think of the woman who said she could never go to one of the largest megachurches in the country because they don't have a Cross on stage. She declared they must not really be a true Christian. Only God can judge if that was an idol worshipper statement. The Cross is simply a reminder. We never pray to a Cross or have even cared whether one was displayed while worshiping. It is merely a symbol, much like the ichthus on the back of a person's car or the "coexist" bumper sticker.

Now, there's a controversy in Christendom over the use of other symbols. The largest of which is Protestant/Catholic dispute over the crucifix (with the image of Jesus on the cross) versus just a cross. Many Protestants view this very specifically as an image of God, since Jesus is the eternal, pre-existent Son of God. As a result, many Protestants will never use the crucifix in any decorations at all for the very specific reason that it has in it the image of God. Sacramentalists stand in the middle of the road claiming the object ought to be treated with reverence out of respect for what it symbolizes.

So, to be clear, symbolism is *not forbidden* in Scripture, and there is a precedent for having symbolic things in a place of worship (lampstands represent Light of the world, Showbread (loaves on the altar) that represents Bread of Life, the other old temple items pointing to Jesus as the Son of God). However, we must remember we serve a God who is jealous (Exodus 20:5; 2 Cor. 11:2).

God's jealousy is not like our self-centered love. His heart expresses His protective zeal for those who are His by creation and salvation. He made us and rescued us to know and enjoy Him forever. How could we ask for anything more than a God who is so zealous — and jealous — for our happiness? How should we best represent God in the world? What is the true image of God?

When God commanded Israel not to make images, He did so because God had already created images that were to represent Him. Where can we find such images? Go look in a mirror.

You and I are God's image on earth. When God created man, He said something about man that was very revealing. Listen carefully to these words from the book of Genesis:

> Let Us make man in Our image, according to Our likeness; and let them rule over the fish of the sea and over the birds of the sky and over the cattle and over all the earth, and over every creeping thing that creeps on the earth. God created man in His own image, in the image of God He created him; male and female He created them. Genesis 1:26-27 (NIV).

We don't need false idols or images. God is saying that we are created to be his image on earth. This does not mean that we are to be worshipped. Man is not the one true God. But it does mean that we are to represent him in our character. We are designed to think what God thinks, feel what God feels, and do what God does. We are to be like him. The Apostle Paul put it in this way: "We are ambassadors for Christ" (2 Cor. 5:20 NIV). An ambassador represents something or someone greater. He or she is to reflect all that is best and the principles He represent. We, as the living images of God are to represent Christ in everywhere. We are to point other people to Jesus Christ.

There is a big difference between an idol and an image in the biblical sense. However, as Bob Dylan once famously sang, *"You gonna serve somebody."*

The group discussion guide for this topic is in Appendix A on page 408.

RENEW

CHAPTER 49

CULTS

*A cult is a group that teaches doctrines, that, if believed,
will cause a person to remain unsaved.*

What is a cult? A cult is more narrowly defined, and the word refers to an unorthodox sect whose members distort the original doctrines of the religion. The word cult has three definitions:

1. It's simply be a group that loves something. When people refer to an "Elvis cult" or "The O.C. cult," they mean really devoted fans.
2. It's a religion whose beliefs differ from the majority around them. In the Roman Empire, Christians were sometimes considered a cult because they worshiped Jesus rather than the Roman gods.
3. It's a religious group that is:
    a. Exclusive. They may say, "We're the only ones with the truth; everyone else is wrong; and if you leave our group your salvation is in danger."

    b. Secretive. Certain teachings are not available to outsiders or they're presented only to certain members, sometimes after taking vows of confidentiality.
    c. Authoritarian. A human leader expects total loyalty and unquestioned obedience.

Experts who watch for dangerous or harmful religious groups now use the term new religious movements.

Why would someone join a cult?

One of the strongest attractions of the cults — authoritarian leadership — is also one of the clearest evidences of error. People are attracted to cults because they find authoritarian leadership, a leadership which they desire, but which is unbiblical. The difficulty is that all too often, truly evangelical churches and causes are led in the same dictatorial fashion as cults. In an article entitled "The Power Abusers," Ronald Enroth wrote:

> The popularity of evangelical gurus, new-age cults, and super pastors says a number of things about our society as well as rank-and-file evangelicalism. First, there are many people in our rapidly changing and often confusing world who have real dependency needs. They are attracted to authoritarian movements, Christian or otherwise, because these movements offer black and white, clear-cut answers (or systematized approaches) to life's problems. Moreover, the leaders of such organizations convey a sense of solidity, a feeling of being on top of problems, of being in control of the situation. In a word, these groups offer security. For people who have lacked

positive structure in their lives, who have difficulty making decisions or resolving conflicts or who are just plain uncertain about the future, these movements/churches/programs are a haven.

Bob Deffenbaugh wrote a great set of articles on cults for bible.org. In it, he clarifies that biblical leadership is as different from cultic leadership as authoritarian leadership is from that which is authoritative. The ministry of our Lord and of His apostles was authoritative, but not authoritarian.

> When He taught, the result was awe. Take, for example, Jesus' teaching entitled "the Sermon on the Mount." He was teaching them as one having authority, and not as scribes (Matt. 7:28-29; Luke 4:32). He didn't have to force a viewpoint or coerce his followers. He never demands anything from them.
>
> Jesus found His authority in the Scriptures and in the fact that He was obedient to the will of His Father, while the scribes maintained their authority as the interpreters of the Scriptures. Jesus had authority because He was in submission to authority. He was in submission to the will of the Father. He neither did nor taught anything contrary to the will of His Father (cf. John 8:29, 38, 42, 54). He was also subject to the law (cf. Matt. 17:24-27; Gal. 4:4). He acknowledged the authority of the government, even to carry out execution (John 19:8-11). Jesus even spoke of the scribes and Pharisees as having certain authority (Matt. 23:1-3).

The issue of authority versus authoritarianism was one that our Lord spoke often about with His disciples. Their authority as His apostles was to be evident in a different kind of leadership:

> You know that those who are recognized as rulers of the Gentiles lord it over them; and their great men exercise authority over them. But it is not so among you, but whoever wishes to become great among you shall be your servant; and whoever wishes to be first among you shall be slave of all. Mark 10:42-44 (NIV)

The kind of leadership our Lord summoned was such that no man would take upon himself the authority, the honor, or the obedience which was due Him: "But do not be called Rabbi; for One is your Teacher, and you are all brothers. And do not call anyone on earth your father; for One is your Father, He who is in heaven. And do not be called leaders; for One is your Leader, that is, Christ" (Matt. 23:8-10).

How do we recognize a cult?

As Christians, the definition of a cult is, specifically, "A religious group that denies one or more of the fundamentals of biblical truth." A cult is a group that teaches doctrines that, if believed, will cause a person to remain unsaved. A cult claims to be part of a religion, yet it denies essential truth of the religion.

The two most common teachings of Christian cults are that 1) Jesus was not God and 2) that salvation is not by faith alone. A denial of the deity of Christ results in the view that Jesus' death was insufficient to pay for our sins. A denial of salvation by faith alone results in the teaching that salvation is achieved by our own works. The apostles dealt with cults in the early years of the church. For example, John addresses the teaching of Gnosticism in 1 John 4:1-3. John's litmus test for godly doctrine was: "Jesus Christ has come in the flesh" (Verse 2) — a direct contradiction of the Gnostic heresy (2 John 1:7).

Be wise, ask questions and look for clarifications on items that seem unbiblical. Remember, cults are deceptive, manipulative through fear and overly controlling. When analyzing their beliefs and tactics, assess the following:

1. The Teaching: Even if a leader acknowledges Christ as Savior, they will say that you need something else before you can get into heaven. Cults often teach that salvation comes through Christ, plus their own little unique way. Some may make Jesus co-equal with their religious teachers or with certain great men of history. The quickest way to recognize a cult is by its treatment of Jesus.

2. The Conformity: Cults frequently attempt to instill fear into their followers. The followers are taught constantly that salvation comes only through the cult. "If you leave us, you will lose your salvation," they say.

3. The Leadership: They exalt the leader of the cult. Cults often center around a man or woman who is trying to gain power, money or influence from manipulating people.

4. The Aim of Discipleship: A final mark of a cult is the unwillingness of the leaders to let the people grow up. A true shepherd will do everything he can to

bring Christian people to maturity as quickly as he can. He will not seek to avoid necessary teaching, nor will he try to keep people from maturity. Many cults perpetuate spiritual dependence so that their followers lose the ability to make independent, rational decisions.

The two most well-known examples of cults today are Jehovah's Witnesses and Mormons. Both groups claim to be Christian, yet both deny the deity of Christ and salvation by faith alone. Jehovah's Witnesses and Mormons believe many things that are in agreement with or similar to what the Bible teaches. However, the fact that they deny the deity of Christ and preach a salvation by works qualifies them as cults. Many Jehovah's Witnesses, Mormons and members of other cults are moral people who genuinely believe they hold the truth. As Christians, our hope and prayer must be that many people involved in cults will see through the lies and will be drawn to the truth of salvation through faith in Jesus Christ alone.[140]

The group discussion guide for this topic is in Appendix A on page 409.

---

140 https://www.gotquestions.org/cult-definition.html; http://www1.cbn.com/questions/church-or-cult; http://www.christianitytoday.com/iyf/advice/faithqa/what-is-cult.html

CHAPTER 50

KINDNESS

Kindness and entering into a relationship with Jesus both begin with a relatively small change in our belief system that eventually will change everything.

What does it mean to love someone? A group of children were once asked a similar question, "What does 'love' mean?" Here are some sample answers:

Rebekah, 8, said, "When my grandmother got arthritis, she couldn't bend over and paint her toenails anymore. So, my grandfather does it for her all the time — even when his hands got arthritis, too. That's love."

Billy, 4, said, "When someone loves you, the way they say your name is different. You just know that your name is safe in their mouth."

Bobby, 7, says, "Love is what's in the room at Christmas, if you stop opening presents and listen."

Tommy, 6, says, "Love is like a little old woman and a little old man who are still friends even after they know each other so well."

Cindy, 8, says, "During my piano recital, I was on a stage, and I was scared. I looked at all the people watching me, and I saw my daddy waving and smiling. He was the only one doing that. And I wasn't scared anymore."[141]

The most interesting word in the English language might be the word love. People have tried to define it for years. Poets write about. Singers sing about it. Painters paint it. Even the Bible has four different Greek words we translate using the English word, love. There is Agape (spiritual or unconditional), Eros (physical love), Philia (mental love or friendship) and Storge (affectionate love or parental love). When we say we love somebody or something, what do we really mean by it? Does loving a burrito from Chipotle mean the same as loving God or loving others? The answer is no. The former is about a strong preference, whereas love of God and others is about a reciprocal commitment.

In 2009 ESPN aired a story about Dartanyon Crockett and Leroy Sutton, two high school students in inner city Cleveland. Crockett and Sutton were teammates on Lincoln West High School's wrestling team. Crockett, who is legally blind, was often filmed carrying Sutton, a double leg amputee, on his back. The show was produced by Lisa Fenn, an ESPN veteran who had done stories about famous athletes like Michael Jordan and Derek Jeter. But when she finished the piece about Crockett and Sutton she couldn't leave their lives. Fenn took it upon herself to help "the one with no legs, being carried by the one who could not see" get to college. She raised donations from around the world,

---

141 Mark Buchanan, in the sermon "The Greatest of These," PreachingToday.com

coordinated college visits and ensured that the boys were well fed every day. Thanks to her efforts, Crockett became a bronze medalist in judo at the Paralympic Games in London; Sutton will become the first member of his family to graduate from college. After the media hoopla died down, Leroy Sutton quietly asked her, "Why did you stay?" She said, "I love you." Sutton pressed, "That's what I thought you'd say. But ... why ... why did you stick around and do everything you did?" Lisa Fenn wrote: "I grew up on the other side of Cleveland. The white side .... My parents scrounged up the money for private school to protect me from the public schools and 'those people' .... But Dartanyon and Leroy eased me in graciously .... They opened up about their struggles — Dartanyon with great eagerness, as I think he had waited his entire life for someone to want to know him, to truly see him. Leroy's revelations emerged more reluctantly. He had been emotionally abandoned too many times before .... But both began to believe that, perhaps, I genuinely cared. I stayed because I would not be next on the list of people who walked out and over their trust .... I stayed because we get only one life, and we don't truly live it until we give it away. I stayed because we can change the world only when we enter into another's world. I stayed because I love you."[142]

Staying to love requires real honesty with oneself. Why am I in this relationship? Is this about what I get or what I give?

Jesus had a counseling moment around this concept of self-honesty and true unconditional love when I young man came to him looking for direction. The scriptures report:

---

142   Adapted from Matt Patrick, "The One With No Legs, The One Who Could Not See, and The One Who Stayed," Mbird blog (7-10-13)

*¹⁸ A certain ruler asked him, "Good teacher, what must I do to inherit eternal life?"¹⁹ "Why do you call me good?" Jesus answered. "No one is good—except God alone. ²⁰ You know the commandments: 'You shall not commit adultery, you shall not murder, you shall not steal, you shall not give false testimony, honor your father and mother.'" ²¹ "All these I have kept since I was a boy," he said. ²² When Jesus heard this, he said to him, "You still lack one thing. Sell everything you have and give to the poor, and you will have treasure in heaven. Then come, follow me." ²³ When he heard this, he became very sad, because he was very wealthy. ²⁴ Jesus looked at him and said, "How hard it is for the rich to enter the Kingdom of God!²⁵ Indeed, it is easier for a camel to go through the eye of a needle than for someone who is rich to enter the Kingdom of God." ²⁶ Those who heard this asked, "Who then can be saved?" ²⁷ Jesus replied, "What is impossible with man is possible with God." ²⁸ Peter said to him, "We have left all we had to follow you!" ²⁹ "Truly I tell you," Jesus said to them, "no one who has left home or wife or brothers or sisters or parents or children for the sake of the Kingdom of God ³⁰ will fail to receive many times as much in this age, and in the age to come eternal life."
Luke 18:18-29 (NIV)*

The story itself is also told in Matthew's gospel and is probably the only place where someone came to Jesus and left disappointed. He came to the right person, asked the right question, received the right answer and made the wrong decision. Why? Because he was not honest with himself.[143] He knew what it meant to talk the talk but not walk the walk.

The scripture starts out with the young ruler using the word "good" when speaking to Jesus. Good was a word reserved for God alone. Jesus asked him why he called him good because he wanted to see if he would profess his belief in Jesus as God. And yet, the young man answered the question by bragging on his ability to follow the law, not on knowing God. Jesus then challenged him to let go of his covetousness (Exodus 20:17) — a love of money — which he could not do. As the disciples watched the man walk away, they started to panic. Because they believed material wealth was sign of God's blessing. Now what? Is wealth bad? No. However, coming to know Jesus begins a relatively small change in our belief system that eventually will change everything. It's called the butterfly effect.

Have you ever heard of the butterfly effect?

On an ordinary winter day in 1961, an MIT meteorologist named Edward Lorenz ran some routine experiments and found some unusual results. Lorenz discovered that seemingly tiny and insignificant changes in his data could produce huge differences in the final result. At first, Lorenz and other scientists in the field of chaos theory called this: "the sensitive dependence on initial data." Fortunately, later on Lorenz used a simpler term — the butterfly effect. In 1972, Lorenz presented a scientific paper entitled "Predictability: Does the Flap of a Butterfly's Wings in Brazil Set off a Tornado in Texas?" According to Lorenz's theory, the butterfly's wing-flapping doesn't cause a tornado, but it can start a chain

---

143   *New Testament Commentary*, Warren Wiersbe, Moody Publishing, Chicago, 2010, p248

reaction leading to giant changes in world-wide weather patterns. In other words, even tiny, insignificant movements or actions can produce huge changes that affect millions of people.

The Bible often describes a similar "butterfly effect" for the spiritual life. When we begin to realize our role in this life, our purpose is to partner with God for the healing of the world in Jesus' name and to proclaim His reign, to become missional; our actions begin to change the world.

According to Jesus, the spiritual butterfly effect occurs when we do small things—making a meal, visiting the sick, befriending the lonely, opening our home to a guest, praying with a friend — for "insignificant" people, which makes a huge difference in God's eyes. But, according to Jesus, there's also a reverse butterfly effect: Consistently failing to display small acts of kindness (i.e. living an unkind lifestyle) has a profound loss of opportunity in the spiritual realm.[144]

A blessing is now given by God, not for one's own benefit, but for the blessing of others so they will come back to Him. So, what will you do with your blessings from God this week? How will you show genuine love to those around you?

The group discussion guide for this topic is in Appendix A on page 411.

---

144 Kenneth Chang, "Edward N. Lorenz, a Meteorologist and a Father of Chaos Theory, dies at 90," NewYorkTimes.com (4-17-08)

CHAPTER 51

VIOLENCE

While Jesus forbids the use of the sword as a means to advance the Kingdom of God, the New Testament does not teach an absolute or principled pacifism.

Violence — we are a culture awash in it. Violence is on our TVs and devices, whether in the form of entertainment or the nightly news. We can't go a day without hearing some new statistic about the death rates in Chicago or about another ISIS moment in the Middle East. For many of us, we have had enough. Our hearts just can't take it anymore. Where is God? How can religion even help? Or maybe, religion is at fault for all the violence. Why doesn't God do something?

The truth is, He did. It just happened to be in a way no one expected. It happened in a moment similar to one that lives in business folklore.

Standard Oil was once one of the biggest companies in the world, led by the famous John D. Rockefeller. On one occasion, a company executive made a bad decision. It cost the firm $2 million. This was the late 1800s and $2 million was a huge sum.

Edward Bedford, a partner in the company, had an appointment to see Rockefeller. When he entered Rockefeller's office, he saw his boss bent over a piece of paper, busily scribbling notes. When Rockefeller finally looked up he said to Bedford, "I suppose you've heard about our loss? I've been thinking it over and before I ask the man in to discuss the matter, I've been making some notes." Bedford looked across the table and saw the page Rockefeller had been scribbling on. Across the top of the page was the heading, "Points in favor of Mr. _____." Below the heading was a long list of the man's good qualities, including notes on three occasions where he had made decisions that had earned the company many times more than his error had lost.

Bedford later said, "I never forgot that lesson. In later years, whenever I was tempted to rip into anyone, I forced myself first to sit down and thoughtfully compile as long a list of good points as I possibly could. Invariably, by the time I finished my inventory, I would see the matter in its true perspective and keep my temper under control. There is no telling how many times this habit has prevented me from committing one of the costliest mistakes any executive can make — losing his temper."[145]

God took stock of the world we see in the Old Testament. He saw our ability to make a mess of it all. He took our animal nature struggling against our human nature at the expense of our Spiritual nature and He responded. God's response to violence is found in the life, death, resurrection and the teachings of His Son. The truly innocent suffered for the guilty. This is where we see God. This is His answer. But how do we even begin to make sense of this?

---

145   Reported in Bits & Pieces, September 15, 1994

Most religious pacifists, and even some Christian Pharisees, ground their convictions in a purported nonviolent "love ethic" of Jesus that is understood to be the teaching of Matthew 5:38-42. They will claim it is a directive of Jesus to always turn the other cheek when wronged. But is that true? Should Christians always respond non-violently?

Matthew 5:38-42 referenced is just one of six case illustrations of Jesus' teaching on the law (Matt. 5:17). With the other five, Jesus affirms and confirms the ethical requirements of Old Testament. Each affirmation uses a similar formula where Jesus says: "You have heard that it was said ... But I tell you ... "

I understand there will be some Bible scholars who don't see it as I do. However, scripture is meant to be taken in context and interpreted considering other thoughts given in the living word. Jesus cannot contradict Himself or the Father. This is one of those areas.

In the Sermon on the Mount, Jesus is not setting aside the idea of restitution, nor the "law of the tooth" (the lex talionis as a standard of public justice). Rather, Jesus is challenging His listeners to consider their attitudes so that they respond properly to personal injustice or insult. Insult that is personal versus public assault is at issue in the passage. And it's clarified thereafter in the words, "If someone wants to . . . take your tunic, let him have your cloak as well" (Matthew 5:40). Handling insults and matters of clothing (a basic human need) are not in the realm of public policy.

In truth, all four illustrations of non-retaliation — turning the other cheek, offering the shirt off your back, carrying someone's baggage an extra mile and lending to the one asking — correspond to the private injury. These are issues of personal inconvenience or abuse, not matters of public policy; they're insulting, yes, but they don't rise to that of assault.

In truth, all of the Sermon on the Mount (Matthew 5-7) is not a statement on the role of government but rather, it concerns issues of personal discipleship. It's more most closely aligned with scripture from Romans 12:17-21, than Romans 13:1-7:

> *Do not repay anyone evil for evil. Be careful to do what is right in the eyes of everyone. If it is possible, as far as it depends on you, live at peace with everyone. Do not take revenge, my dear friends, but leave room for God's wrath, for it is written: "It is mine to avenge; I will repay," says the Lord. On the contrary: "If your enemy is hungry, feed him; if he is thirsty, give him something to drink. In doing this, you will heap burning coals on his head." Do not be overcome by evil but overcome evil with good.*

In "Why I Am Not a Pacifist," C. S. Lewis considers Jesus' injunction regarding "turning the other cheek," which he believes cannot be intended to rule out protecting others. "Does anyone suppose," he asks, "that our Lord's hearers understood him to mean that if a homicidal maniac, attempting to murder a third party, tried to knock me out of the way, I must stand aside and let him get his victim?"[146]

If Jesus is calling for absolute nonviolence based on Matthew 5:38-40, then we would be under obligation to turn the cheek of a third party. Lewis prefers to accept the plain reading of this text.

"You have heard that it was said, 'Eye for eye, and tooth for tooth. 'But I tell you, do not resist an evil person. If anyone slaps

---

146 https://www.crossway.org/articles/why-c-s-lewis-wasnt-a-pacifist/

you on the right cheek, turn to them the other cheek also. And if anyone wants to sue you and take your shirt, hand over your coat as well" (Matt. 5:38-42).

In the end, the Christian is called to resist evil when and where it is possible, as saint's past and present always have understood. And the apostle Paul states in no uncertain terms that the magistrate exists precisely for this divinely instituted function:

For rulers hold no terror for those who do right, but for those who do wrong. Do you want to be free from fear of the one in authority? Then do what is right and you will be commended. 4 For the one in authority is God's servant for your good. But if you do wrong, be afraid, for rulers do not bear the sword for no reason. They are God's servants, agents of wrath to bring punishment on the wrongdoer. (Romans 13:3-4)

Even when Jesus forbids the sword to advance the Kingdom of God, the New Testament does not teach an absolute or principled pacifism. Nor does it forbid the Christian from "bearing the sword" — or serving as a magistrate, for that matter — in the service of society and the greater good of the community.[147]

Animal nature is raw and violent. Spiritual nature is thoughtful and kind. Human nature is the struggle between the two. Through Jesus' example we understand the perfect response — love in all its forms.

The group discussion guide for this topic is in Appendix A on page 412.

---

147   https://www.crossway.org/articles/what-did-jesus-teach-about-violence-and-turning-the-other-cheek/

RENEW

CHAPTER 52

COMPLACENCY

Complacency is more harmful to one's spirituality than any other spiritual sickness because we are lulled into believing everything is as it should be.

I've been having a lot of conversations lately and asking what the greatest challenge in our community is. The greatest response after the basics of food and shelter has been the recognition of a need for a spiritual revival. A renewing of the connection with God and the principles that foster it.

Complacency is defined as: A feeling of smug or uncritical satisfaction with oneself or one's achievements. Synonyms: smugness, self-satisfaction, self-congratulation, self-regard.

The consistent word in the synonyms is self. Complacency has been around since the moment Adam and Eve and they were so complacent with living in the garden of Eden, they made the decision they wanted the same knowledge of the creator. Notice I didn't say wisdom. Knowledge and wisdom are different. The latter is the intelligent use of the former.

In our humanness, we struggle to be self-reliant, often stepping over a very dangerous line. A line detailed by one of Jesus' closest companions, John, in the book Revelation. It comes as John reveals God's displeasure with the seven churches. The number seven represents completeness. In these descriptions of church communities, we see all the largest manifestations of "self" that permeate the church. The two I'd like to highlight are from the third chapter of Revelation. They are the churches of Sardis and Laodicea.

> The Lord said to Sardis:
> [2] Wake up! Strengthen what remains and is about to die, for I have found your deeds unfinished in the sight of my God.
> [3] Remember, therefore, what you have received and heard; hold it fast, and repent. But if you do not wake up, I will come like a thief, and you will not know at what time I will come to you. (NIV)

> The Lord said to Laodicea:
> [15] I know your deeds, that you are neither cold nor hot. I wish you were either one or the other! [16] So, because you are lukewarm—neither hot nor cold—I am about to spit you out of my mouth. [17] You say, 'I am rich; I have acquired wealth and do not need a thing.' But you do not realize that you are wretched, pitiful, poor, blind and naked. [18] I counsel you to buy from me gold refined in the fire, so you can become rich; and white clothes to wear, so you can cover your shameful nakedness; and salve to put on your eyes, so you can see. (NIV)

The first letter to Sardis highlights a complacency that comes when the work is sort of done and everyone believes it's good enough even though there is more to do. In Laodicea, complacency comes when we truthfully have more than enough to make life comfortable. Both forms permit a false sense of security and make a life of living for the Lord more risk averse.

Life is constantly changing. Any point in which we begin to stand still, we have made a decision to give credence to the status quo. I'll always remember a coffee with an articulate and talented leader in the ministry who was in the valley. She was sharing her pain of doing ministry and failing to sense God in her ministry as before. Her whole ministry up to this point had been connected to her emotional experiences with God. He was silent, and she was wondering if it was a time to stop. I knew this pain and often talked about it as a valley. Every ministry leader does. Mother Teresa felt it. Popes have experienced it. I asked her what she was doing to improve her ministry and rejuvenate her passion. Her facial response to my questions was so telling I asked, "Are you leading your ministry on how you feel, or what God is doing through you for the advance of His Kingdom?" Complacency often masks itself in the life of a believer and leader. It justifies itself with our feelings, excuses and self-knowledge.

The book of Proverbs provides the following wisdom:

For the waywardness of the simple will kill them, and the complacency of fools will destroy them (Prov. 1:32 NIV).

There are a few signs to watch for that let you know if you have a spiritual life moving towards complacency:

1. *Far Too Easily Satisfied.* The words "good enough" and "I'll be fine without 'x'" are a constant.
2. *Quick to Make Excuses* about why it's okay to not be growing spiritually. Challenges can become obstacles, obstacles allowed to become barriers, and barriers allowed to become excuses. It becomes easy to hide out behind such excuses and accept the status quo.
3. A. The greatest of which for this age is: "I'm so busy or there's never enough time." There's the facade of activity and busyness, but it is seldom meaningful Kingdom or spiritually challenging activity.
4. *No Longer Teachable.* In truth, you have become obstinate and defiant regarding any suggestions. Even the best of ideas to release the former passion are discarded for various reasons. All of which leave you as the expert. In a single word: pride. It's the place of failing to implement anything substantively new, and cling to the old ways.

Content with Early Success. Often, early success in any adventure can challenge individuals with the question, now what? Is this all there is? In a sense, the failure to continue to dream circumvents the motivation to continue moving forward.

They say the average pastor in America lasts 7-8 years before they move on. I would say volunteer ministry leaders have an even shorter span of service. Why? Discipleship takes time and rarely do admit we have a personal interest in the success of our ministry actions. However, when success is slow in coming, we allow ourselves to begin to drift and slip away.

How do we snap out of these spiritual low points?

If you are currently in this valley, the good news is there is help to renew your zeal for the Lord. The scriptures point to it. The recovery programs demand it. The traditions offer the following answer:

1. The first step is to admit there is a problem.
2. Confess it to a trusted confidant.
3. Ask for God's help to begin walking in a new direction.
4. Finally, find an accountability partner and begin discovering a life worth living again.

Remember, Complacency is more harmful to our spirituality than any other form of spiritual sickness because we are lulled into believing everything is as it should be. However, God is never done creating. The heavens show us that. His loving word shows us that. He loves us too much to ever leave us where we are. He longs to help us become the person He created us to be. He wants to renew you and those around you.

The group discussion guide for this topic is in Appendix A on page 413.

RENEW

APPENDIX A

DISCUSSION GUIDE QUESTIONS

The purpose of these discussion guide questions is to seek in the life of Christ principles to guide our lives. The principles revealed over the next few weeks are from His life, His culture, His country and His time. He shared freely and loved unconditionally. We live in another age, and the methods and problems of our life are different; but the same principles which guided Him are to guide us. We will work to open God's word and apply it to our lives. The principle of worship, humility and service should rule us now as it ruled Him then.

The true way to answer the question, "What would Jesus do?" is to study the principles of Jesus' life and teaching. And then, intelligently strive to do whatever He did. There is no greater opportunity to grow and become more like Christ than to undertake a bible study such as this. After all, comparing the shifting opinions of men to the solid judgements of Jesus leads us to pursue the true meaning of our lives where hopeful ideals are matched with an equal set of ideals.

1. RENEW: MISSIO DEI
- What was the coolest building you have ever been in or seen and why?
- Define the word "church" to someone who has never been.
- What are the excuses you have used to justify not attending a house of worship? What is the best you have ever heard or used?
- What's the mission of the church?
- We will read Matt. 28:18-20 aloud and discuss at the tables.
- What did you hear that was unique? Does it change or modify your table's understanding of the mission?
- Think of your closest friend(s). Who are they? Where do you meet at? How often do you talk?
- How do you define the word "love"?
- We will read 1 John 3:17-5:5 aloud and discuss at the tables. What did you hear that was unique? How would you apply it to your life?
- How would your life look differently if you lived "love" as a lifestyle?
- Do all relationships require trust formed through personal contact? If not, what helps you form better relationships?
- What's an event or situation in your life in which your friends made the largest positive impact? Please focus on what they did or said that helped.

Assertion: The mission of God is to make disciples by teaching them to obey all the commands.

2. RENEW: UNCONDITIONAL LOVE

- What is the best book you have ever read?
- As heard in the author's story, have you ever wandered away from God?
- Have you ever memorized a poem or a song or story?
    - Why did you memorize it?
    - Could you repeat it now if asked?
    - How long did it take to memorize it?
    - What was the process?
- Review and discuss the following scripture from Mark:
    - [28] One of the teachers of the law came and heard them debating. Noticing that Jesus had given them a good answer, he asked him, "Of all the commandments, which is the most important?" [29] "The most important one," answered Jesus, "is this: 'Hear, O Israel: The Lord our God, the Lord is one. [30] Love the Lord your God with all your heart and with all your soul and with all your mind and with all your strength.' [31] The second is this: 'Love your neighbor as yourself.' There is no commandment greater than these." [32] "Well said, teacher," the man replied. "You are right in saying that God is one and there is no other but him. [33] To love him with all your heart, with all your understanding and with all your strength, and to love your neighbor as yourself is more important than all burnt offerings and sacrifices." [34] When Jesus saw that he had answered wisely, he said to him, "You are not far from the Kingdom of God." And from then on no one dared ask him any more questions.

- The greatest commandment from the leader of the Christian faith comes out of the Old Testament writings from the book of Deuteronomy. Any good Jew would know these words. The words had meaning because they came from God through Moses. They were called the Shema. Shema ("hear") is the Hebrew word that begins the most important prayer in Judaism. Read Deuteronomy 6:4 and discuss.
- Read 2 Tim 3:16-17 and discus. Why did Paul make this statement to Timothy and all of us?
- What part of this statement from Greg Ogden's book *Discipleship Essentials* do you find refreshing or troubling: "Because the Scriptures of the Old and New testament are the uniquely inspired revelation of God and the standard of truth in all matters of faith and practice, a portion of each day should be set aside to read study and meditate on God's word. The Bible is to the spirit what food is to the body."[148]
- Read Psalm 119:1-16 and discuss the following questions:
    - What are the different words or phrases for the Law?
    - What is suggested to us regarding following the law?
    - The 11th verse provides one reason for memorizing Scripture; can you think of any others?

---

148 *Discipleship Essentials*, Greg Ogden, 2005

3. RENEW: FATHER
- How did Jesus perceive of His relationship with His Father?
- Let's look to the Scriptures: Matt. 11:25; 26:39, 42; Luke 23:34, 46 and John 11:41; 17:5.
  Hint: "Abba" is a key reference from these passages. There are no references of Jesus addressing God as Almighty God or Infinite or Eternal One.

<u>Jesus and the Father's Core Statement</u>
Jesus understood God in a Fatherly manner. He chose to live in this type of relationship fully knowing God's creative power, as well as His omnipotent dignity.
- Let's read John 17:11, 25.
- Did Jesus' words here claim anything other than reverence?
- Let's read John 6:38; 8:29.
- Do these words tell us anything more about Jesus' relationship with the Father?
- If Jesus understood the relationship with the Father to be intimate and reverent (or filled with awe), How does this affect the way you are currently connecting with God? How might you adjust?
- Let's read John 8:48-59 and Matt. 5:17-30 together.
- What do these passages tell us about Jesus' identification with God? Also, what other characteristics of Jesus' relationship do they reveal?
- How many times in John 5-8 does Jesus refer to himself as "sent?"
- How do you apply these teachings to your daily life? If you haven't, how might you in the future?

4. RENEW: PRAYER

- Have you ever prayed for something or someone only to have the prayer seemingly go unanswered? How did you reconcile your request with the reality of the situation?
- Are there conditions for our prayers being answered? In your opinion, what are they?

Jesus and Prayer Core Statement
Jesus maintained a sense of God being near, as well as a life of love and devotion to the Father through a life of prayer.

- Let's read Matthew 5:8. What seems to be a condition of a prayer request? Leader Note: Purity of heart is essential in prayer. However, it is not the only condition noted by Jesus.
- Let's read Matthew 5:23-24 - What is the condition being specified in this scripture? Leader Note: Restitution and reparation for wrongdoing.
- Let's read Matthew 6:12-15. What is the condition highlighted by Jesus? Leader Note: Forgiveness of the heart.
- Let's read Matthew 17:20. What is the condition highlighted here? Leader Note: Faith and trust are important.
- Let's read Matthew 18:19-20. What is the condition of the heart? Leader Note: Unity of desire with others.
- Let's read Luke 11:5-8. The condition? Leader Note: Honest longing.
- Read Luke 18:9-14. The condition? Leader Note: sincere humility.

- If Jesus understood the relationship with the Father to be intimate and reverent (or filled with awe) and we are told prayer is the way to stay connected, how is it with your soul today as you go before the Father? Are you pure in heart, cleaned your side of the street, forgiven others, trusting in Him, desiring the best for others and oneself, and are you seeking Jesus with all humility?
- Let's read Matt. 5:43-48; 9:37-38; 26:41; 21:22. Leader Note: Enemies, Laborers, Temptation, Right Desires?
- Have you been praying for these three items? What do these passages tell us about Jesus' thought process?
- Let's read Matt. 6:7-8; 7:5-6; Luke 18:1; Matt 26:41. After we have read each one, please come up with a single word that sums up the point. Leaders Note: Simple, secret, constant, vigilant are important aspects of our connection to the King of Kings.
- The promise of prayer is the assurance of three distinctive benefits. They are summarized in the following scriptures:
    - Matt. 7:9-11 — Assurance of the Father's love is greater than an earthly father
    - Matt. 18:19-20 and John 16:23-24 — Jesus Himself hears our prayers
    - Matt. 6:8 — Our Father knows our heart already, loves us and wants a relationship with us in all our activities in this life
- If we are to emulate Christ in our prayer life, we should review how, when and where He prayed. What were

the times you can recall reading Jesus that prayed?
- Let's review scripture these answers: Mark 1:35, 6:45-47; Luke 6:12; John 18:2; Luke 5:16, 6:12. Time and place are key in these. Matt. 14:23-33; Luke 6:12-13' 9:18-20; Matt. 14:23; Mark 1:32,35; Luke 3:22. Before, during and after big events in His life, He prayed.
- Do you pray about all your daily situations? Why or why not?
- Have you ever thought about why Jesus prayed? If ever there was a man who didn't need to pray, it was Jesus. What did He lack? What did He need to communicate to the Father?

5. RENEW: WILL OF GOD
- Have you ever wondered what God's will was for your life? How did you figure it out?
- What do you think God's will was for Jesus?
- Let's read John 6:35-40 (Key Verse 40): "For my Father's will is that everyone who looks to the Son and believes in him shall have eternal life and I will raise them up at the last day."

Jesus and the Will of God Core Statement
Jesus maintained a connection with the Father so He would remain devoted to doing God's will. The will of the father from the scripture is to help everyone believe in the son and enter eternal life.

APPENDIX A

- Let's read Matthew 6:7-14 (Key Verse 10). In Jesus teaching of how to pray, he shares with us what is most important to pray for. Leader Note: Jesus was making sure the disciples knew the main aim was to do the Father's will on earth.
- Do you have fear about doing the will of God on earth?
- Let's read Luke 12:7, 32. Leader Note: God tells us and plenty of prophets to "fear not." The evil one prays on our emotions to create doubt and uncertainty. However, God can and will free us from this when we trust in His love for us.
- Do you believe that when you do the will of God you will have peace?
- Let's read John 18:33-38; 19:9-12. The will of God lifts us from our own thinking.
- Do you believe when you are doing God's will that he supernaturally equips you with power to accomplish the task?
- Let's read Matt. 9:6-8, 28:18. Leader Note: When we say we are doing God's will then we must understand that we are in a partnership with Him to accomplish His goal. However, just having a supernatural dose of God's power is not the only sign you are in God's Will. The angel of darkness has power as well, so we must be careful.
- If you are wondering if you are doing the will of God, you can check yourself by asking:
  - Does this cause me to sin? 1 Thess. 4:3; Heb. 10:10

- Does it enhance our relationship or detract from it? Col 1:9; Phil 2:13
- Does the action align with my prayer life? 1 John 5:14
- Do my actions help another come to know Him? 1 John 2:17
- What is an area of your life where you would like to know God's will? Leader Conclusion: The overall arching will of God is for all his creation to know Him and live accordingly. We often want a more personal answer of how God wants us to use our lives. This is selfish and self-centered. God's will is for all to come to him — now and throughout eternity.

6. RENEW: HUMAN SOCIETY

- How many friends do you have who are not Christian?
- How many activities do you do with people not associated with the church?

The Holy men of the middle ages deemed the deepest knowledge of God incompatible with a free life among men. They withdrew, accordingly, from the movements of the world, and in cloister, cell and cave sought the Holy life. "The greatest saints," says Thomas a Kempis, "avoided the society of men when they could conveniently and did rather choose to live to God in secret." And he quotes the

APPENDIX A

saying of Seneca, "As often as I have been among men, I returned home less a man than I was before."[149]

While for many of us in the room, this is a true statement, is this the example of Jesus?
- How did Jesus interact with the society at large?

<u>Jesus and Society Core Statement</u>
Jesus maintained a connection with the Father, so He would know the highest and the best. As such, he moved freely among all men and seemed comfortable in all of creation's presence.
- Let's read John 2:1-11. Is it okay to go a party with people doing things you wouldn't approve of?
- Let's read Luke 15:8-10, 14:34-35; John 2:24-25. Did Jesus love all men in the same way His Father did? Do you think he would be called people watcher?
- Let's read Luke 5:29-30, 15:1-2; Matt. 11:19; Luke 7:34. What were the criticisms of Jesus?
- Let's read Luke 7:36-50. How did Jesus act with those he did not hold a high opinion?
- Leader Note: He never compromised his standards for their respect.

Leader Conclusion: The overall arching will of God is for all his creation to know Him and live accordingly. Our role as we emulate Him in the world is to live among the individuals he places in our lives to demonstrate His love!

---

149   Robert Speer

7. RENEW: DEFECTS OF CHARACTER
- Have you ever heard the devil made me do it? Do you believe the devil makes you sin? If not, where in the world does sin come from?
- If Jesus never sinned as written in 2 Cor. 5:21 and claimed by Jesus in John 8:46, is it possible for us to live like Christ in this world for a minute, an hour, a day, a week? Leader Note: We all have fallen ... defective. It's important to remember this as part of our make-up. As Paul says in Romans 3:23, "We all fall short of the glory of God ..." which in turn sets up our need for him.
- Let's read Luke 5:17-25. How did Jesus' view of this man differ from that of the Pharisees and the legal experts? Leader Note: The word translated to "forgive" in the gospels means literally "to send away' or in other areas "to let off."

<u>Jesus and Defect of Character/Sin Core Statement</u>
Sin is not merely a sickness or a disease (although it has those characteristics). It is God's gifts gone astray in their use. The New Testament word for it is "missing the mark."

- Let's try and list all the time Jesus loosens sin's hold on his followers in scripture. Leader Note: Obviously, sin is not something to be playing around with. We need to take a negative view of it if for no other reason to keep it from creeping in and then taking over our lives.
- Let's read Matt.. 4:1-11. How did Jesus deal with sin as it approached? Leader Note: Three of four of the gospels share this story (Mark 1:12-13, Luke 4:1-13).

- If you were going to divide the story up into three temptations, how would you categorize them? How are they different? Which type of sin was the temptation trying to elicit?
- What did Jesus say about sin? Read John 8:31-38. Leader Note: Jesus called sin slavery; he came to free us from it. Sin is repugnant because it stifles our liberties and our understanding of the world.
- Let's read John 5:24-30. When you read Jesus is the judge of our lives, our sins and our eternal destiny, does that change your perception of His role in your life? Leader Note: While Jesus is the judge, He is also our redeemer. He agrees to make right your affront to the father by paying your penalty in advance.
- Do you have any stories where someone helped you out of a situation you put yourself in?

Leader Conclusion: Sin is a want of perception. It is a want for completeness of life, a want for a change of environment, a want for a connection with something greater. Sin is a search for perfection in an imperfect world and body. Sin is the refusal of the offer of all He came to earth for. It is open rebellion and an affront to God that only Jesus can forgive when we are willing to confess and be accepting His forgiveness.

8. RENEW: TEMPTATION

- Have you ever thought about temptation? What aspects of this life tempt you most: food, money, sex, power, being right, control, reputation, comfort, security, etc.?
- Why do you think we are shy about talking about what tempts us? Does just speaking of temptation give it power over us? Leader Note: We all have fallen ... defective. It's important to remember this as part of our make-up. As Paul says in Romans 3:23, "We all fall short of the glory of God ..." Which, in turn, sets up our need for him. In the last chapter, it describes Jesus facing temptation in the desert. We will all face temptation.
- Do you believe Jesus was tempted in the same ways we are? Why or why not?
- Leader Note: The definition of temptation is: a desire to do something, especially something wrong or unwise.
- Let's compare the three temptations of Christ in the wilderness from last week with three temptations describe in 1 John 2:16.
- "For everything in the world — the lust of the flesh, the lust of the eyes and the pride of life — comes not from the Father but from the world."
- What were Christ's temptations as he worked out his mission? Let's classify these by reading the following together: Matt. 16:1; 19:3; 22:18, 35; John 8:6.

Jesus and Temptation Core Statement

Jesus never sought temptation, but it came. We should be aware that temptation is a part of this life and being connected to the Father insures our strength to preserve.

- We pray as parts of the Lord's prayer "lead *us not into temptation.*" Does God lead us into temptation? Why do you think Jesus taught us to pray this way or to be aware of temptation?
- Look back on your day or week; where or when did temptation come? Did you learn from the experience? Do you think you would have been better off if you had never succumbed to the experience? Leader Note: Robert Speer once wrote, "The might of innocence will always be greater than the might of experience of sin."
- Were the disciples tempted? When? What were the results? Luke 22:28. Leader Note: Peter? Thomas" Judas?
- How do we not yield to temptation? 1 Cor. 10:13; James 1:2,12; 2 Peter 2:9
- Leader Conclusion: We must always remember the claims of Hebrews 2:18-19, God can and will help those in temptation. Temptation is a part of the journey of a follower.

9. RENEW: POLITICS

- Has anybody ever heard the comment "religion and politics don't mix"? Where do you think this comes from? Leader Note: It's hard to say for sure. However, the largest collection of writings on this topic come about as part of Germany's rise to power during Adolph Hitler's reign. It was the idea that nationalism supported by religion creates a rationalization for extremism in the name of God.

- Why do you think people are timid in discussing these two topics together? Why in a society with freedom of speech, as well as freedom of religion, do we find the discussion so uncomfortable? Leader Note: In an article from 2005, Fritz Stern wrote about the mixing of politics and religion. In it, he says that a key lesson of Germany's history is that civic passivity and willed blindness were preconditions for the triumph of National Socialism.

- Do you believe Jesus had to overcome the same political uncomfortableness or are we in a different time? Leader Note: The most interesting part of Jesus' ministry is the constant juggling he had to do as it intersected the powers of His day. Jesus dealt with three powers in his ministry. The Pharisees were the religious government of the day. The majority were hoping for an independent state from the occupiers and the Herodians. The Herodians were the original dictator/leaders of the day. They ensured family succession and leadership for the nation. The third governmental power of the day was Rome itself.

APPENDIX A

Jesus had to toe a fine line between all three entities. There was seriously tension in the air. Today, we only have two parties and we still can't get along.
- The larger question is should we as Christians be involved with the process of our government or be passive knowing that God is in control and we are not citizens of this Kingdom? How did Jesus move in the society he was a part of? Can you think of any instances where Jesus acted in the political realm while he was present? Leader Note: Jesus never violated any ordinances of the Jewish state or Roman Empire. He was accused unjustly in both.
- Let's read about Jesus in his religious trial and his civil trial. - Mark 14:53-72 and Luke 23:1-25
- Leader Note: Jesus never violated any ordinances of the Jewish state or Roman Empire. He was accused unjustly in both.
- Let's read about the Pharisees and more trickery in Matt. 22:17-21 (Taxes to Caesar), John 6:15-21 (Christ the King?) and Jesus and the devil temptations (Matt. 4:8)
- What do the readings say about Jesus relations with the authorities and His intentions?
- Does being a Christ follower mean we are to avoid evil (turn the other cheek) or even allow it to exist?

RENEW: Politics Core Statement
The people of Jesus day didn't have the freedoms we have today. Life was solely from the top down. However, Jesus came to give

us His power and as such, we are accountable to set wrongs right and continue building the Kingdom he began.

- Let's read Matt. 19:17-21; Mark 10:43-45; Luke 10:25-37.
- The two greatest commandments are to Love God and Love others. With this as a guide, what do you believe your responsibility is as it relates to our governing bodies?

10 RENEW: CHURCH

- What is the first thing you think of when I say the word church? Leaders Note: The Bible only uses the word church three times. (Matt. 16:18, 18:17)
- What church did Jesus attend? Leaders Note: Jesus trained the new church within the old. His formal relations were to the Jewish church.
- What do you think Jesus thought of the church of his devout parents?
- Let's read Luke 2:41-51 - Leaders Note: Jesus displayed his reverent and earnest interest in the institutions of his people. Jesus loved the church. He went there daily to teach.
- Read Luke 4:16, Matt. 12:9; Luke 4:33, 44; John 6:59; Matt. 26:55 -Leaders note: Jesus was often in the house of God.

- Why did Jesus get upset when he enter a house of worship?
    - Bartering in sanctuary – John 2:14-15, Mark 11:15-16
    - Pretension in worship – Matt. 6:1-6
    - Formal Repetitious – Matt. 6:7
    - False Holiness – Matt. 6:18-20
    - Enslavement of Tradition – Mark 7:1-8
    - Shows of Piety – Mark 7:10-13
    - Emphasis on Externals – Mark 7:18-23
- Read Ephesians 5:25-27. What Christ desire for His church?
- What would Jesus say about the church of today? Leader Note: Jesus distinguished between the Church and the abuses that disfigured it, and did not let His love for the former suffer because of His aversion to the latter.

11. RENEW: ENEMIES
- Have you ever really disliked someone? Who were they? Do you still carry those feelings?
- Jesus had enemies (1 John 3:12-13). Can you name any of them? Leader Note: A Pharisees (Mark 12:22-37; Matt. 12:38-45.Why were they upset with Him?
- Has anyone ever really disliked you? What happened? Did you do anything about the issue?

- Who is your greatest enemy today?
- Did Jesus ever provoke His enemies (John 7:1; 8:37-40; Luke 11:37-52)?
- How does He expect us to treat our enemies? Jesus (John 7:25-26, 11:56-57).

Leader Note:
- ◦ Goodness is no guarantee a man will have no enemies.
- ◦ God's will is to dissuade men from their evil purposes (John 8:37-40). We are to resolutely move forward in the face of opposition and even despite it (John 7:25-26).
- ◦ We are to love our enemies. We are to be gentle in our suggestion they need to correct error to be just (John 18:19-24).
- ◦ No enemy can conquer a Christian — *except* an enemy from within (1 Cor. 15:25; Rev. 3:21).

RENEW: Enemies Core Statement
"To stand with defeat behind us, and to face Godward, knowing that every sin has left an impress on character that will need vigilance of the awakened manhood to overcome, and yet know that the soul never stands alone, that the power to overcome is always within the grasp of the man who fights to win, gives victory."[150]

---

150   P.56 Robert Speers

12. RENEW: FORGIVENESS
- When you hear the word forgiveness, what or who do you think of?
- Have you ever forgiven someone without telling them?
- Have you forgiven a person and they continue to do the same actions?
- Is there an offense against you that you don't believe you could forgive?
- Have you ever committed this same offense against someone else?
- Repeat the Lord's prayer together. What do the words, "forgive us our trespasses as we forgive those who trespass against us" mean for you and your errors in life?
- Have you ever confessed your sins with another person? How did the experience make you feel? Did you change your actions as a result? Why not?
- Read Matt. 18:21-22; Luke 17:3-4 and discuss.
- Read John 21:15-19 and answer the question: How do you think Peter felt?

13. RENEW: ERROR
- As you read the chapter, what thoughts came to mind?
- What cultural idea was Jesus trying to debunk and what is the lesson we should understand?

Matt. 5: 13-16	Matt. 5: 17-20
Matt. 5: 21-26	Matt. 5: 27-30
Matt. 5: 31-32	Matt. 5: 33-37
Matt. 5: 38-42	Matt. 5: 43-48
Matt. 6: 1-4	Matt. 6: 5-15
Matt. 6: 16-18	Matt. 6: 19-21
Matt. 6: 22-24	Matt. 6: 25-34
Matt. 7: 1-6	Matt. 7: 7-14
Matt. 7:15-20	Matt. 7: 21-23
Matt. 7: 24-27	

- What cultural misunderstanding do you identify with? Why?
- What is new to you in these teachings of Jesus?

14. RENEW: UNBELIEF

- What in your reading of the manual was a unique or interesting thought?
- How did Jesus react to those who did not believe in God the Father or His connection to Him?

RENEW: Unbelief core concept

Jesus spoke of "believing in Him" in several scriptures (John 3:18, 36; 6:29, 35, 40; 9:35). He was clear that all who accepted His understanding as true would surrender their life to Him. Unbelief was a refusal to accept Jesus' declarations (John 8:45).

- Unbelief was an important — as well as offensive — decision to Jesus (John 3:18).
- What does this scripture say about belief in God?

- What did Jesus think of unbelief? (John 16:9, Mark 16:14)
- Where does unbelief come from? (John 5:44, John 10:26-27)
- What does our unbelief affect? (Matt. 17:20)
- Read Luke 12:35-48. How does this parable classify those who do not believe? What were the consequences?
- Read John 8:24 and John 5:31-47. Leader Note: John 14:1, John 5:38, 40.
- Compare the passages from Luke 9:50 and Luke 11:23. Do these passage conflict? Why or why not? What do they say about belief in Him?

15. RENEW: FRIENDSHIP
- Read John 17 out loud. What were some of the main points which were new to you?
- Did Jesus hate anybody?
- Did Jesus have authentic friendships?
- Would Jesus have a Facebook page? What would it say? Pictures?
- What was the main principle of Jesus' friendships?
- Who were Jesus' friends?
- Did Jesus hold his friends accountable? How? When?

16. RENEW: MARRIAGE
- Read Eph. 5:18-33 and discuss.
- How does society think of marriage?
- What does Google say the definition is?
    - Do you agree or disagree?
- What does Jesus say about marriage?
- What is the purpose of marriage?
- Did Jesus allow divorce?
    - Read Matt. 5:27-30.
    - Read Mark 10:11.
- Does Christianity allow Polygamy?
    - Read Matt. 19:3-12.
- Is marriage only for this portion of our lives?
    - Matt. 22:30-33
    - Luke 20:34-36

APPENDIX A

<u>Good Marriage Books:</u>
The Meaning of Marriage – Timothy Keller
The Five Love Languages – Gary Chapman
Love and Respect – Emerson Eggerichs
Highly Happy Marriages – Shaunti Feldhahn

17. RENEW: FAMILY

- Do you remember this family song?

Show me the way to go home
  I'm tired and I want to go to bed
  I had a little drink about an hour ago
  And it's gone right to my head
  Wherever I may roam
  On land or sea or foam
  You can always hear me singing this song
  Show me the way to go home.

- Do you know the history of that song?

<u>Leader Note:</u>
"Show Me the Way to Go Home" is a popular song written in 1925 by the pseudonymous Irving King (the English songwriting team James Campbell and Reginald Connelly). The song is said to have been written on a train journey from London by Campbell and Connelly. They were tired from the traveling and had a few alcoholic drinks

during the journey, hence the lyrics. The song is in common use in England, Ireland, Scotland and North America. It has sold millions of copies.[151]

- Read and discuss John 7:48-52.
- Read and Discuss Matt. 10:34-39.
- Let's look at the lessons from Jesus' interaction with family:
    - He spoke to God with the love and respect of a son (John 2: 16; 5:17, 10:15, 11:41, 12:27-28
    - He gave glimpses to others of real intimacy and closeness he had with "Dad" — Abba (John 5:35; 5:20, 26;6:57;8:28, 38; 17:5)
    - He strove to be like His Father (John 5:19)
    - He thought of heaven as a home (John 14:2)
    - He related to others in a family way (Eph. 3:15)
    - Attended the family events — wedding, etc. (Luke 9:42, John 2:1-11)
    - Connected to the appeals by family members (John 4:49)
    - He was always aware of his parent's feelings (Luke 7:11-15)
    - He spoke of a Father's unconditional love (Luke 15:18
    - He appreciated the family home and the importance of those closest to Him (John 19:27; 20:10)
    - He found rest in the family circle (look at Bethany)

---

151   Wikipedia 2017

18. RENEW: WOMEN
- What do you think of the statement: Many women equated oppression with religion or spirituality?
- What do you think of Islam's founder *Muhammad, as well as Aristotle and Charles Darwin?*
- What does the founder of Christianity say and demonstrate about God's view of women?

Review Jesus' words and deeds to understand His view of women.
- He made them His friends (Luke 10:38, John 11:5).
- He answered their questions (John 4:9-11).
- He heard their cries (Luke 11:27).
- He offered His sympathy (Luke 23:28).
- He healed women (Luke 8:2).
- He praised their faith (Matt. 15:28).
- He included them in His teaching and vision (Matt. 15:38).
- He cared for them (Luke 13:11).
- He spoke of their noble qualities (Luke 18:1-8).
- He commended a woman's loving service of God (Luke 21:1-4).

Review Paul's statement in Galatians 3:28. What did Paul think of women?

Core Learning:
Jesus never recognized inferiority of women and his actions demonstrated equality.
- In the *Principles of Christianity*, Robert Speer said, "Jesus presented the gospel equally as masculine in its strength and just as feminine in its tenderness that the equality of the two sexes in the highest matters must be recognized at once ..." Do you agree or disagree with his perception? Why or Why not?
- What is the difference between leadership or headship?
- Read Matt. 5:1-11. What do you find interesting about the contrasts?
    - The Beatitudes fits both sexes (all who claim Him as Lord and Savior) to be under the law of service to God and others.

19. RENEW: WRATH
- Have you ever felt God had his wrath upon you? Why? When?
- Open and discuss the following scriptures: Luke 16:19-31; Romans 5:6-11; Romans 2:5-6; John 3:36.
- Did you know that God's wrath was connected to the Old Covenant? .What do you think of the statement: God did not pour out His wrath on Jesus on the cross?
    - Thought: The cross was not the punishment for sin, but a way for God to forgive sin by cutting a New Covenant of forgiveness.

- What do you think of the idea that the New Testament references to wrath are primarily speaking of the destruction of Jerusalem that was coming in A.D. 70?
  - Thought: This was the final pouring out of God's wrath on the earth. The first-century Jews who received witness of their Savior, but refused to accept Him, were the "children of disobedience." They clung to the Law and the Old Covenant and, therefore, chose to be judged with it, bringing the wrath of God upon themselves.
- The Old Covenant and the New Covenant coexisted during the New Testament (A.D. 30-70), in the time between Jesus' death and resurrection (inauguration of the New Covenant) and the destruction of Jerusalem (elimination of the Old Covenant). How much do you think the old Covenant understanding affected the new covenant understanding? Some of the statements in the New Testament were written from the perspective of the Old Covenant and the Law rather than the gospel of grace.
- What do you think of the idea that the Old Covenant was forever destroyed by the destruction of Jerusalem in A.D. 70 (as described in Rev. 15:1 and Matt. 24)?
  - Thought: Revelation 15:1 indicates the complete removal of God's wrath and the passing away of the law. God does not have any more wrath to pour out on the earth, ever. (All that remains is the final judgment before the throne of God.)

Core Learning — When a believer sins, God responds with grace, not judgment.

20. RENEW: RICHES
- Did you know the poverty level threshold in Will County, Illinois is $24,250 for a family of four?
- What do you consider rich in terms of income?
- How much more, by percentage, would your family income need to increase for every need to be satisfied? 10 percent, 20 percent, 50 percent, more?
- How could you cut your current income by the same amount you would like to see it increase? What would be required to spend the less?
- Read and study Luke 12:13-20 and Luke 16:1-15.
- What are the curses of riches?
    - Matt. 6:19-34 and Rev. 3:17-18 (distraction)
    - Luke 21:1-4 and Mark 12:41-44 (privilege of sacrifice)
    - Are there other ways in which riches can be a curse?

21. RENEW: POVERTY
- Which is more dangerous, poverty or wealth?
- Have you ever been poor? Please share the story.
- Would you take a vow of poverty if being a Christian required it?
- Let's review Mark 1:20, 14:3; Luke 14:13. What do these verses tell you about Jesus' friends?
- Let's look and discuss Luke 21:3.
- How did Jesus teach those who were poor?

- How did Jesus feel about those who were wealthy or who had possessions?
  - Jesus steadfastly refused to allow class hatred or political rebellion (John 6:15). He encouraged those with power and money to experience a life without burden or guilt (Luke 19:8).
- Read and Discuss Luke 18:18-30.
  - How would you have reacted hearing these words?
  - Could you give up all you have to follow Jesus? All the comforts of home?

Core Learning:
Jesus deemed the perils of wealth worse than the perils of the poor.
- What does Matt. 16:26 and 10:28 say about giving of the stuff of this life?

Leader Note:
Any wise man will give all that he has for his life. Possessions can't add to this life. Time cannot be added either.

- Did Jesus ever suggest an economic platform for Christians to follow?
- How do you respond to Mark 14:7; John 12:8?

22. RENEW: GIVING TO MAN

- What did you learn from the Contemporary Samaritan Story?[152]
- How would you define virtue?
- How does the current virtue of definition from Merriam-Webster compare with yours?
    - *conformity to a standard of right: morality*
    - *a moral excellence*
    - *a beneficial quality or power of a thing*
    - *manly strength or courage: valor*
    - *a commendable quality or trait: merit*
    - *a capacity to act: potency*
    - *chastity, especially in a woman*[153]
- Read Matt. 6:1-4 and discuss.
- How would you define charity?
- The word "charity," according to the definition from Webster's dictionary of 1828 (Walking Lion Press, 2010) means, "A disposition of heart which inclines men to think favorably of their fellow men and do good. In a theological sense, it includes supreme love to God and universal good will to men." How does this definition compare with your definition of charity?

Core Learning

The virtue of Christian giving to another person includes giving of oneself. Or, as good friend once said, charity begins when we give from within to recognize the greater value of the person before us.

---

152 https://owlcation.com/humanities/The-Unscrupulous-Lawyer

153 https://www.merriam-webster.com/dictionary/virtue

- Read Luke 10:30-36 and discuss the Parable of the Good Samaritan
  - What are the lessons Jesus was trying to impart to the Jewish audience?
- How does the parable and Jesus' assertion apply to your giving to others?

23. RENEW: GIVING TO GOD

- What was the best gift you ever gave someone else and why it was special?
- What has been the best gift you have ever been given? Who was it from?
- What is your favorite charity and why?
- Corban is "a Hebrew word, meaning that which is brought as an offering." Jewish people would sometimes claim an item or a resource was "corban" to avoid giving it to a parent or another person in need. Whatever might be required by a parent is refused, claiming it has a prior and more sacred destination. This sin was particularly disgusting to God. Why do you think so?
- Read Acts 5:1-11 and discuss.
- Read Luke 21:1-4 and discuss the widow's action.
- How does the widow's response contrast with the rich young ruler?
- We never read what happens to the rich young ruler. Do you suppose he followed through or lived out his existence without Christ?

- Professor's Paul Piff's researched giving: *His experiment primed subjects by showing sympathy inducing videos and encouraging them to imagine themselves in different financial circumstances. That changed their reactions — for both sets of subjects. In other words, the poor, imagining themselves rich, became less altruistic. The rich, imagining themselves poor, became more generous to the destitute and ill.* Piff concluded: "*Empathy and compassion appeared to be the key ingredients" in the generosity of the poor."* Do you agree or disagree with his findings?
- Do you think people who have a faith are more generous? Why or why not?

24. RENEW: WAR
- Is war inevitable?
- Let's read Matt. 5:38-48 and discuss.
- Should America be involved in armed conflict — why or why not?

Just war theory is defined as:
- "All forms of Just War Theory provide guidelines that fall into two categories: justice in entering a war, and justice in waging a war. (These two categories are known as jus ad bellum, and jus

> *in bello, respectively.) Broadly speaking, Just War Theory holds that a nation can go to war only in response to the impetus of a "just cause," with force as a "last resort," after all other non-military options have been considered and tried—with its decision to go to war motivated by "good intentions," with the aim of bringing about a "good outcome." And it holds that a nation must wage war only by means that are "proportional" to the ends it seeks, and while practicing "discrimination" between combatants and non-combatants. Finally, in a requirement that applies to both categories, Just War Theory holds that the decision-making power for when, why, and how to wage war—including the declaration of war—must rest with a "legitimate authority."*

- What are your thoughts of this statement?
- What are your thoughts about Augustine's proposal that acts of aggression are okay if they are used to protect the rights of others? Does that align with Jesus' words?
- *Miriam-Webster Dictionary* defines altruism as the belief in or practice of disinterested and selfless concern for the well-being of others. Is it possible for human beings to ever act without a selfish motive? Why or why not?
- Compare the words of Jesus in Matt. 26:52, John 18:36 and Luke 4:17-21.

- What do you think of the assertion "The "Church" has never been called to go to war? Governments have and invoked God's name in the process. Does God call His person to involve themselves only when evil is to be thwarted or justice for the powerless is the aim?"

25. RENEW: NON- RESISTANCE
- Let's read Matthew 5:38-39 and discuss.
- Have you ever been bullied? Please share about the situation.
- Let's review the scriptural basis for tonight's non-resistance talk:
    - When people threatened to stone Him, he made no resistance and simply walked away (Luke 4:29-30; John 8:59, 10:39).
    - He disapproved of His disciples' use of violence when he was arrested (Matt. 26:52).
    - He refrained from use of His power to get rid of his enemies (Matt. 26:53-54)
    - When unjustly accused and tried, He endured insult without a word (Matt. 26:67; Mark 14:65; Matt. 27:30).
    - When confronted with torture and death, He did not resist (John 19:17).
    - He told his disciples to act in a similar fashion when both rejected from a village (Luke 9:54-55) and welcomed negatively, just let it go and move on (Matt. 10:23).

- Was the Lord of life in Luke 12:14 legislating only the inward spirit of mankind?
- What do you think of Woodrow Wilson quote: "The only use of an obstacle is to be overcome. All that an obstacle does with brave men is, not to frighten them, but to challenge them."
- Let's review and discuss Matt. 18:15-18; Psalm 101 and Gal. 6:1.
- What do you think of the idea of binding evil?
- What do the following scriptures indicate about the authority handed over to Christians when confronting evil?
  - To overcome all the power of the enemy (Luke 10:19)
  - The forces of evil in society (Eph 6:13)
  - James and Peter tell us to resist the devil (James 4:7; 1 Peter 5:9)
  - Winning the ultimate battle over the enemy (Col 2:15).
  - Are you good at setting boundaries in your life? Why or why not?

26. RENEW: RIGHTS
- What stands out from the articles of human rights handout from the UN? Is there any right you feel is absent?
- What kind of right is "the pursuit of happiness"?

- In looking at society, what rights are they most concerned about? Why?
- What American right is more important: freedom of religion or freedom of speech? Why?
- Are there any rights that come with declaring oneself a Christian?
- Let's read 1 Cor. 9:4-27 and discuss the implications.
- Let's read 2 Thess. 3:9; Matt. 17:25-27; 1 Cor. 9:4-27 and discuss.

27. RENEW: CHARACTER

- The concept of externalism is defined by *Oxford Dictionary* as excessive regard for outward form in religion. "religion needs to be questioned for its negative attitudes, hypocrisy, and externalism."[154]
- The scripture associated with it most often is:
  - "Beware of practicing your righteousness before men to be noticed by them; otherwise you have no reward with your Father who is in heaven" (Matt. 6:1 NIV).
- How would you define the externalism principle in your own words?
- Where in the American church do you see this today?
- What influences your thoughts and actions most (John 7:17)?

---

154   https://en.oxforddictionaries.com/definition/externalism

- Are our thoughts or our actions more damaging?
- Let's read Matt. 5:27-28. Does this change your answer to our last question?
- Read the following scripture: Matt. 5:44-45; John 12:36, 15:8. Who are we called to be on earth?
- Read John 10 about the Good Shepherd and discuss.

28. RENEW: DEATH

- Are you afraid of dying? Why or why not?
- Had you ever considered Jesus was not afraid of his death only the means the Romans would use to hasten it? How does this inform your understanding of the garden moment?
- What do you believe happens when we die? Where do we go? Do we just stop existing? Are there any qualifiers to moving to the next plane of existence?
- Read each of the following scriptures and discuss: Psalm 23; Psalm 77; Psalm 139; Isaiah 43:1-4; Jeremiah 17:5-8; Luke 12:13-34; Romans 8:18-39; 1 Cor. 15:51-57; John 14:1-10.
- Do you view death as the gateway to a greater life with the creator or the end of your existence?

29. RENEW: LOVE
- How do you understand the phrase, "God is love?"
- How is Christian love different from love in society at large?
- Read Matt. 22:37-40 and discuss.
- An expert in the law tried to test the Lord Jesus by asking Him to declare what was the greatest commandment in the Law of Moses. In one masterful statement, Jesus condensed the entire law that God had given Moses: "You shall love the LORD your God with all your heart, with all your soul, and with all your mind. This is the first and great commandment. And the second is like it: 'You shall love your neighbor as yourself.' On these two commandments hang all the Law and the Prophets."
- Let's read what Jesus is referring to:
    - "When you reap the harvest of your land, you shall not wholly reap the corners of your field, nor shall you gather the gleanings of your harvest. And you shall not glean your vineyard, nor shall you gather every grape of your vineyard; you shall leave them for the poor and the stranger: I am the LORD your God. You shall not steal, nor deal falsely, nor lie to one another. And you shall not swear by My name falsely, nor shall you profane the name of your God: I am the LORD. You shall not cheat your neighbor, nor rob him. The wages of him who is hired shall not remain with you all night until morning. You shall not curse the deaf, nor put a stumbling block before the blind, but

APPENDIX A

shall fear your God: I am the LORD. You shall do no injustice in judgment. You shall not be partial to the poor, nor honor the person of the mighty. In righteousness you shall judge your neighbor. You shall not go about as a talebearer among your people; nor shall you take a stand against the life of your neighbor: I am the LORD. You shall not hate your brother in your heart. You shall surely rebuke your neighbor, and not bear sin because of him. You shall not take vengeance, nor bear any grudge against the children of your people, but you shall love your neighbor as yourself: I am the LORD" (Leviticus 19:9-18).

- What do you notice about the verse and how it would apply today?

Leader Note:
Loving our neighbor would include:
1. sharing with the poor and the alien;
2. compassion and absolute honesty and justice in our relationships with others; impartiality;
3. a refusal to be a party to gossip or slander;
4. an absence of malice toward anyone and a refusal to bear a grudge;
5. taking care never to put another's life at risk and never taking private vengeance upon another.
6. If we have an issue with anyone, we should strive to make it right by going to him or her directly. James calls this the "royal law" (James 2:8).

- Let's read John 13: 34-35 and discuss.
- Let's read 1 John 4: 8 and discuss.
- How has today's reading of scripture informed your understanding of what it means to love as a Christian?

30. RENEW: WORK

Work was established as an activity to bring ourselves and others into relationship with Him.

- What are the more positive aspects of your work life, whether that be in an office, home or school?
- What are the more negative aspects for you for your work life?
- Read and discuss Genesis 1:27-28 as well as Genesis 2:15.
- How have you ever tried to see God at work?
- Are there any Christians in your workplace? How do you know?
- Read and discuss John 9:1-12. (Verse 4 in particular.)
- Does God care about what we do for a living? Why or why not?
- Read and discuss Colossians 3:23-24.

31. RENEW: TEACHING
- Who was your greatest teacher, how did you come together and why?
- What is your preferred way of learning?
- Are you currently trying to learn anything new in your life?
- Read and discuss the meaning of Proverbs 11:14 and Proverbs 24:6.
- Have you ever had a mentor? How did you come to ask him or her to come alongside you and counsel you?
- Read and discuss Exodus 18:1-24.
- What do you think of his father-in-law correcting him in this passage?
- How have you experienced critique in life? Is there a person who you always listen to?
- Jesus taught people: Mark 1:21-22; 2:13; 4:1-2; 6:30-34; 9:31; 10:1; 11:17; 12:35. What do you make of these scriptures?
- What do you make of the figures Jesus used in His teaching in: Matt. 5:14; John 3:8; 4:34-35; 6:35; 7:37-38; 8:12; 15:1-7?

32. RENEW: DISEASE

- Do you ever wonder why God chooses to heal some sick people and not others?
- What about tonight's message struck a chord in you?
- Read Luke 7:1-17 and discuss.
- Do you believe God heals miraculously today?
- Review 1 Cor. 12:9 and James 5:14. Discuss how these scriptures inform your understanding of healing.
- Have you ever wanted to have the gift of healing?
- Have you ever thought of modern medicine as the hand of God at work?
- Do you know anyone who has been, or have you ever been healed miraculously?
- What do you make of these references to the finger of God — Exodus 8:19, Exodus 31:18; Deut. 9:10; Luke 11:20?

33. RENEW: KINGDOM OF HEAVEN

- Do you believe in heaven? Why or why not?
- Have you ever wrestled at a funeral, wondering if the person is in heaven?
- Do you know of anyone who has had a near death experience?
- Why do you think Jesus spoke in parables?
- Heaven description scriptures for review aloud:
  1. Isaiah 25:8-12, Ezek. 2824-26; Matt. 5:17-20; 7:13-15; 19:17-19; 22:29-33

APPENDIX A

2. Luke 13:29-33; John 14:2-4; Col. 3:1-7; Rev. 7:13-17; 21:4-8
- Let read the parables from Matthew 13
  1. Matt. 13:1 - 23 The Parable of the Sower
  2. Matt. 13:24 - 30 The Parable of the Weeds
  3. Matt. 13:31 - 33 The Parable of the Mustard Seed
  4. Matt. 13:33 - 35 The Parable of the Yeast
  5. Matt. 13:44 The Parable of the Hidden Treasure
  6. Matt. 13:45-46 The Parable of the Pearl
  7. Matt. 13:47 - 52 The Parable of the Net

- Why would Jesus teach the disciples to pray for the: "Kingdom to come and they will to be done on earth as it is in heaven"?
- What are your thoughts about the scriptural references to who will be in the Kingdom of Heaven? Leaders Note:
  1. believers in Jesus and His work on our behalf (Matt. 4:17; 7:21,10:7)
  2. poor in spirit (Matt. 5:3)
  3. persecuted for righteous sake (Matt. 5:10)
  4. Obedient to living for Him and His will (Matt. 5:19)
  5. Humble in serving others especially those whom compassion is hard (Matt. 5:45; 18:1-10)
  6. Selfless (Matt. 11:11)

34. RENEW: HELL
- What do you believe about heaven and hell?
- What do you think about the idea of purgatory? Definition below from Merriam Webster's' dictionary:
    - *an intermediate state after death for expiatory purification; specifically: a place or state of punishment wherein according to Roman Catholic doctrine the souls of those who die in God's grace may make satisfaction for past sins and so become fit for heaven*
    - *a place or state of temporary suffering or misery*
- If hell exists, what do you think happens in hell and who ends up there?
- Read Revelation 21:8 and discuss.
- Read Romans 3:23-24 and discuss
- Do you believe in tonight's assertion that "Hell is the default destination for humanity?"
- What do you think of CS Lewis statement that *"Hell is a door locked from the inside?"*
- What do you think of Preacher/Theologian JD Greear rationalization for Hell's existence in his statement: "... *Hell magnifies for us the love of God by showing us how far God went, and how much he went through, to save us?"*
- What do you think of the idea that a sin is greater depending on the person it is perpetuated against?
- What are the differences in the words used in the scriptures for hell - Hades and Gehenna?

35. RENEW: FALSHOOD

- When was the last time you lied to avoid a troubling situation? Why did you lie?
- Scott Peck classified lying into two types: the black ones of which we know is not true and the white ones which are also false but still leave a significant part of the truth. Is it ever okay to lie?
- Read and discuss John 8:44-45 and 1 Peter 2:22, 3:10
- In Martin Scorsese's film *Silence*, missionaries were asked to step on an icon of Jesus to recant their faith, if they chose not to, others would die and they would have to watch. How would you respond? What about if your family or friend's life depended on it?
- What do you think of the Muslim view on lying as outlined below?
    - Taqiyya - Saying something that isn't true as it relates to the Muslim identity.
    - Kitman - Lying by omission. An example would be when Muslim apologists quote only a fragment of verse 5:32 (that if anyone kills "it shall be as if he had killed all mankind") while neglecting to mention that the rest of the verse (and the next) mandates murder in undefined cases of corruption and mischief.
    - Tawriya - Intentionally creating a false impression.
    - Muruna - Blending in by setting aside some practices of Islam or Sharia in order to advance others.
- Have you ever thought of lying as a coping mechanism and a survival technique?

- As Robert Speer shares, "If it is impossible or wrong for God to lie, it is impossible and wrong for us to ever lie as well." He also asserted the devil was the father of lies and He did not make room for some lies which did not bear the stamp of the devil's paternity. How do you understand this statement?
- Let's read John 7:8-10 and Luke 24:28 and discuss your view of Jesus' actions.

36. RENEW: JUDGEMENT

- Have you ever felt judged? When and for what?
- Have you ever judge someone else incorrectly? When and how?
- Do you agree or disagree that Christians are more judgmental than non-Christians?
- Read and discuss Matthew 7, focusing on the juxtaposition between Verse 1-2 and Verse 24.
- In what circumstances is it okay to judge someone else?
- What do you think of the statement by Mishnah: "Judge everyone favorably," because every person is believed to have some goodness in them?
- Do you agree or disagree with Gandhi's statement: "It has been my experience that I am always true from my point of view, but am often wrong from the point of view of my critics? I know we are both right from our respective viewpoints of view. ... The seven blind men who gave seven different descriptions of the

elephant were all right from their respective points of view and wrong the viewpoint of one another and right and wrong from the point of the view of the man who knew the elephant."
- Review John 5:30 and discuss. All judgement must pass through this lens.
- Let's review the following scriptures with regard to judgment
    - "I judge no man" (John 8:15; John 12:47; Luke 12:14)
    - Jesus judges the multitudes (Luke 12:57 and John 7:24)
    - Jesus curses the Pharisees (Luke 11:42; Matt. 23:27,33)
    - Jesus claims he came to judge the world (John 9:39)
    - Jesus claims his judgement is right (John 5:30)
    - Jesus approves of certain behaviors (Luke 21:3-4 "the widow")
    - Jesus disapproves of a disciple's behavior (Matt. 16:23)
        - *Let's continue reviewing what God's word teaches:*
    - Superficial judgement is wrong (Prov 18:13, Luke 7:36-50)
    - Hypercritical judgement is wrong (Matt. 6:2, 5, 16)
    - Harsh and unforgiving judgement is wrong (Titus 3:2)
    - Self-righteous judgement is wrong (James 4:6; Luke 18:9-14)
    - False judgement is wrong (Prov. 19:5; Titus 3:2)

37. RENEW: FAITH

- What do you think of the definition: Faith is an intelligent and reasonable confidence in God which provides absolute assurance of the truth of God's way in us and the world around us.
- What is one person, place and thing you have faith in? Why have you given them your trust?
- After hearing the four elements of faith, how would you classify your faith in God?
    - **Aim capable of embracing life as a whole**
    - **Conviction the aim will be realized**
    - **Belief in the mission**
    - **Consciousness of God's oversight**
- Let us review the Hall of Fame of Faith (as it's called in scripture) — Hebrews 11. What are the qualities listed for the people of faith?
- Let's look at the list of other scriptures and see the positive effects of faith in our lives:
    - Faith eradicates fear from our lives (Luke 5:10; 8:50; 12:7 Matt. 8:26)
    - Faith is a sister to joy (1 Peter 1:8) and hope (1 Peter 1:21)
    - Faith is the secret to victory over the world (1 John 5:5)
    - Faith removes the shame and failure our of life and fills us with confidence (1 Peter 2:6; Heb. 10:22; Rom. 9:33)
    - Faith begets patience and content (2 Thess. 1:4; Rev. 2:19; 13:10)

- Faith unlocks the future and us perfect assurance in it (2 Tim. 1:12)
- Faith speaks of rest and removal of our burdens (Heb. 4:3; Matt. 11:28)

38. RENEW: SACRIFICE

- In the movie *Hacksaw Ridge*, the main actor would chant "just one more" when he went back into the battlefield to save another life. What did you think about when Desmond Doss went to help the Japanese soldier?
- Let's read the scriptures and discuss: Rom 12:1; Eph 5:2; Phil 4:18.
- What's your definition of a sacrifice? To who? Why?
- How do you feel when you are asked to sacrifice?
- Has anyone ever sacrificed for you? If so, how did it make you feel? Did it change your perspective of the person?
- What is the most valuable possession in your life?

The definition of sacrifice from *Merriam Webster Dictionary* is:
1. *an act of offering to a deity something precious*
2. *destruction or surrender of something for the sake of something else*

Robert Speer's suggestion is that sacrifice really means: *"rendering to God that which has never been consecrated to Him before"* (POJ p.199).

- Would you be willing to sacrifice your greatest possession in your life if a friend asked you to? A boss? A relative? A child? An enemy? Your God?
- Let's look at what the New Testament says about sacrifice. Let's read and discuss: Mark 12:33; Luke 2:24; Acts 7:41-42; 1 Cor. 10:18; Heb. 9:9, 10:1.
- Let's look at Jesus' example of sacrifice:
    - He came to do God's will (John 6:38)
    - He yielded Himself to the Father and His purpose (John 7:29, 17:4)
    - He surrendered what He might have accomplished on earth for what was accomplished for others (Mark 15:31)
    - He fulfilled the Old Testament requirements completely, concluding with being the Passover lamb for our sin (1 Cor. 5:7; Heb. 10:12-18)
    - He made the only true sacrifice of a humble and contrite spirit (Ps. 51:17)
- Let's look at Jesus' statements about his expectation of their commitment to Him:
    - Homes (Luke 14:26)
    - Occupations (Luke 5:10, 27)
    - Possessions (Luke 14:33)
    - Comfort and Ease (Luke 9:57-62)
    - Jesus said, "If any man come after Me, let him deny himself and take up his cross daily and follow me" (Luke 9:23-24).
- What do you think of the statement: "Sacrifice in the sense of self-denial lays the emphasis on what we

leave behind. However, sacrifice in the sense of self-devotion is focused on what we move towards"?
- Read and discuss Luke 5:10 and Matt. 19:29.

39. RENEW: HOLY SPIRIT

- Have you ever had an encounter with Holy Spirit? What happened?
- Read Acts 2 and discuss.
- How would you describe the Holy Spirit?
- Read and discuss John 14:15-18 and 16:5-15.
- As Christ-followers, we know from the scriptures: The Spirit descended on Jesus at His baptism (Matt. 3:16), made Him unique to the Prophet John the Baptist (John 1:33-34), led Jesus in the wilderness (Luke 4:1), gave Him power in service (Luke 4:14) and moved Him through the rest of His ministry (Matt. 12:28; Luke 4:18). Do you believe the Holy Spirit is available to you in the same way? Why or why not?
- Let's read and discuss the following Scriptures: John 20:22; Luke 24:49; Acts 1:8.
- When you get to heaven, how will you describe the Holy Spirit's role in your life; have you ever grieved the Spirit?
- Read and discuss Eph. 5:1-20.
- Let's read and discuss John 3:34.

40. RENEW: PLEASURE
- When I say the word pleasure, what do you think of?
- Let's look at Luke 8:4-15 and discuss the Parable of the Sower.
- Sigmund Freud was the first to coin the phrase the "pleasure principle" to characterize the tendency of people to seek pleasure and avoid pain. Freud argued that people will sometimes go to great lengths to avoid even momentary pain, particularly at times of psychological weakness or vulnerability. Does the idea of the pleasure principle have some merit? Why or why not?
- Let's review Matt. 6:18-34 and Luke 12:19-21 and discuss the core idea.
- Have you ever found yourself like Phil Jackson, wondering if this all there is to life? Please share the experience with the group.
- I will re-read the list of possible questions when we meet God in heaven; are any of them particularly convicting or troubling?
  - *God won't ask what kind of fancy car you drove. He will ask how many people you took to church who didn't have transportation.*
  - *God won't ask the size of your house. He'll ask how many people you helped who didn't have a house.*
  - *God won't ask how many fancy clothes you had in your closet. He will ask how many of those clothes you gave away to those who didn't have any.*

APPENDIX A

- *God won't ask what social class you were in. He will ask what kindness you displayed.*
- *God won't ask about your material possessions. He'll ask whether those possessions dictated your life.*
- *God won't ask what your highest salary was. He'll ask if you trampled over anybody to obtain that salary.*
- *God won't ask how much overtime you worked. He will ask if you worked overtime for your family.*
- *God won't ask how many promotions you received. He will ask what you did to promote others.*
- *God won't ask what your job title was. He will ask if you performed your job to the best of your ability.*
- *God won't ask how many promotions you took to chase a dollar bill. He will ask how many promotions you refused to advance your family's quality of life.*
- *God won't ask how many times you didn't cheat on your spouse. He will ask how many times you lusted after another.*
- *God won't ask your degrees. He'll ask how many people you thanked for helping you get those degrees.*
- *God won't ask what your parents did to help you. He will ask what you did to help your parents.*
- *God won't ask what you did to help yourself. He will ask what you did to help others.*

- *God won't ask how many friends you had. He will ask how many people you were a friend to.*
- *God won't ask what you did to protect your rights. He will ask what you did to protect the rights of others.*
- *God won't ask what neighborhood you lived in. He will ask what other neighborhoods you visited.*
- *God won't ask how many times you told the truth. He will ask how many times you told a lie.*
- *God won't ask about the color of your skin. He will ask about the color of your heart.*
- *God won't ask how many times your deeds matched your words. He will ask how many times they didn't.*
* Let's review and discuss the following three scriptures: 1 Tim. 4:8; 2 Tim. 1:1; 1 Cor. 3:21-23; Matt. 6:33.

41. RENEW: PURPOSE

* Have you ever struggled with what your purpose is in life?
* Let's read the scriptures: John 13:1-15; Mark 10:45; Acts 20:35.
* Of the three quotes, which do you identify with? Or is there another you prefer?
  - "The purpose of life is to live it, to taste experience to the utmost, to reach out eagerly and without fear for newer and richer experience." — Eleanor Roosevelt

- "The human race is a monotonous affair. Most people spend the greatest part of their time working in order to live, and what little freedom remains so fills them with fear that they seek out any and every means to be rid of it." — Johann Wolfgang von Goethe, The Sorrows of Young Werther
- "The purpose of life is not to be happy. It is to be useful, to be honorable, to be compassionate, to have it make some difference that you have lived and lived well." — Ralph Waldo Emerson

* How do you think the world would react to the statement: The purpose of life is to be in service of God (Matt. 6:24); in love (Mark 12:30); and in holiness (Matt. 5:48). And our fellow man (Matt. 10:28; Luke 22:26-27); in love (Mark 12:31); and in humility (Matt. 20:26).
* What do you think of the statement: One's life is not for one's own gain but to use as a sacrifice for greater significance? What are you doing to apply this understanding today?
* Let's review the significance found in a relationship with Jesus (Read scripture and narrow the answer to the one listed or another word.):
  - Purity (Matt. 5:8; James 1:27; 2 Tim. 2:22)
  - Freedom (John 8:31-32)
  - Unconditional love (John 13:1, 15:13)
  - Strength (Eph. 6:10; 2 Tim. 2:1; 1 John 2:14; 1 Cor. 1:25)
  - Eternal Life (1 John 2:17)

- Motivation (John 6:38; Heb. 10:7)
- Fulfilment (John 6:51;4:34)
- What were Jesus' actions while physically present on this earth? What did he do?
- Can you find scriptural references for Jesus' actions of:
  - Renew lives through love
  - Forgive sins
  - Offer compassion (healing)
  - Comfort the sick and mourning
  - Be a peacemaker and joy giver
  - Live unselfishly in all areas of life
  - Stay focused on the spiritual
  - Declare the immortality of life
  - Give glory to God in all things

42. RENEW: JESUS

Jesus is God?

1. How would you answer the question, "Who is Jesus to you?"
2. Why do you think the name "Jesus" causes negative reactions?
3. What do you think of the Muslim and Jewish understanding of who Jesus is?
4. What do you think of Isaiah 40:31 " ... but those

who hope in the Lord will renew their strength. They will soar on wings like eagles; they will run and not grow weary, they will walk and not be faint"?

5. Read Matthew 11:25-30 aloud and share your thoughts
6. When you hear Verse 30 read: "For my yoke is easy and my burden is light," does his yoke seem easy and light to you? Why or why not?
7. Please read Matthew 16:13-20. What do you think of Jesus response?

43. RENEW: MORAL

- Before reading this topic, what are a few things you believed were moral?
- What is the current dictionary definition of morality? Please read it aloud to the group and discuss.
- What are your guiding values today? Would an inventory of your time, talent and resource expenditure over the last ninety days demonstrate that?
- The big question to consider: If you could change one aspect of the current world, what would it be? How would you answer?
- Let's read the Sermon on the Mount together, noting all the big ideas being offered to us: Matt. 5-7.
- After reading the Sermon on the Mount together, is being perfect possible in this life? If so, how? If not, why try?

- On a personal level, perfection is a disciple who embodies the teacher (like 5:48, 6:40). It's the goal of all spiritual life: To attain a level of understanding and submission to a greater ideal.
- On the communal level, it's the idea of a community with the goal of an all-encompassing love being the singular focus (John 17:23).
- On a worldly level, it is the idea of a world remade complete (2 Cor. 7:1; James 2:22; 1 John 4:17-18; Heb. 2:10, 5:9). It's the idea of a world with no pain, no tears, no selfishness, perfect in all aspects (Rev. 21:1-4).

- Are we our brother's keeper?
- What do you think of the statement "Jesus was not social reformer"?
- How do you practically live the great commission of Jesus?

44. RENEW: GOSPEL
- Of all the ideas about the gospel, which one did you connect with?
- Read Romans 8 and discuss.
- What do you think of the statement: "The gospel is called good news because it promises the power of the living Christ is at work in human life reproducing itself."

- Had you ever heard of Moralistic Therapeutic Deism before today?
    - "A god exists who created and ordered the world and watches over human life on earth."
    - "God wants people to be good, nice and fair to each other, as taught in the Bible and by most world religions."
    - "The central goal of life is to be happy and to feel good about oneself."
    - "Good people go to heaven when they die."
    - "God does not need to be particularly involved in one's life except when God is needed to resolve a problem."[155]
- The Christian creed most often recognized as the faith is: "He came, He suffered, He died, He rose for the forgiveness of sins and life eternal." It's a simple statement (creed actually) with profound reverberations. How does it inform your understanding of the Gospel?
- What are your thoughts on Robert Speer's comments from 1908, *"All other religions are separable from their founders. ... To remove the Christological element is radically to alter its character, to destroy the class in which it stands by itself and to reduce its in kind to the level of other religions. It is to rob it of its power. ... The human heart needs the personal experience of God and if it is denied the joy of merging itself in God in Christ and still preserving personality, it will seek the*

---

[155] http://www.albertmohler.com/2005/04/11/moralistic-therapeutic-deism-the-new-american-religion-2/

sense of divine unity and will secure it at the expense of the personality and responsibility, safeguarded to us by the historic doctrine of the Christian faith (POJ 253-54).
- Hugh Halter, in his book entitled *Flesh* (P.180-181) said: *"Jesus came to change everything you don't like. And everywhere He went, He talked about a Kingdom of God coming into the Kingdom of darkness and winning out. The Kingdom of heaven simply means that the way things are in heaven can begin to change the way things are on earth. You probably know that He died on a cross and that is a key part of the story, but the reason He did that was so that something incredible could happen to His people."* How would you express what that incredible happening is for you?

45. RENEW: SUPERNATURAL
- Have you ever had an experience with the supernatural in your life? What happened? How did you know it was from God?
- After watching the video clip about the supernatural from the filmmaker for *The Finger of God*, do you believe in supernatural events or not?
- Read Acts 2 and discuss the supernatural happening within the chapter?
- Have you ever considered that when you pray for a

miracle, you are asking God to suspend the laws of nature for your desire or someone else? How do you think God receives such requests?
- Have you ever thought about the stories of Jesus as supernatural? How does that inform your witness of Him to the world around us?
- Discuss the three aspects of Jesus' supernatural presence: Birth into human form (Luke 1:26-28, Matt. 1:18-25); constant connection with God (John 10:30); and His resurrection and ascension to heaven. How would we perceive such events today?

46. RENEW: TECHNOLOGY

The simplest answer to the question of technology and whether it is a good tool or not is: "Knowing the nature of God, would this be honoring to Him and the message He wants for us to live and offer to others?"
- Let's read scripture — Tower of Babel Genesis 11:1-10.
- How have you seen technology change your life for the better? For the worse?
- Do you believe the advancement of technology has changed our thought patterns?
- Had you ever heard the term "FOMO" (Fear of Missing Out)? Does it explain anything happening in your life?
- Have you ever considered the intersection of theology and technology? " ... Do we resist it, with the hope of preserving an older memory? Do we harness it, with

sure confidence that it is a gift from God? Or do we find ways to critically, but realistically, engage?"
- Do you believe there are a new set of *expectations that have slid into place without much conversation, resistance or notice?*
- Has technology ever caused a relationship problem for you at home, at work or in your social life? How?
- What are the benefits of technology for the Kingdom of God?

    Leader Assistance: Technology overs five distinct benefits for the Kingdom: 1) it amplifies the voice of God's message through the preacher's ability to share the gospel to more individuals through presentation both in person as well as electronically. 2) It increases the availability of good teaching 3) It shortens the discipleship cycle from immaturity to maturity due to the constant availability of teaching 4) it offers multiple worship experiences 5) it provides grace to those in the minority or with communication issues.

- What are the issues of the use of technology for the expanse of the Kingdom of God?
    - Leader Assistance: The issues technology creates for the Kingdom are: 1.) The ability to distract from God's a greater purpose and connection with Him. 2.) The ability it provides for people to isolate. 3.) Its failure to create a Christian community. 4.) Its ability to reduce worship to a theatrical event for the enjoyment of the followers, not God. 5.) It advances the culture outside the doors of the church to redefine and reshape those inside the

church. 6.) It fosters complacency in the pursuit of a relationship with God and others.[156]
- What do you think of the minimalist's saying, "Love people, use things. Don't use people and love things."

47. RENEW: SEX

Jesus did not come to abolish the law but fulfill it. He calls on us to live understanding heterosexual relations are for the purpose of creating, understanding relational intimacy and continuing God's will in the world

- Read the Scriptures and discuss: Matt. 5:20-48; John 8:2-11.

    Leader Assistance: Adultery does not just consist of the final act. A man who eyes a woman with lustful intent commits adultery with her. The tense is significant.
- What do you think of the statistics from 2009:
    1. Did you know that couples who cohabitate prior to marriage have a 46-50 percent higher divorce rate than the rest of the married population (whose divorce rate is 40-50 percent anyway)?
    2. Did you realize that the divorce rate among Christians is as high or higher than the general population?
    3. Are you aware that in 1960 single women accounted for just over 5 percent of the babies

---

[156] http://www3.dbu.edu/Naugle/pdf/The%20Effect%20of%20Technology%20on%20Christianity2.pdf

born in the United States? Did you know that by 1985, the rate had grown to 36.8 percent, and by 2005, 70 percent of African-American, 46 percent of Asian-American and 25 percent of white infants were born to single women?
4. Did you know there are 1.37 million abortions in the United States every year? What do you think of the statistic that 93 percent of all abortions occur not because of medical problems, but for "social reasons," that is, the child is not wanted?
5. Did you know there are over 420 million porn websites?
6. What do you think of the idea that 2.8 percent of males and 1.4 percent of females identify themselves as homosexual? Did you think this number was higher or lower?
7. What do you think of the statistic that less than 2 percent of homosexuals are monogamous, and the average number of lifetime sexual partners is 50.

- How would you respond to the person who claims the restrictions in scripture regarding sexual behavior are dated and based on a former cultural understanding of sex?
- How do you feel about the sexual restrictions on:
  1. Contraception: God's disapproval of this is implied by his condemnation of Onan to death for regularly practicing coitus interruptus with his brother's widow (Gen. 38:8–10). While his crime was partly that he failed to fulfil his duty by his brother of producing

offspring for him (Deut. 25:5–6), this was not his whole crime, for, under the law, failure to fulfil this duty, while being regarded as a serious offence, did not carry the death penalty (Deut. 25:7–10).

2. Nudity: Before the Fall, Adam and Eve were not ashamed of being naked (Gen. 2:25). After the Fall, they were, and used leaves to cover themselves (3:7). God subsequently provided them with garments of skin (3:21). From this point onward, exposure of nakedness has been regarded as shameful (9:20–27; Exod. 20:26, 28:42–43).

3. Polygamy: Though practiced in the Old Testament, this goes against the basis for marriage set out in Genesis 2:18–24. While Solomon had many wives and concubines (1 Kings 11:1-3), in the Song of Songs, he discovers the joy of having one lover (Song 6:8–9).

4. Self-gratification: God's disapproval of this is implied by his condemnation of Onan (Gen. 38:8–10). He does not, however, condemn those who do this involuntarily (Lev. 15:16–18; Deut. 23:9–11).

48. RENEW: IDOLATRY
- Do you have any idols in your life?
- If we were to judge your idol worship on where you invest your time and money, where would we see you invest the most?
- Read Exodus 20:1-15 and Leviticus 26:1 and discuss.
- Why do you think God wants us to only worship Him?
- Read 1 Cor. 10 and discuss.
- What do you think of Nancy Pearcy's definition: *"An idol is anything we want more than God, anything we rely on more that God, anything we look to for greater fulfillment than God. Idolatry is thus the hidden sin driving all other sins."*
- Are there any other items we worship in the church or in the community?
- Read and discuss, 1 Thess. 1:9; Romans 1:22-25.
- What is your first reaction to God being a jealous God (2 Cor. 11:2)?
- How does it feel to think you are God's image on earth (Genesis 1:26-27)?
- Do you ever consider yourself an ambassador of God? How does that understanding change your willingness to live your life differently (2 Cor. 5:20)?

APPENDIX A

49. RENEW: CULTS
- Begin with scripture: Gal 1:6-9, 2 Peter 1:20-21
- When you hear the word cult, what do you think of?
- What did you think of the religious defining factors?

Leaders Assistance:
1. *Exclusive. They may say, "We're the only ones with the truth; everyone else is wrong; and if you leave our group your salvation is in danger."*
2. *Secretive. Certain teachings are not available to outsiders or they're presented only to certain members, sometimes after taking vows of confidentiality.*
3. *Authoritarian. A human leader expects total loyalty and unquestioned obedience.*

- What do you think of the fact that the strongest attraction to a cult is authoritarian leadership? Why do you think that is in a society where individuality is prized?
- Let's read the following scriptures and discuss: Ephesians 2:8-9; John 20:31; 1 John 4:1-3, 5:11-12; 1 Cor. 2:10-12; Heb. 1:1-2, 9:24-28; John 3:16
- Read Mark 10:42-44 and discuss.
  1. *The issue of authority versus authoritarianism was one that our Lord spoke about often with His disciples. Their authority as His apostles was to be evident in a different kind of leadership: "But do not be called Rabbi; for One is your Teacher, and you are all brothers. And do not call anyone on*

409

earth your father; for One is your Father, He who is in heaven. And do not be called leaders; for One is your Leader, that is, Christ" (Matt. 23:8-10).

- The two most common teachings of Christian cults are that 1.) Jesus was not God and 2.) that salvation is not by faith alone. Are you familiar with any organizations who have taught either of these?
- Let's look at what Jesus' disciples dealt with. The apostles dealt with cults in the early years of the church. For example, John addresses the teaching of Gnosticism in 1 John 4:1-3. John's litmus test for godly doctrine was "Jesus Christ has come in the flesh" (Verse 2) — a direct contradiction of the Gnostic error (2 John 1:7).
- Let's use our smartphones and look up two of most well-known examples of cults today: Jehovah's Witnesses and Mormons. What are some of their claims?

Leaders Assistance:
Both groups claim to be Christian, yet both deny the deity of Christ and salvation by faith alone.

- What is another cult you have come into contact with and want to investigate?

50. RENEW: KINDNESS
- What does it mean to love someone? Who was your first love? Who loves you the most?
- When we say, we love somebody or something, what do we really mean by it? Does loving a burrito from Chipotle mean the same as loving God or loving others? What's the difference between preference and reciprocal commitment?
- Have you ever researched the four words translated for love in Greek?

<u>Leader's Assistance:</u>
Even the Bible has four different Greek words we translate using the English word love. There is Agape (spiritual or unconditional), Eros (physical love), Philia (mental love or friendship) and Storge (affectionate love, parental love).
- Read Luke 18:18-29 and discuss
- Have you ever heard of the butterfly effect? What is your thought on the reverse butterfly effect?

51. RENEW: VIOLENCE

- Have you ever been in a physical altercation (a fight)? Why and what happened?
- Have you ever been in a rage (uncontrolled anger)? What happened?
- Read Matthew 5 together and discuss. Key verses are Matthew 5:38-39.
- What do you think of C. S. Lewis' conjecture: *"Does anyone suppose,"* he asks, *"that our Lord's hearers understood him to mean that if a homicidal maniac, attempting to murder a third party, tried to knock me out of the way, I must stand aside and let him get his victim?"*
- Compare Romans 12:17:21 and Romans 13:1-7.
- What do you think of the conclusion that: "Even when Jesus forbids the sword as a means to advance the Kingdom of God, the New Testament does not teach an absolute or principled pacifism?"
- "Animal nature is raw and violent. Spiritual nature is thoughtful and kind. Human nature is the struggle between the two. Through Jesus' example we understand the perfect response — love in all its forms." What should be our loving response to the violence of the world around us?
- How will you implement the learnings on violence in your life and your community?

52. RENEW: COMPLACENCY

- Read Revelation 3 and discuss your thoughts.
- Have you ever been complacent in your life or in your spiritual life? What happened and what was it like?
- Do you agree or disagree with the assertion: Complacency is more harmful to one's spirituality than any other spiritual sickness because we are lulled into believing everything is as it should be. Why or why not?
- Complacency is defined as:
1. *a feeling of smug or uncritical satisfaction with oneself or one's achievements.*

    Synonyms: smugness, self-satisfaction, self-congratulation, self-regard.
2. Would you add or subtract anything from the definition?
- What's your impression of the following Scriptural references:

A) The idea of spiritual complacency: Zep. 1:12; Luke 12:19. See also Deut. 8:14; 2 Ch. 20:33; Ps. 10:4; Isaiah 43:22; Isaiah 64:7; Jer. 10:21; Eze. 33:31; David 9:13; Hos. 7:7; Zep. 1:6; Heb. 6:12; Heb. 12:25

B) The examples of complacency: Jer. 6:14; Ob. 3; 1 Cor. 5:1-2. See also Pr. 30:20; Isaiah 16:6; Eze. 28:2; Hag. 1:2; Mal. 1:6-14; Matt. 7:26; Matt. 22:5; Matt. 26:33; Luke 12:47-48; Luke 14:18; 1 Cor. 4:8; Rev. 3:15-17

C) The warnings against complacency: Am. 6:1; 2 Cor. 13:5. See also Pr. 1:32; 10:4; 12:27; Ecc. 10:18; Isaiah 32:9,11; 47:8-9; Eze. 30:9; 1Cor. 10:12; Heb. 2:3

- *Are there any other signs of complacency in addition to those shared?*
  1. Far too easily satisfied
  2. Quick to make excuses of why it's okay to not be growing spiritually
  3. No longer teachable
  4. Content with early success.
- *What are your thoughts on the process of renewing your zeal from complacency?*
  1. The first step is to admit there is a problem.
  2. Confess it to a trusted confidant.
  3. Ask for God's help to begin walking in a new direction.
  4. Finally, find an accountability partner and begin discovering a life worth living again.

www.ingramcontent.com/pod-product-compliance
Lightning Source LLC
Chambersburg PA
CBHW030105100526
44591CB00009B/286